Creative Truth

Creative Truth is your playbook for starting, building, and enjoying a profitable design business. Whether you're a solo freelancer working from home or a small group of creative entrepreneurs ready to get to the next level, this is your roadmap to success. You're the CEO, CFO, CTO, Secretary, Janitor, Office Manager, and everything in between. Finding a balance between running the business and doing great creative work is a constant struggle. From learning how to price your work and manage your time, to setting up your business and defining your market, Brad Weaver covers everything designers need to know to run a studio without losing heart.

Highlights:

- Real numbers, real tools, and best practices that you can start using immediately in your business.

- A companion website that offers up-to-date resources, articles, tools, and discussions, allowing readers to continue learning as they grow.

- Practical tips for getting clients, being more profitable, building your network, managing your operations, getting things done, hiring help, managing contractors, and finding joy along the way.

Brad Weaver is a Managing Partner & Chief Experience Officer at Nine Labs in Atlanta, GA. He went to school to be a lawyer, then came to his senses and has spent the last 18 years as a UX generalist with a geek's heart of gold. Brad's professional experience includes product development, interactive, branding, and market segmentation for clients including IHG, Verizon, Bank of America, AT&T, ESPN, Disney, NATO, The PGA, and Coca-Cola. Along the way, he's been the big cheese, the plebeian, the middle manager, and the class clown. Not one to shy away from hard work or his blue collar upbringing, he's also folded clothes, pumped gas, bagged groceries, sold cell phones, and climbed the Great Wall of China. His likes and loves are design, film, whiskey, Oxford commas, and Jesus, but not in that order.

Creative Truth

Start and Build a Profitable Design Business

Brad Weaver

Routledge
Taylor & Francis Group

New York London

First published 2014 by Focal Press
70 Blanchard Road, Suite 402, Burlington, MA 01803

and by Focal Press
2 Park Square, Milton Park, Abingdon, Oxon OX14 4RN

First issued in hardback 2017

Focal Press is an imprint of the Taylor & Francis Group, an informa business

Library of Congress Cataloging in Publication Data
A catalog record for this book has been requested

ISBN 13: 978-1-1388-4489-6 (pbk)
ISBN 13: 978-1-1384-7537-3 (hbk)

Typeset in Minion Pro and Agilita LT Sans
by Designers Collective Limited

Contents

1. Full Measures: The Creative Business Mindset 1

2. Rookie of the Year: Pushing the Start Button 13

3. The Hunt: Sales, Marketing, and Getting Client Work 39

4. Basic Rocket Science: Pricing Your Work 71

About the Author

"The best prize life has to offer is a chance to work hard at work worth doing."

Theodore Roosevelt, speech to farmers at the New York State Agricultural Association,
Syracuse, New York (7 September 1903)

Brad Weaver's first job was stocking beer coolers at age twelve. Ever since then, he's had a paying job. After going to school to become a lawyer, he came to his senses and has spent the last eighteen years as a designer & user experience generalist. His experience includes product development, interactive, branding, and market segmentation.

He founded Suckerpunch Studios in 2007, after working on the development of early Online Media programs at Verizon Wireless. Currently, he is the co-owner and Chief Experience Officer at Nine Labs.

Brad's professional experience includes product development, interactive, branding, and market segmentation for clients including IHG, Verizon, Bank of America, AT&T, ESPN, Disney, NATO, The PGA, and Coca-Cola. Along the way, he's been the big cheese, the plebeian, the middle manager, and the class clown. Not one to shy away from hard work or his blue collar upbringing, he's also folded clothes, pumped gas, bagged groceries, sold cell phones, and climbed the Great Wall of China. His likes and loves are design, film, whiskey, Oxford commas, and Jesus, but not in that order.

He lives and works in the heart of the South, Atlanta, with his gorgeous wife and two adorable yet destructive sons.

Why This Book, Why Now?

Over the Thanksgiving holiday of 2009, my first son was born and my largest client went bankrupt. Within six weeks, two additional clients informed me they wouldn't be renewing retainers with my company for 2010. My quarterly revenue dropped from $120,000 to $16,000. I was about to lose everything.

The following March, I sold a set of $500 Alessi side tables for $50 to an interior designer at my empty office. I sat on the cold floor with my laptop and waited for him to arrive. I clicked profile after profile on LinkedIn looking for my next client. He arrived, I loaded the tables in his car, and then stared at a hollow space.

I turned out the lights, locked the door, and turned my back on everything I had built. I put $15 of gas in my car and drove to a free networking luncheon. There, I presented my business, made notes, and looked for anyone that I could get work from immediately. As people spilled out of the room, I passed out cards, got names, and set up coffee meetings.

Driving home to work out of a spare bedroom, I ran through the names of those I met and thought about the emails I'd send to ask for new business. I had three websites due within the week, and none of them was over half done. Even worse, that wasn't enough business to cover upcoming bills. Here I was, four months behind on my mortgage and I still owed backed payroll to my former employees.

I needed to borrow money, but my credit was maxed-out, so I called my mother. Here I was, thirty years old, and asking my lower-middle-class parents for a loan. I was broken and ashamed. My mother agreed to the loan, fully supportive as always, and said to just let her know if I needed anything. Before saying goodbye, I paused, not finishing the call just yet.

I needed to rant, and my mother was there to listen. I was tired and scared. I couldn't take the grind anymore. I was a great designer and I knew what I was doing. I couldn't understand why things fell apart. I couldn't understand why more people weren't hiring me. Sure, the economy had tanked, but there was still a lot of work out there. I should be the one getting it, not the other guys. They were in it for the wrong reasons. I was passionate. I took the time to get it right, and I cared. I felt that I was doing everything right, yet the economics were all wrong. She listened, let me rant for a while, and told me that no matter how things turned out, she and my dad were there to help.

My work was good, yet I wasn't getting hired. Therefore, I must not be any good; me, the person, not the work. I just wasn't going to get the "big" work. I'd always toil away doing projects for a few hundred or maybe a few thousand dollars, and this was as good as it was going to get. I thought that there was something fundamentally wrong with me that I would never overcome.

For the next several weeks, I went on a few hours' sleep here and there, got a few more below-average clients, and survived. Enough money came in to keep the lights on. I was always on the edge of default. I went on like this for over a year and a half. I took any project I could get. If a client said I was too expensive, I negotiated down to get the work. I sent in low-ball quotes to anyone from whom I could get a request for proposal. I couldn't risk getting outbid and losing the job. I worked seven days a week as my son grew up and missed most of it.

Rock Bottom

In September of 2011, eighteen months after cleaning out my office and breaking my lease, my wife was rushing me to the Emergency Room. I spent several days in the hospital and the following weeks going to several specialists. I was diagnosed with a host of medical conditions. I was an active athlete with 10 percent body fat, yet I had the medical profile of a sixty-year-old diabetic with congestive heart failure. I was diagnosed with anxiety, depression, compromised immunity, asthma, and high blood pressure. I had destroyed my mind and body in the fight to stay afloat.

Friends and family advised me to shut down my business. Their advice was to let go and let someone else handle the stress. I should get a regular nine-to-five job and file bankruptcy. They felt that another chance could come someday down the road, but now it was life and death. I had to settle down.

A Stubborn Bastard

Before I started my company, I had a substantial and stable paycheck for creative work at a growing company. That didn't make me happy, so I left to start my own business. Now that I was sick and broke, I probably should have fallen into regret and despair. I was already depressed, so it couldn't get much worse. Somehow, I was still happy being on my own. It seems crazy even today, but the pain and suffering were still worth it for the freedom of owning my creative business. I knew that if I were to quit and return to a nine-to-five, I would never try again. I had come too far, and I couldn't let go.

I took a hard look at every aspect of my business. I pushed my creative books aside and turned to economics, psychology, and business management resources. I tore my business down to the foundation to find the cracks and start rebuilding the right way. Through this "last chance", my wife supported me and made it clear that a house and two cars weren't as important as my pursuit of the life I'd set out to build. I surrounded myself with the right people and the right advice. I took on the mantle of business owner first, designer second. My life and my business were fundamentally changed.

What I Learned

- I learned that I didn't have to love every aspect of my business and that I didn't have to do everything I loved in my business. (Chapter 1)

- I learned that I could, and should, start over and build for long-term sustainability. (Chapter 2)

- I learned the difference between work and clients and the value of working relationships. (Chapter 3)

- I learned that clients want to talk about money, they just don't know how. (Chapter 4)

- I learned that I am a professional, and there's a right way to run a creative business for stability. (Chapter 5)

- I learned that frequent and transparent communication with my clients would make or break my business. (Chapter 6)

- I learned to set boundaries and stick to them if I'm ever going to do meaningful work. (Chapter 7)

- I learned that collaboration is the key to falling in love with what I do and with whom I work. (Chapter 8)

- I learned that everyone's idea of growth isn't the same and that there was no perfect creative business. (Chapter 9)

- I learned that you have one life, but endless opportunities at creative life. (Chapter 10)

This is the advice I desperately wish someone had given me over a decade ago.

What Came Next

The change from borderline failure to sustainable business didn't happen overnight. But within a year, I had built a profitable business. Over the next few years my business and I grew, and I took on staff and partners. I landed some of the dream clients I'd always wanted. Now, I can take vacations and weekends off, experiment with new creative ideas, and even take the time to write a book!

The truth that came from lessons learned wasn't easy to swallow, but it saved me. I'm still learning, but I've been given the chance to share what I've learned so far. My hope is that you'll avoid much of the pain I endured. We're going to slow down and go through the experience piece by piece, sharing the hard truth about what it takes to survive and thrive in a creative career.

"Running the business is your first priority. Your success (and financial stability) will come from expertly running your business—not writing copy, rebranding your client's website, teaching yoga, podcasting, or making jewelry. In other words, you will spend 15% of the time doing what you love (your gift ... in my case coaching and writing) and 85% of the time marketing, administrating, selling, strategizing your business, and answering a shitload of email. Survival will totally hinge on how quickly you adopt this role of Business Owner first, creator of pretty things, second."

Stephanie St. Claire[1]

On Creative Courage

You're taking a tremendous risk by starting a creative business. My guess is that the people you most admire are risk takers. They are titans of industry, artists, musicians, activists, martyrs, and philanthropists—they're the crazy ones. This line of work isn't safe or for the faint of heart. There are no guarantees with your time, your schedule, or your income. What you can bet on is one hell of a ride. Whether you do this for one year or thirty, it's the best job on the planet. Making something—giving an idea life—is the ultimate challenge. It's worth all of the heartache. But you have to be brave, you have to be courageous, and you must respect yourself.

Your creative courage comes from being self-aware. You will get nothing out of this book if you aren't willing to stop and take a hard look at yourself. You must be prepared to acknowledge your strengths and weaknesses, your passion and apathy, and your real motivations. If you're in this to make a lot of money, then be willing to go broke. If you're in this to get famous, be willing to be ignored. Whatever your motivation, you will hit walls over and over again that will discourage you.

We're going to be candid, you will see inside my life and my business as we go along. My motivation is to save your life. I mean that with all sincerity. You may only get one shot. If you let it pass you by, the weight of responsibility and commitments may never let you try again. You've picked up this book, and you're serious about making a living as a creative. I want to help you be courageous, to be brave, and to take the leap.

" The three most harmful addictions are heroin, carbohydrates, and a monthly salary."

Nassim Nicholas Taleb[2]

There's More Online

Visit **thecreativetruth.com** for links to tools and resources, additional articles and insights, and community discussions for creative business owners.

Notes

1. https://medium.com/i-m-h-o/11-things-i-wish-i-knew-when-i-started-my-business-3dc264023df5.
2. https://twitter.com/nntaleb.

Acknowledgments

Books are finished by those who have zero commitments or lots of support. Since my calendar looks like a Christmas tree, I needed the help. The most important source has been the love of my life and star in my sky, Lisa. From words of encouragement to clearing my personal calendar to allow marathon writing sessions, she made this book happen.

My two wonderful boys have understood despite their youth and managed to let their dad finish something. When they get around to reading this, maybe they'll feel some of the responsibility for it not being as good as it could have been.

My loving, tough as nails, and incredibly sharp father never let me settle for mediocre. My loving, brilliant, and endlessly sacrificial mother is the reason I'm here. They're amazing, and I'm so lucky to have parents who care so much. My brother Russ always made me work harder because he's smarter than me, so thanks for that. Love you all (tap tap).

My business partner and dear friend, J. Cornelius, has been a source of knowledge and strength. I'm truly grateful we get to work together without wanting to kill each other.

Becky Simpson brought this book to life with her out of this world illustrations. She is an absolute delight and someone I'm beyond lucky to know. Dave Bevans, Mary LaMacchia, and Sean Connelly at Focal Press have been a fantastic crew with which to work. This book wouldn't be happening if Dave hadn't wandered into my conference talk in Portland, so Dave, I still owe you a beer.

Ilise Benun, thank you from the bottom of my heart for being straight with me on the first draft. This book wouldn't be half as good without your help.

Writing a book is one of the hardest things I've ever done, and none of it would have happened without going on the strength of the Lord Jesus. And whiskey, lots and lots of whiskey.

FULL MEASURES

THE CREATIVE BUSINESS MINDSET

"I flew the Atlantic because I wanted to … Whether you are flying the Atlantic or selling sausages or building a skyscraper or driving a truck, your greatest power comes from the fact that you want tremendously to do that very thing, and do it well."

Amelia Earhart[1]

Follow Your Passion, Fall Off a Cliff

In May of 2014, actor Jim Carrey gave the commencement address at a small University in Fairfield, Iowa. The speech went viral thanks to Carrey's remarks about following your dreams, taking risks, and doing what you love. Social feeds were full of people waxing poetic about "following their passion." The world was one big poster with eagles and mountains underscored by the word "DREAMS." I wanted to join in and sprinkle pixie dust on the conversation, but it honestly made me want to punch a kitten.

People readily latch on to the idea of finding one's calling in life and pursuing it to the ends of the earth. While the earth isn't flat, there are cliffs, and blindly pursuing a passion is bound to take you over more than one. In an age where overnight celebrity and wealth are becoming increasingly common, the adage "follow your passion" is a message of hope that everyone loves to embrace. But it's a terrible business strategy. Not every passion can earn you a paycheck.

DREAMS

Follow your passion and your life will be perfect.*

*If you work your ass off for decades, get really lucky, inherit a fortune, and have great hair.

When we're in the thick of it, and doing the work, that fire isn't burning as bright. We're tired of doing yet another repetitive task for a client that asks for ridiculous revisions. We have half the budget we need to do a quality job, so we cut corners and turn in another final product that isn't worthy of our portfolio. A few months or years go by, and you haven't done anything "meaningful." What happened to that passion? What happened to that fire? Now, it just feels like a job.

I love it when someone brings a deep and personal passion together with good business sense. People like Sara Blakely, Richard Branson, Tori Burch, Walt Disney, Jeff Bezos, Elon Musk, and Tony Hsieh come to mind. They did the work as business people first in order to sell creative and innovative ideas. They all had talent, but their focus was always on getting the solution into people's hands. They knew that no matter how fun or enjoyable the work, if no one used it, it wouldn't be around for long. We expect others to be infected by our passion. Typically, that isn't the case. You have to sell your ideas, your solutions, and yourself. It's no surprise that it requires a lot of hard work and energy to do so. It's laborious.

"Work is what we do by the hour. It begins and, if possible, we do it for money. Welding car bodies on an assembly line is work; washing dishes, computing taxes, walking the rounds in a psychiatric ward, picking asparagus—these are work. Labor, on the other hand, sets its own pace. We may get paid for it, but it's harder to quantify … Writing a poem, raising a child, developing a new calculus, resolving a neurosis, invention in all forms—these are labors. Work is an intended activity that is accomplished through the will. A labor can be intended but only to the extent of doing the groundwork, or of not doing things that would clearly prevent the labor. Beyond that, labor has its own schedule."

Lewis Hyde[2]

The Pursuit of Happiness

We're raised to believe that tasks producing income are work, and anything else is playing. So when we spend our time doing something we don't enjoy, like waiting tables or selling insurance, we're unfulfilled. We feel that our work is distracting us from our true calling. Throughout our monotonous workday, we long to rush home and labor at our side projects and creative pursuits: our passions. We hear speeches and read articles that fuel the fire to quit our jobs and pursue our passion. We search desperately for ways to do what we love and have it be our primary source of income. So we tear off that apron, slam it on the table, yell "I quit" and go home to open a graphic design business.

And then six months later we're on food stamps.

Maybe that's a bit harsh, but it happens. The reason for failure probably wasn't a lack of passion or even a lack of talent. Most likely, it was a lack of income. Reconciling something we've always done for fun to our financial livelihood isn't easy. The truth is that most people who set out to make money pursuing their passion end up disillusioned, disappointed, and underemployed.

But why?

Get Your Mind Right

In the words of Young Jeezy, "you gotta get ya mind right." A creative job will follow you everywhere you go. Being a garbage man or customer service rep isn't likely to do so. You finish your work and you go home, there is no "labor." We need garbage men, but "if we believe that personal fulfillment is really the ultimate purpose of labor, then who do we expect to do all the other jobs that are not so existentially fulfilling?"[3]

Garbage men and customer service reps aren't defined by their jobs. The garbage man may be an incredible woodworker on the weekends and the customer service rep a great jazz singer at local clubs. Neither of them may harbor a desire to make a living at their creative pursuit. For them, a job is a job, and love is love. "It makes it seem like work is a very important if not primary source of love, and if you aren't deriving pleasure from your work that there's something wrong with you or something wrong with the choices you've made in your life—I absolutely reject that."[4]

You don't have to turn your passion into your career, but if you're going to do so, know that there are challenges along the way. Turning your passion for creative into a bad business will suck out every ounce of joy. But that's what we're here to fix, so don't be sad! I promise, I'll put you on the back of a magical unicorn that's riding through candy mountain—you just have to climb on.

If you get into this line of work because you believe it's going to fulfill you or give your life meaning, prepare for war.

The pursuit of passion and great work is part of finding happiness in a creative business. The key is to change your approach and let the passion come from the work.
"Don't follow your passion, follow your effort."[5] If you get into this line of work because you believe it's going to fulfill you or give your life meaning, prepare for war. It's hard to be financially stable and find meaning from a creative business unless you learn to treat the work as a deliverable. You're only a few pages in, so there's still time to run away. If, however, you're still with me, I want to help you do what you feel you must do and make a decent living along the way.

You, Defined

In "When You're At the Crossroads of Should and Must," artist Elle Luna asks a profound question, "what if who we are and what we do become one and the same? What if our work is so thoroughly autobiographical that we can't parse the product from the person? What if our jobs are our careers and our callings?"[6] Your life as "you," the person and your creative life are then one and the same. The work is the outcome of your efforts, so it is your energy and your time being traded for an end product. You are the equipment, the tool, and the machine. Just like a factory, if a piece of equipment is used at full speed without rest, maintenance, and care, it will break. Getting to a place where we can relax and enjoy the fruit of our labor means being smart about how we work.

"A master in the art of living draws no sharp distinction between his work and his play; his labor and his leisure; his mind and his body; his education and his recreation. He hardly knows which is which. He simply pursues his vision of excellence through whatever he is doing, and leaves others to determine whether he is working or playing. To himself, he always appears to be doing both."

L. P. Jacks[7]

Business in the Front, Creative in the Back

What stands out among my successful creative colleagues is a dedication to the creative work and business operations that run in parallel. They are intentional about their day, week, month, and year as a business owner first, then a creative. They're focused and tactical. When things go wrong, they aren't lost without a map. They've developed systems and methods for working through the inevitable creative and business challenges. Those systems, as boring as they may sound, won't stifle the creative fire. In fact, they make it possible to keep it burning for years to come.

In a creative business, misguided passion can be poison. Holding too tightly to your vision, your design, and your opinion can cost you clients, money, and personal peace. In the past, if your creative pursuits were just for play, the pressure was off. Now, it's what keeps the lights on. Your attitude regarding your creative work changes when it becomes your job; it's unavoidable. You have to become pragmatic, which doesn't come easy for many creatives. Pragmatism means using success and experience to determine what works. It means being practical, which at times is the opposite of passionate.

It's Just Business, Baby

Business, business, business. There, you said it. Your creative endeavor is a business, through and through, whether you're working on the side for a few hours a week or full-time.

No matter how and when you start, having the business mindset from day one is critical for longevity.

But what is a business mindset?

- **Strategic thinking**. It's knowing what you want, what you need, and how you're going to get it. It's being intentional with your time, energy, and resources to move your business forward rather than reacting to whatever comes your way.

- **Making money.** You have to earn money to keep a business open. There are a lot of ways to make money in your business, but the most common is to exchange your time and effort for client revenue. So you have to be strategic about where money is going to come from. It also means you intend to be profitable.

- **Having a vision.** You're getting away from mundane tasks and finally doing something you enjoy, so don't muck it up by doing a bunch of mundane tasks! Dedicate time on a regular basis to think about where your business is going long-term and how your daily decisions affect that vision.

- **Marketing**. You have to talk about what you do to people who may hire you to do that thing. That may be in person, online, or through other media channels.

- **Being uncomfortable**. You will have to make sacrifices to keep your business growing. Being willing to make business decisions, fueled by pragmatic thinking, can be the difference between success and failure.

So, here's your first hard truth: this shit is hard. It never gets easy. There may be times when things are going well, and all seems right. Enjoy it, because darkness can and will come. You can't avoid every single pitfall that comes from owning a small business; it's impossible. Success and sustainability come from mitigating risk and lessening the impact. Think of it as wearing a bulletproof vest but still getting shot. Above all, you have to create the maximum opportunity for optimism. The more control you have over the business side of things, the less panic you'll feel when things go wrong.

Sold Out, Not Selling Out

How do you find the balance between doing great work and making money? And not just some money, not just enough money, but the money you need to find your level of happiness and fulfillment? Money doesn't equal happiness, I believe that. But I can tell you that barely making it from month to month doesn't equal happiness either.

Holding yourselves up by the bootstraps for years on end will result in your feet falling off.

Some artists wear perpetual financial struggles on their sleeve like a badge of honor. Small design shops shake their heads at the big conglomerate agencies. No self-respecting web designer or developer would work with Microsoft products! There is a beauty in the bootstrap culture that prevails in our industry today, but holding yourselves up by the bootstraps for years on end will result in your feet falling off. At some point, you have to let go and start walking the walk.

How would it feel to be as passionate about business growth as you are about the creative work?

You should never start a business by purely thinking about the financials. Most of us started this because we had kick-ass band posters on our wall, we got our hands on a copy of *Made You Look,* or we finally realized that Massimo Vignelli and Milton Glaser may not have been from this planet. That passion for creating something amazing is innate in the creative soul; the passion for making money doing it is, if anything, the antithesis of creative passion.

Those who focus on the fundamentals are the most likely to get noticed and get to keep creating good work indefinitely. The hardest thing I had to realize is that I am not, and never will be, the best designer in the world; I'm not even the best designer in my zip code! There are some people who are so talented that work will find them. For the rest of us, we're not going very far if no one knows who we are. Getting that recognition, and the clients and cash that come with it, starts with focusing on the business first.

It's No Longer a Hobby

Once you get started, it's important to be clear with everyone whom you interact with, that this is your job. As you transition into working full-time in your creative business, "the work" and "your work" collide. In the past, there's most likely been a difference. For some, there are personal projects that you do on the side—maybe for a freelance client—and then the work you do at your day job. Your creative work that is now your business felt like an escape from your day-to-day when it was "personal work." Now *that* work is your day-to-day grind.

It's critical that you establish escapes from what was, in the past, your hobby. It sounds insane, I know, but you can't sustain a lasting love with creative client work without an external outlet. That may mean something that is different from your creative roles such as music or writing. Your family and relationships are not those outlets. For the creative mind to thrive, you need constant growth and that only comes from external pressure.

Some of my most successful creative friends' hobbies include surfing, gardening, triathlons, go-kart racing, teaching yoga, and interior decorating. Regardless, it's important to make the time for hobbies early on, even when you're in those sleepless start-up days. The quality of your work will suffer if the type of creative work you perform in your daily business is all that you do, all the time. I can tell you from personal experience, it's exponentially harder to wedge in a hobby once you've gotten used to giving your business every waking hour.

Every Project is a Transaction

It's also important to treat every project as a business deliverable. Even the simplest things, such as a quick polish on a past project or throwing together a one-page flier for a friend's small business, should be treated as a business transaction. It goes without saying that you should bill for all of your work, but even more importantly you have to treat every client, regardless of size, as a business customer. When you're freelancing on the side, you throw together things for friends. I often did mini sites for friend's tiny business ideas or whipped up small flyers for local non-profits free of charge—it's a good way to get practice and to establish yourself in the community. When you decide to turn this into your real, income-generating business, there are no more hobby projects. We'll cover *pro bono* work later; there is a time and place for it, but it can't be all the time.

To this day, when working for a close friend or family member (which I don't rec-ommend), I do provide discounts and have even bartered for work a couple of times. It should be rare because it's rarely fun or successful. Just as you wouldn't walk into your friend's business and ask them to give you their time or product for free, neither should they ask that of you. There are always exceptions, but, above all, make it clear to those around you that this business is how you make a living, and you charge for it; it's no longer your hobby.

Another Creative Business? Really?

So you may be asking yourself if you should be adding yet another web design firm or blog to the world at large. My answer will always be "yes, you should." Most peo-ple who are starting a new business are doing so because they believe they can do something unique. The problem is that the word "unique" has been hijacked. The better word is "distinctive," which means "characteristic of one person or thing, and so serving to distinguish it from others." The difference is that it revolves around the characteristics rather than the action. You don't have to have an original idea, but you have to be an original person. There is no other "you" in this world; you're the only one. So "you" are what's unique. You, the unique individual, can be found at the center of a business much like thousands of others and create something truly special.

"Nobody gets to be you, except you. Nobody has your point of view, except you. Nobody gets to bring to the world the things that you get to bring to the world—uniquely get to bring to the world—except you. So saying there are enough writers out there, enough directors out there, enough people with a point of view—well, yeah, there are—but none of them are you, none of this them is going to make the art that you're going to make, none of them will change people and change the world in the way that you could change it. So if you believe somebody who says, 'No, no, we've got enough of those,' then all it means is you're giving up your chance to change the world the way only you can change it."

Neil Gaiman[8]

Don't worry about whether you'll be able to compete in your market and if there are too many businesses doing the same thing in your zip code. If your desire is to move to an underserved area and open a web design shop in a small community in Montana, then please do so. Everyone deserves good design. But don't let the fact that you live in Austin or San Francisco, where you'll find a creative business on every corner, keep you from bringing your distinctive offering to the world.

There's Plenty of Room, So Jump In

Stephen Covey coined the phrase "abundance mentality"[9] to contrast the "scarcity mindset," which is the prevalent school of thought when it comes to founding a business. The idea of scarcity means that if someone else wins, you lose. So if they're getting clients, you're losing those same clients. The abundance mindset, in which there are plenty of resources and successes to share with others, is alive and well in the creative industry. There simply aren't enough good creatives out there to take on the millions of projects that need help. Everything needs good content, design, coaching, and marketing. There's quite possibly no end to the amount of work awaiting us!

So, if you predicate your business strategy on being exclusive, you've already lost. Services are almost impossible to protect from competition and copying. No matter your idea's originality or difficulty in execution, if it's good, someone else will find a way to duplicate it. You may be the first to market, but that won't protect you from being surpassed by the competition. No one can duplicate your individual personality. The more of "you" found in your business, the more distinctive it will be. The bonus is that you'll love it so much more when it feels like a part of who you are.

Recalibration Isn't Forever

As I shared in my story, I had to strip my business down to the foundation to find the cracks. What I found was a business started out of passion, but running with a complete lack of direction. The change in mindset to business first, creative second was hard to swallow. It felt wrong for quite some time, but it saved my life. My work is better than before because I have so much more freedom to work on meaningful pursuits. I can spend more time getting projects right because I'm charging clients more. Most importantly, I enjoy what I do because I'm not always struggling to find out from where my next project is coming. I feel the freedom to make mistakes, say no to work that isn't interesting, and to pursue work about which I feel passionate.

I know what it's like to take this approach, to strip away the love and the passion. You don't have to do that forever, just long enough to recalibrate your approach to your creative business. Sometimes the truth hurts, but in the end it's worth it.

Notes

1. http://explore.brainpickings.org/post/37916180672/i-flew-the-atlantic-because-i-wanted-to-if-that.
2. Lewis Hyde, *The Gift: Creativity and the Artist in the Modern World.*
3. Miya Tokumitsu, http://jamesshelley.net/2014/03/do-what-you-love/.
4. Miya Tokumitsu, http://jamesshelley.net/2014/03/do-what-you-love/.
5. Mark Cuban, http://blogmaverick.com/2012/03/18/dont-follow-your-passion-follow-your-effort/.
6. Elle Luna, https://medium.com/@elleluna/the-crossroads-of-should-and-must-90c75eb7c5b0.
7. *Education through Recreation.*
8. http://neil-gaiman.tumblr.com/post/37350257826/advice-to-aspiring-artists-this-is-very-short.
9. Stephen Covey, *The 7 Habits of Highly Effective People.* Habit number 4.

CHAPTER 2

W-4

1099-MISC

ROOKIE OF THE YEAR

BUSINESS DEBIT CARD

CLIENT MEETING RECEIPT

PAPERLESS BANK STATEMENT

PUSHING THE START BUTTON

ATTORNEY FEES

CPA DOCUMENT

DBA APPLICATION

LIBRARY CARD, JUST BECAUSE

CLIENT CONTRACT

BANK STATEMENT

You'll Never Be Ready, But Do It Anyway

Big changes are never easy—whether it's changing careers, opening a business, having a child, or jumping out of an airplane. At some point, you either do it or you don't. If this is important to you, if you really want to start, then just start. There is no better time than today.

" Start before you're ready" Steven Pressfield[1]

The first step is to determine that this is, in fact, your job now. You've chosen a creative career, and it's no longer a hobby. Starting today, you're a professional. This chapter is your step-by-step playbook for starting your business. Here's what we'll cover:

- How to start

- When to start

- How to build relationships

- How to get your first clients

- Business plans, education, and documents

- Your professional helpers: accountants, attorneys, bankers, and insurance brokers

- Where to work

- The difference between freelancing and small business

- Lessons learned on starting and rebuilding

How to Start

Dive in Head First, But Wear a Helmet

The easiest way to start your creative business is just to start selling your services. If you don't have a job or you have few financial obligations, there's no reason to wait. It is as simple as getting some business cards and a website and selling your services to clients. If you can get someone to give you money to do something creative for them, you've got a creative business. The complete lack of barriers to entry is what makes creative life so attractive.

Yes, there are tons of financial and legal steps you need to take, and we're going to break all of them down. But, you can work on the legal and financial side of things while you're finding clients. Just don't go out and sign a huge client without taking the steps to secure your business. You can sort out the rest while you're building your brand. Step one is to tell people you're in business and available for work.

Are You Ready to Do the Side Hustle?

The side hustle is how I started. It's a dance-oriented way of saying "a job on the side." You've got a job, maybe even a semi-creative job, that pays your rent and keeps the fridge stocked. Walking away from that job to start a creative business with no clients, no portfolio, and no idea what you're doing sounds like suicide. For some, it can be; for others, it's the only way they'll ever start. Either way, starting out "on the side" or as a side-hustle is the prevailing advice for transitioning into a creative career. Why? Because you need to know that you can make money at this before you fully commit.

This isn't exclusive to creatives, I have a good friend with a stable job who wanted to open a pastry shop. She started baking out of her kitchen at night and on weekends, selling at farmers' markets and making deliveries on her lunch break, and eventually she moved into her pastry business full-time and quit her job. I've had friends do the same with everything from iPhone apps to custom woodworking to family counseling. If you want it, you'll put in the work to make it happen.

How Long Should It Take?

Typically, this means you ramp up your business on the side while working your current job, probably at night and on weekends. The goal is to grow your side hustle to a level that replaces your regular income, or at least enough to warrant making the switch.

Discussing his move from one creative endeavor to the next, Sean McCabe says, "once you've gained momentum and traction in that area, you can start to phase out your previous job gradually. Every vocational transition for me has been a slow process where I have been working on that pursuit for some years in my nights and weekends first."[2]

It may take years of side hustling to get out of your job and into your business full-time. You may take a lighter "day job" to focus on the creative business more, but still not be in a position for it to be your only source of income. The more baggage you carry, the more difficult the switch will be. If you have a mortgage, children, debt, or other responsibilities, it's going to be hard. You and only you can decide when to take the leap.

There is no magic number that will tell you when to make your move. We will, however, break down some guidelines for how you could move from side hustle to full-time in the next section.

When to Start

Some of us are "lucky" and are pushed off the cliff into full-time creative work. Maybe you're laid off from your job, fired, or your pay is cut. The rest of us have to decide when to take the chance and quit our jobs. For me, it was terrifying. Walking away from a stable salary, retirement funds, and top-notch health benefits wasn't easy. But I did it, and I'm so glad that I did.

Signs It May Be Time to Make the Move

- When you have so much business in your side hustle that you can't take on any other work

- You have more prospects interested in working with you, and you can't serve the ones you have

- You're making close to enough money in your side hustle to get by without your day job income

- You're working so many hours that you can't physically go any further, yet the creative business is what you want more than financial assurances

- You've saved enough money on which to live for a while as you get more work

No matter the sign, the feeling of bending at the block, of being at the starting line, gets the butterflies going, and the sweat starts to pour. "Is it time? Do I start now? Am I ready?"

Enough to Start

There is no perfect formula, but you're asking yourself, "okay, but when do I actually start?" The best guideline is when you have enough money so that you can pay your bills and get by for at least two or three months. It doesn't have to be all cash. It can be a combination of bank balance/savings, invoiced work that has checks coming your way, and contracts on the books that will pay out in that timeframe as long as you complete the work. If you need $4,000 a month to get by, can you come up with $12,000 over the next ninety days? If so, you're ready.

How to Quit Your Job

Quit your job with grace, respect, and honesty. Don't burn bridges. Believe it or not, I ended up doing freelance work for my old employer a few years after I left. Had I left on bad terms, that wouldn't have been possible. It's also possible that current co-workers may end up becoming clients or referral partners down the road as they move on to different jobs. If anything, keeping them as connectors in your network is just one more person that can help you get to potential clients. Once you've made the decision to move into your business full-time, be open and honest with your employer.

Hopefully, you're not violating any non-compete agreements or taking any intellectual property with you, but you do need to be forthright in your reason for departure. If you work at Starbucks or a shoe factory, they probably don't care. But if you're in a job where your co-workers and supervisor will continue to be LinkedIn connections and are in your local business community, it's best to tread lightly.

You may have stocks or retirement accounts tied to your employer. Typically you can move them to free-standing accounts with the same service providers your employer is using. You may even be able to continue making contributions from your small business. It's best to get the advice of a financial advisor, but at the very least find out from the HR department at your employer who you need to contact to learn more.

If you plan to take any work or clients with you, be sure that you can legally do so. You're better off facing the awkward conversation with your boss now than in a courtroom. The same goes for equipment, software, or tools. Often these are licensed to your employer and aren't yours to keep.

Build Relationships Before You Start

Hopefully, you're not in a situation where you have to be publicly discreet about your goal to quit your day job. I've had friends who were already creatives and employed full-time striking out on their own, so letting everyone know that they were planning to do so was impossible. In that case, you can still build trust with others outside of work and find out who can support you in the transition. Get them to help you line up possible clients.

However, if you can be open about your plans to leave, please do so. Start networking and build your book of business so that you've got clients lined up. Mark a target date and push to get as much work as possible as you get closer to that date.

Getting Your Next Client Fast

Many small service-oriented businesses fail within the first several months, and that momentum you have from your initial orders quickly dies as you work to fill them. So filling your pipeline has to be a primary focus—up to half of your time—right after you start.

Go after one type of client initially. Casting a wide net won't work. Instead, focus on particular client markets and networks, such as healthcare or legal, to maximize closing projects fast.

Get booked through staffing firms. Staffing firms aren't for everyone, and you lose some of your pay to their fees, but they can find substantial work for you quickly. It's okay to combine staffing agency work with direct client work as well, even if they need you to be onsite with the client.

Work for other creatives or large ad agencies. One of the easiest ways to get creative work when you first start is to work for other creatives. They may be overbooked, and they may need your skill set since it replicates their own. You may be cheaper than they are, and they need to make a little markup on a lower-cost project. They are also much less concerned with your existing body of work and thus more likely to give you a shot.

Use job boards. Don't wait for client work to come to you; go out and find it as you build your network. Having a portfolio, and being able to articulate your reasoning behind your work, are most important in getting hired from job boards. If you don't have any clients, you're only out the time it took to respond to the post. You're learning what others are looking for, and if they're kind enough to send a rejection, you're getting valuable feedback from the people who will eventually hire you. **AuthenticJobs.com** is our job board of choice.

Ask your mom's friends. Seriously, ask your personal network to connect you with their friends and family who fit your target audience. It's not sleazy, it's business. If you can't ask relatives, then you certainly can't ask strangers. Get used to it.

Write and share. If three people read something you wrote on Medium or another website, that's three people who didn't know about you before. Unless you go on a reality show, audiences don't happen overnight. You have to build them. You don't have to wait until you have numerous clients or awards to start writing. If anything, write questions. Go on Quora or Reddit where your peers and potential clients hang out and ask questions. If they see your name, and then you ask them for something later, that connection could result in them responding vs. hitting delete.

Do *pro bono* **work**. Working for free when you're in need of clients, and otherwise sitting around, can be a smart move. The key is to get something instead of financial payment for it. Make it clear what you can do, how much you can work, and set expectations in writing. Don't just drift along working aimlessly for free at the client's whim. Get a commitment from them that they'll supply feedback and a testimonial in the end and possibly referrals. If it's a non-profit, ask if you can present the work to their board and meet the board members (who will likely be prospective target clients). Make sure they know what you charge, and that you wish to become a paid vendor as they grow. If they don't have funds, offer to help them find ways to get funding to pay you such as helping them do creative work for their grants or presentations. Only do free work for clients who are your exact target type such as healthcare or legal. If you're interested in doing work in the healthcare space, it probably doesn't make sense to do a children's clothing website pro-bono.

Do I Need a Business Plan?

The standard advice is to devise a business plan with projections and forecasts before you get too far along. I had spent months on my business plan before I moved from side hustle to full-time creative. While it was a valuable exercise to determine what it was going to take to build a business, it was wholly unnecessary. I do believe you need to know what kind of business you want to make, but it's premature to expect a creative to forecast where they'll be in three to five years.

I applied for bank loans when I started, which required the business plan. I didn't use the money wisely and shouldn't have had it. If possible, don't take on debt at all when you start out. At most, you need computers and a place to work, and a credit card should be adequate for those purchases. Anything significant enough to require a bank loan can most likely wait.

A basic roadmap won't hurt. You can build one by asking yourself a few simple questions:

• Do I want to have the maximum flexibility or a higher income?

• Do I want to have partners or peers that sit at the ownership level someday?

• Do I want to have full-time employees and create a company culture?

- Do I want to work from home always or am I more interested in having an office?

- What would make me want to stop working in the business?

- What would it take for me to walk away from the business for something "better"? How would that look?

- How long do I want to do this?

You don't have to buy a template or do financial projections; this can be a few pages in your notebook or a simple journal entry you write to yourself with your fiscal and creative goals. It doesn't have to be a formal business plan that fits the standard template used by franchises and car washes.

Do I Need to Go to School or Get a Degree?

For most of the careers that we call creative, not everyone has a certification or degree. You may decide to pursue an undergraduate degree in a liberal arts school, or there may be some courses you can take online. You may attend a private, for-profit art school. Those paths are a great way to go if you're able. I came into creative through self-guided learning. I thought I wanted to do something completely different when choosing a college major.

Unlike medicine or law, there is no board of review to determine who is and is not qualified to be a creative. There may be a piece of paper or an organization you can join that says "I know what I'm doing" by taking a test to prove your aptitude. But those carry little weight in the direct-to-client world of creative services. Even with art degrees in hand, we often shift our focus from what we studied, such as photography, to something that grabs us, such as illustration. For our creative careers, many of us simply started doing it one day.

If your goal is to work at a large agency or inside a corporation, a degree could be crucial. Not all organizations can hire based on a portfolio. While some publications hire writers based on samples, it's unlikely that the most venerable newspapers are hiring many people without journalism degrees. There's something to be said for learning the fundamentals of your craft from an academic professor. I hate to admit that I didn't read *Meggs' History of Graphic Design* until I'd been practicing for almost seven years.

If it means taking on $150,000 in student loans to get a degree, you have to decide if it's worth it.

Art school can be expensive, and the added pressure of student loans when you're first starting your creative business, can be a heavy burden. The best answer is that you need to do what feels right for you. "Making a college degree standard for artists just creates a barrier of entry for people who can't afford them."[3] If it means taking on $150,000 in student loans to get a degree, you have to decide if it's worth it. If you do take on those loans, you should be prepared to work for someone else at an agency or company for a while to pay your debt. You don't need a degree to start, and it shouldn't hold you back from pursuing your dream right now, but if you can afford an education, it's not going to hurt.

Who You Need (Your Services Army)

Protecting yourself, your assets, and your family (not to mention your clients) is important. "You" the person and "you" the business are two separate entities and there are certain steps you should take to make the separation clear. It means assembling a small army of service professionals to help you along the way. It's the one thing that you should try to do before you make significant income as a creative. If you have zero seed money to start with, then plan to pull a portion of the income from your first few jobs to pay for hiring your professional service advisors.

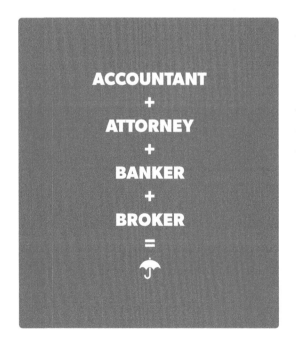

Finding these four critical partners shouldn't be left to search engines. Ask your friends and colleagues who they use for these services. They don't have to be fellow creatives, just small business owners. You're entrusting your business to each of these partners, so you'll want someone who's proven their worth with your trusted contacts.

Service Soldier #1: Your Accountant

Hire an accountant first. Don't wait until you need to file taxes or can't handle your books anymore to hire one. Most accountants for small businesses will work on a flat rate or hourly, without the need for expensive retainers. You don't need to hire a major accounting firm. There are work-from-home small business accountants or multi-service shops that will fit your budget. There are even some accountants who specialize in working with creative service professionals only.

Your accountant will save your ass more times than you can possibly imagine. From filing paperwork on time to advising you on what you can and can't do with that car you are trying to justify as a business expense, they are your first line of defense against later headaches. Most small business accountants are almost like a part-time CFO. They can advise you on the ins and outs of purchases, write-offs, and when to hire your first employee.

Finding an accountant is not hard, but finding the right one may be a process. Each accountant has their own style and spin on certain deductions and methods. My first accountant was very aggressive, and while I like to push close to the line, he was too much for my comfort. My current accountant isn't conservative, but she pulls me back more than I push her. It's important to find someone you trust and enjoy working with because they will have access to your books—how you spend, live, and behave.

You may have to file annually to register your business with your local or state/provincial government plus your municipality. You should have a business license in most cities but for services work it gets a bit gray. It's best to speak with your accountant about what's best for you and your business type. Sales tax in the USA or VAT in Canada and similar taxes in Europe also get dicey with services. For most American creative businesses that aren't selling a physical product, sales taxes aren't required, but it's becoming more common for individual cities and states to enforce them. Having an accountant who understands your business and what you're actually doing can accurately advise you on what to collect on which services.

My accountant serves as my bookkeeper as well. You can hire a bookkeeper separately, but I want my accountant to know everything coming in and out at all times. Even with powerful online accounting tools like Xero, Less Accounting, and Quickbooks Online, I couldn't keep up. I think most of us still need the guidance of an accounting professional to help make decisions big and small. It's a complete waste of your time to do this sort of work when you can spend a few hundred dollars a quarter to have a professional do it for you in a tenth of the time. Hiring a bookkeeper can give you back ten hours a month.

However, don't simply hand over your books and ignore them. Meet with your accountant at least quarterly and always check your books at least once a month. I have had friends completely misread what was going on and be shocked by tax bills, litigation, and other issues because of failing to communicate with their accountant.

Do your own invoicing or at least have your accountant copy you on all invoicing and communication. Using apps like Harvest or FreshBooks to know your cash flow situation is necessary for staying on top of your business. Devote an hour or so each week to reviewing the reports and sending your accountant a note with any questions.

Service Soldier #2: Your Attorney

Establish a business entity rather than conducting business as an individual. Many freelancers operate as an individual rather than a business. In the USA that's often a 1099 contractor. While freelancing is okay, it's not entirely safe until you separate your operations and finances. In the United States, it really is about a number. You, the person, have a social security number and you, the business, will have a tax ID number. That needs to happen quickly for your protection and growth potential.

In the USA, we have a few different setups for small businesses with the most common being an LLC or Limited Liability Corporation. There's also the S-Corp (Sub-Corporation), which is very similar. With both types of entity, the owner(s) of the business are responsible for paying any applicable income taxes the business incurs as individuals on their personal tax return. It creates a layer of insulation between you and your clients or customers. In the event that something goes wrong, and your business is sued or faces financial damages, the business is held accountable instead of you, the person. This means if you are sued, they can't take your house or first-born from you.

Many solo creatives establish Sole Proprietorships. They're easy to establish, but oh so dangerous for services work. There is no legal separation between you and the business and in the event that the business faces any legal action or financial hardship, you—and everything you own—are in jeopardy. There are some tax advantages that accountants will bring up with this entity, but they just aren't worth the risk.

Don't stress about finding the perfect name before filing. You can call your business Judy Smith, Inc. for now. It's a simple set of forms to establish a DBA (Doing Business As) name once you come up with a catchy marketing-savvy name and logo.

Most attorneys will require a retainer of at least $500 to $1,000 to start. You may not have that in the bank. For your incorporation, especially if it's just you and no partners or property are involved, it's perfectly okay to use a service like Legal Zoom. You can always have your incorporation paperwork amended or adjusted by an attorney as your revenue grows.

An attorney can help you with contracts and agreements, both in preparation and in the unfortunate event that you enter litigation with a client or contractor. Having an attorney you can call upon when things go South is helpful. If you are creating work that needs copyright protection, hiring an intellectual property or copyright attorney is also essential.

If a particular project calls for unusual help from a lawyer, build the cost of your attorney's services into your client costs. Using an agent, especially for illustrators or photographers, can cover this base somewhat but you should still have an attorney on call. Your agent is not your lawyer; you still need someone who is sworn to be on your side.

Service Soldier #3: Your Banker

The very first payment you get for any creative services work should go in a separate bank account. Even if you haven't set-up a business entity yet, separate your business income and your personal income from day one in a separate checking account. As soon as you do have a legal entity established, getting a business account is very easy with almost any bank. It requires a few forms, a small deposit, and an hour or less of your time. You will save yourself, and your accountant, endless headaches by having everything separate.

Also, get a separate credit card, debit card, and check book for your business and use them only for business. The biggest challenge most creatives face is having enough money to run the business and live. Your personal account has $30 in it, your business account has $300 and you need to buy groceries; so you just use the business debit card until you can pay yourself. No, no, no! Not only can this get you in tremendous tax trouble, but it's just bad form. You may be the sole owner and employee of your business, but you still have a job and an employer. You must pay yourself as an employee and operate separately. Avoiding the mixed up accounts is a combination of living within your means, paying yourself and your taxes before your bills, and other tactics we'll cover later on.

Work with a bank that allows you to actually meet a human who isn't two lollipops shy of jumping off a bridge. Local credit unions or community banks are much nicer to small business owners. I love the mobile deposit tools of the big banks, but over time working with a community bank outweighs the inconvenience of depositing checks in person. Having a business checking and savings account also allows your business to build its credit. That means you won't have to use your personal credit down the road if the business needs a loan for office space, materials, or lines of credit against invoices.

Your banker meets other business owners all day, most of them starting new businesses or growing existing ones. Often their customers are in need of your services. Your banker can be one of your best referral partners by recommending you to those business customers. I've had this happen several times. Needless to say, my business banker gets a holiday basket every year.

Paying yourself doesn't have to go through a payroll service, it can just be an electronic transfer between accounts. You will need to pay taxes quarterly, but your accountant can handle this with forms and services. Only when you have employees or contractors should you look into the added expense of a payroll service. If you do need it, using your bank's basic services is typically enough.

As you grow, one alternative to expensive HR systems is co-employment. This means that you and your employees join a large "corporation" of other small business owners who share health insurance groups and payroll services. You then have access to the same tools and rates as Fortune 500 companies without the astronomical fees. We've been using co-employment for a few years, and it's been great for our employees when it comes to expanding families and getting mortgages.

Service Soldier #4: Your Insurance Brokers

Insurance, at least for health, is critical for your long-term protection. Depending on your country of residence, health insurance can be very simple or exorbitantly complex. In the USA, it's downright enigmatic.

Insurance brokers are free to you, they make their money from insurance commissions, so don't try to figure out your insurance on your own—get help. Health insurance brokers help you review and compare plans to find the best fit for your needs. They handle all of the paperwork and research and present you with options for which you qualify. You can buy insurance directly from providers, but the savings aren't always guaranteed. There's also the option of marketplaces and exchanges, which do a great job of comparing plans available to you. Brokers use tools very similar to the marketplace, but I prefer having that extra layer of advice readily available.

If you are providing any creative services, you need General Liability (GL) and Errors & Omissions (E&O) insurance. You'll purchase this through a Commercial Insurance Broker. Insurance will protect you if you're sued for negligence, as in you did something wrong, and your client's business is now suing you for it. GL insurance can also protect you if you are sued by employees or contractors. Policies also provide insurance for your equipment and assets. If something's damaged, lost, or stolen, it can be replaced. Two years ago, coffee was spilled on my MacBook Pro at a shop. It fried the computer within hours. I made one call to my insurance company, drove to the Apple store, bought a new computer and, less a $500 deductible, I had a brand new computer in my hands that same day.

Usually a business insurance broker and a health insurance broker are not the same persons, but you may get lucky and find someone who handles both. Regardless, don't put off insurance, it's as critical as your internet or cell phone bill for running your business.

Where to Start (Finding a Home)

For many, the holy grail of creative life is working anywhere, any time, any way. There is an entire movement of suitcase entrepreneurs whose sole motivation is building a business that allows them to be nomadic. The biggest perk of being able to fit your entire toolkit on your back, literally in a backpack, is that you can do it anywhere. As with anything in creative business, there are pros and cons. The flexibility truly does breed freedom, but it makes it exponentially more difficult to keep a schedule and build a local network.

If your dream is to be truly able to work anywhere in the world and any schedule you want, you can have it. That is the honest truth; there are many people living it to the fullest extent. However, you will have to make some concessions. It's possible you'll need to do more production work and be at the mercy of talent scouts or agents. Bloggers and product providers—those who have a paying customer base rather than services clients—are more likely to build a substantial living as a nomad.

If you're running a local creative shop, one that sticks to a certain city where you live and have a permanent residence, there is still a tremendous amount of freedom. For many, the idea of the "freelance designer" at the hipster coffee shop screams "unemployed." Truth be told, as a partner in a very successful design shop, I'm writing these exact words from a coffee shop overlooking a gorgeous rushing river while wearing a t-shirt, jeans, and sneakers; I know that the majority of the people on the street behind me are rushing to and from meetings in heels and suits.

With that freedom, there are still downsides if you aren't managing your time and resources well. Let's take a look at a few of the ways most creatives work and find some ways to improve performance.

Coffee Shops

Thanks to Starbucks and the craft coffee movement you can find a European-style coffee house even in the smallest town, with free WiFi, comfy seating, power outlets, and the nectar of the gods. I love working from coffee shops just to break out of the office. For the majority of my first few years as a solo business, a few local coffee shops were my desk. I had a small home office for production work and then I conducted all of my meetings at coffee shops. I still go to one at least once a week just to break up the monotony. It's been proven that a change of scenery can boost creativity, so even if you have a fixed office space, it's still an excellent way to get out.

A few keys to working from a coffee shop:

- **Go by on a day you aren't planning to work there.** Are there good spots to work? If not, move along. If you get to a shop, and there are no seats, or the vibe isn't right, leave. Never order your coffee first unless the shop requires you to do so; find your spot before committing to work there.

- **Invest in good headphones.** Get comfortable noise canceling headphones. The money is well worth it. Earbuds won't cut it; get over-ears. You will be very glad you did.

- **Cache your music for offline playback.** If you stream, cache it and store it for offline playback; don't rely on the shop's WiFi for streaming.

- **Preload your tabs.** If you must have certain browser tabs open to complete your work, open them before you get there.

- **Learn to love localhost.** If you program or blog, learn to work on localhost; it makes the sporadic dropping of the signal from coffee shop WiFi bearable.

- **Bring the internet with you.** Buy a personal router to use, like Karma or Freedom Pop, if you must get on WiFi and the shop's connection is bad and tethering isn't working for you.

- **Bring an extension cord.** Bring a long cord or at least the one for your laptop charger that triples the length. I'm serious; you're there to work and no one is going to laugh at you for bringing your own power strip or cord. If you can't find a power outlet to work beside, just ask someone beside one who isn't plugged in if you can switch. Surprisingly most people are cool with this, especially if you're in a local shop where others are also trying to work. Even better, just remember to charge your laptop and phone before you leave your house.

- **Don't be an ass.** Buy more than one cup of coffee and tip generously. I tip at least 50 percent; typically I spend at least $5 and tip at least $5 for a half day or more working at a shop.

- **Make friends.** Share your table if someone is wandering around aimlessly looking for a spot. I have found three freelancers, five or more clients, and one very good friend doing this.

Co-working

A shared office environment, or co-work, is an easy way to move into a regular workspace. Typically you pay a monthly fee, with no contract or long-term commitment, to become a member of the co-work. You may be able to get a private office with a door, but at the very least co-works are semi-private, unlike a public coffee shop. A good co-working space should have all of the trappings of a regular office: conference rooms, a secure place to leave your things, printers, more than one bathroom, reliable WiFi, and power outlets. Many also have free coffee, kitchens, and common areas to hang out and meet other members. You may get lucky like me and work in a spot with free beer, free video games, and free parking.

I still run my entire agency out of a co-working space. We have dedicated offices, but we often find ourselves drifting into the open co-working area or working in the lounge rather than sitting at our desks. Co-working is hands down the greatest thing to happen to the creative class since Twitter. We'll chat more about isolation in Chapter 8, but consider co-working the cure for solitude.

Tips for getting the most out of co-working

Be conversational. Don't be "that guy" and don't give everyone else nicknames like "beard guy" or "giant glasses chick"; actually find out who they are and what they do. While you need to get things done and plug in your headphones, use the water cooler just like you would in a regular corporate office and chat with people.

Hire and get hired by people in the space. Working with people in your co-working space is so much easier than working with remote workers. It feels like you're in the same company. You're building your own local network with much greater ease when you work with people you see regularly.

Get involved and share knowledge. Post on message boards (digital and physical) and let people know what you're up to. Ask for help and referrals from the people around you.

Plug in. When you need to work and focus, plug in just like you're at a coffee shop. The unspoken rule with creatives is "headphones on = door's shut."

Get to know the people who own or run the space. They are the ones who get asked about resources and referrals. For example, the co-work owner may get asked by a designer if anyone there is a PHP programmer. If that's you, the owner will remember you and give them your name.

Leverage conference rooms for your heads-down time. Book them and use them; you don't have to have clients coming in. And if someone really needs it for clients and you've already booked it, switching with them will put them in your debt forever.

Get an external monitor and store it there. It will save your neck, literally. Also use cloud services like Dropbox or Box to store your files so that if you forget a hard drive or your regular computer, you can still get to that important file. Some people even keep a cheap laptop or Chromebook at their co-working space for quick drop-in work.

Be tidy. Clean up after yourself and even clean up after others. Good citizens are heroes.

Don't be creepy. Don't look into other people's spaces, linger behind their monitors, or stare at the cute new member. People are there to work.

Office Space

The day I decided to go into my business full-time and leave my corporate job, I started looking for office space. I found a 1,500 sq. ft. studio in the creative, loft-style part of town. I spent about $20,000 on furniture, equipment, paint, and lighting to get it looking perfect. We bought reasonably priced items from Ikea and similar stores, used inexpensive electronics, and even used non-permanent lighting. We did it "right," or so we thought. That was the single worst mistake I made in the first several years of my creative business.

Even if you are starting from day one with twenty employees, hold off on signing a lease. You don't know what you'll need, so give yourself time to determine where you want to be and what kind of environment you need. But, if you feel you need office space from the start, ask yourself these questions:

- Do I need a dedicated place to work other than my home?

- Do I expect clients to come regularly to my office for meetings and I'm having difficulty finding a place to meet?

- Is there co-working with enough room for my business reasonably nearby?

- Is there another company willing to sub-lease space to me without a long-term commitment?

- Am I sure that I can afford to pay for this place for the next few years?

- Is this the location I want to be in for the next few years?

If you still think you need a dedicated office after going through these points, then try your best to find something that provides maximum flexibility. Get creative with your leasing terms or try to take up the remainder of someone else's lease. Work with a leasing agent and be candid about your situation and expectations.

Working from Home

The home-based office is the most common way to work for creatives. There are rather large creative companies whose entire staff work from their respective homes. There are employees of Fortune 500 companies who telecommute. Working from home has become, for many, the ideal situation. There are reasons ranging from being in a different city than your employer/client, having small children, an unrealistic commute to the nearest co-working space, or a medical condition that would lead someone to desire working from home. For some, it's just that desire to be free and not be told when and how to work.

There are downsides to working from home, some you should know before basing your entire creative business around reaching that goal. It's harder to be focused and productive, it's harder to build relationships with colleagues and clients, it can be lonely and depressing, and it can make you feel like you are always at work. The biggest risk of working from home is becoming sedentary. When it's easier just to work one more half hour rather than get out and go to the gym, you can get unhealthy quickly. It's easier to snack and not control your eating, and it's easy to sleep in because you don't have to "be anywhere" at a particular time.

Almost every creative does some work from home, even if it's not their main office. When you are working from home, you have to treat work as work and not let it meander throughout the day and mingle with your personal life. While I believe that there is no such thing as work/life balance (more on that later), you must set boundaries between your workspace and your life-space.

Tips for working from home

- **Establish a workspace that is only for work.** Even if it's one-half of your dining room table, establish a place where your work tools live and nothing else can go there. Ideally it should be a room with a door, but at the very least find a spot that is for work only. Don't make this the overflow junk room, the spare bedroom, or anything else. Give up what you have to, even if it's a guest room or treadmill, to have a dedicated workspace.

- **Set office hours and a schedule.** Establish a time that you start working and stop working and stick to it. Don't wander through the day doing laundry at 11am or watching SportsCenter or talk shows in the middle of your work day. Get up at the same time, stop at the same time, shower at the same time, go to the gym at the same time. If you are at home with kids, structure your schedule the way you structure theirs.

- **Get dressed.** Yes, the whole life without pants, working naked, PJ patrol world is lovely. It's fun, but after a while it's depressing. We work with Fortune 100 clients all the time, and I rarely dress more formally than t-shirts and jeans. You can be comfortable, but you need to put on clothes you would wear in public. This may be yoga pants or sweats, that's fine, but don't wear what you slept in while you work.

- **Get out of the house every day.** If you're in the suburbs and walking to grab lunch or coffee isn't an option, then get a dog. Get something that makes you open the door and face the sun before you turn into a vampire.

- **Do your client work in the morning.** This is mission critical. Working from home almost always ends up breaking in the afternoon as life bleeds in. Anything that's mission critical to deliver that day, get it done early. If you're a late night worker, then "morning" may mean 1pm, but the first two or three hours of your work day should always be set on what you have to get done.

- **Have a do not disturb system.** Hopefully, your home office has a door that shuts, but it may just be headphones on. If anyone else lives with you, there must be a way for them to know you're not available. Get a whiteboard sticker for your laptop or put a red light on it, hang a flag up above your head on a stick, do whatever you must to tell people you're off limits.

- **Be consistent.** You will work from home in the evenings and on weekends, regardless of where your regular office is located. Stick to the workspace, the work rules, and the do not disturb system even during the extended work hours.

- **Invest in good equipment.** Spend a good chunk of money on a nice chair from a manufacturer like Herman Miller. Get a quality desk that you can adjust to the right height for work. Working on a spare couch isn't the best set-up for the long term.

- **Check into zoning laws for home-based businesses.** Believe it or not, some homeowners or tenant associations won't allow you to run a business from home, even if you aren't seeing clients in your space. You could violate your covenants and be subject to fines or eviction. Your city may also require you to acquire a business license and pay certain taxes. Most creatives ignore this, but as you grow, and people start to know about your home-based business, keep this in mind.

- **Take care of yourself.** Network, exercise, shower, and much more that we'll cover later.

You can interface with clients and work from home. Peleg Top loves to cook for his clients and meet around his breakfast table. My friend Sophia Voychehovski holds strategy meetings in her condo and plays host to her clients. Since she's in the trust-oriented practice of user experience strategy, it lowers emotional walls and makes clients more likely to receive her advice.

It's important to be transparent with clients when you work from home. It's normal, it's nothing to be ashamed of, and it certainly doesn't mean you're small or insignificant. If you have children and it's possible they'll barge in during a conference call, it's best that a client knows up front that you work from home so that it's not a shock. It's common practice to hear barking dogs in the background of almost any conference call I'm on now.

Working from home with kids

If you have kids, which I do and struggle with when trying to work from home, here's a few additional tips:

- **Establish a routine around their schedule.** If your children are small and at home all day, you're likely dealing with naps, meals, and snacks. Be intentional about your work time when they will not need you and focus. Don't use the daytime for household chores. The physical work such as laundry, cleaning, and cooking can be outsourced or done at night. You must feed yourself and wash your clothes, you don't have to work if you don't want to, or at least that's what your brain will tell you.

- **Set boundaries.** Set aside time to play with your children, fill up their tanks, and then get back to work. Teach your children to recognize timers that are audible that signal you have to stop playing and go to work.

- **Get help.** If you're doing this, hopefully, you're making enough money to hire someone to take care of your children even while you're at home. Get an au pair or someone who can play with your children and take care of their needs during the day. Even having one for half days, say from eight to noon, can make a huge difference.

- **Hire a cleaning service.** It's worth every single penny.

- **Get out and work out.** Use the childcare at the gym and work out during the much-needed break time rather than vegging out in front of the TV at night.

- **Bring it to your door.** Use delivery and concierge services as much as possible for everything from groceries to washing your car. Use couriers to pick up packages or mail you need sent out. The less time you spend loading and unloading your children to run errands during the work day, the better.

- **Sleep later.** If you are doing creative work full-time, you may have to switch your sleep schedule to work late nights and sleep later until your children are up.

"My advice to other [parents] who are overwhelmed by starting a business while they have small children at home is that it won't be like this forever. Your kids will be in school before you know it. Your business will grow and change in ways you can't even imagine. It's okay to not accomplish as much as you'd like to as fast as you'd like to—you'll get there eventually!"

Sara Tams[4]

Working from home for teams

If you are part of a team distributed across home offices or a mix of offices and coffee shops/co-working, there are great ways to work from home as a team. There are powerful apps that can connect you in real-time so that you feel like you're in the same room. You can also monitor your team's activity if you have trust issues in whether they are working.

At our company, we have a flexible policy on working from home. We require everyone to be on our chat app, Slack, during the primary business hours of ten to four unless they are heads-down on a client deliverable or have something on their calendar. Otherwise, work where you're happy and productive. Certain teams get together at set times and we certainly have our share of client meetings. Outside of what's on the calendar, we don't care what you wear, when you work, or where you are.

The Truth About Starting

Success is Relative

A creative career doesn't ever have to be all of your income. You can always do this as a side hustle, never going full-time. That's okay. You're not excluded from the creative class if you're a bank teller or stay-at-home mom by day. Side businesses aren't a failure if they never turn into full-time businesses. The same attitude, tips, and suggestions we're discussing apply regardless of the income percentage your creative business provides to your overall lifestyle. Sometimes all you're looking for is an alternative from a perfectly good day job, and that's fine! If you've got a creative hobby that people are willing to pay you for, then why not do it? It doesn't mean you have to quit a perfectly good day job.

Sacrifice

Starting a new business or side hustle means giving up most of your free time. It means late nights, early mornings, and giving up weekends. It may mean giving up TV, video games, exercise, or hobbies. My go-to financial guru, Dave Ramsey, says, "If you will live like no one else, later you can live like no one else." Dave is referring to financial responsibility and getting out of debt, but it's the same for starting a business. If you're willing to suffer for a stretch of time to get your business going, you can reap the rewards of finally doing what you enjoy for the rest of your life.

Getting Your Finances in Order Helps

Try to get your finances in the best shape possible before you start. Having savings and reserves to live on as you ramp up, what most business books call your "runway," can keep you from taking the wrong work at the wrong price.

If you can't get debt-free before starting, sell what you can and make cuts. You may have to live lean when you make the jump. As with the side hustle, the general advice is to have three full months of income put away. For many of us, that may take years to save up and delay starting the business. Just do your best. Even if you have a good stable of clients or customers, living on an irregular income is a big change if you're used to paychecks showing up at the same time for the same amount every month.

Financial clean up is also important because having a strong credit score will come in handy. As you grow, you may need loans or a line of credit. Having an irregular income makes it more difficult to borrow money. If you can get those loans done before you quit your job, do it.

Get as much financial breathing room as you can, but I'd be a hypocrite if I said I did a good job myself. When I started my business, I had over $20,000 in credit card debt from years of bad habits. It did not help with my stress levels.

It's Easier To Develop Habits Before You Start

Work on healthy habits while you're doing the side hustle. You're already giving up your free time, so give up a little more by establishing an exercise and good sleep routine now. Don't choose between sleep or the gym and the side hustle, choose between TV and the bar and the side hustle. The more ingrained the healthy habits are when you're working double time, the easier it will be to keep them when you're pulling all-nighters in your creative business full-time.

Start for the Right Reasons

Starting a creative business should come from a positive place, not from a "get me the hell out of here" situation. If you're starting your creative business because you think that it will be easier or more fun than your current day job, please stop.

Running a creative business is hard; really hard. It never gets easy. The grass isn't greener as a creative business owner if you like paid vacations, nine-to-five, and a secure retirement account. It has to be about wanting to do something so much that you're willing to give up your free time, your money, and your sanity to make it happen. If your heart isn't there yet, I strongly advise you to reconsider quitting your day job right now. Take the time to run your business as a side hustle and see if you love the work when there's money involved.

There is a huge difference between building a friend's website on the side for fun and doing it for a complete stranger who has a timeline and specific requirements in mind.

Karim Boubker created an excellent list of reasons why he decided to work for himself:[5]

- You can work from anywhere.
- You can do work you actually enjoy.
- You will create jobs.
- There are no limits to what you can do and earn.
- You don't have a boss.
- You'll become more mature.
- Your skin will thicken (you'll get tougher).

- You can live out your purpose in life (to create meaningful work).

- Your skills will grow.

- You'll be remembered (creating a legacy).

I think Karim's attitude was in the perfect spot for striking out on his own. There's some dissatisfaction here with the status quo, his day job was "sucking the life out of him," but his motivations were going after a better and more fulfilling career. Doing this isn't all rainbows and butterflies—clients can be difficult —but it's worth it if you want to make it happen. Karim followed up on his post several months later with some additional reasons that included understanding the true value of a dollar, becoming more empathetic, becoming more independent, and losing the fear of failure.

In a Forbes interview with Vanessa McGrady, authors of the fantastic book *The One Thing*, Jay Papasan and Gary Keller, said, "Ask yourself, 'Why is it important to do this? What will it do for you? What will it do for your family? What will it do for the world?'" A person who ventures out on her own will face hard times. Business will go up and down. There will be failures. What helps you ride through them is how you answer the question. Then (when you have your answer) "Write it down. Tattoo it on your back. Don't forget it."[6]

What You Actually Need— The Minimal Starter List

- Laptop, preferably a Mac

- Smartphone

- Internet plan for your Smartphone

- Extra chargers for your Mac and Smartphone

- Good headphones—Sennheiser, Bose, or other noise canceling types

- Good notebooks and pens—Moleskines and Muji

- A bag or backpack to put your laptop, phone, chargers, headphones, notebooks, and pens in

- Accountant, Attorney, Banker, and Insurance Broker

- Business bank account and credit card

- Tax ID and Incorporation, i.e. LLC or S-Corp

- Your brain

Just Push Start

So that's how you start. You just go. Start doing the work and call yourself a designer, illustrator, etc. Tell everyone you encounter that this is your job. There is no 12-step program; there is no ritual or internship or anything else required to make you a creative professional. People give you money to use your skills to do the things that you set out to do; now it's your job. Don't let anyone else tell you to spend months or years spinning your wheels. You've got the skills, the drive, and the tools—now let's get to work.

Notes

1. Steven Pressfield, *Do the Work*.
2. https://www.freelancersunion.org/blog/2014/04/04/how-freelancer-sean-mccabe-made-learn-lettering/.
3. http://99u.com/articles/39523/molly-crabapple-the-best-path-is-the-one-you-build-out-of-your-own-dysfunction.
4. http://ohmyhandmade.com/2011/head/businessy-goodness/balancing-parenthood-running-a-small-business/.
5. http://karimboubker.com/quit-your-job/.
6. http://www.forbes.com/sites/vanessamcgrady/2014/11/03/quit-your-job-start-your-business-a-smarter-way-to-make-the-switch/.

CHAPTER 3

THE HUNT

SALES, MARKETING and GETTING CLIENT WORK

TO MEET YOU :) 3745 ✉

SAVE ME FROM THE INTERNET
SEEKING DESIGN + DEVELOPMENT. INTERESTING + ENGAGING PROJECT. I KNOW YOUR WORTH AND WANT TO DOUBLE YOUR ASKING PRICE. 2030

QUILT DIVA 4 HIRE

DESIRABLE DEPENDABLE DEVELOPER
27, 3.5 GPA, HILARIOUS, EXQUISITE TASTE, EARLY DELIVERY, FAVORITE COLOR IS RUBY. SEEKING LONG-TERM CLIENT WITH DEEP POCKETS. GIVE ME A RING AND I'LL SEND YOU A PROPOSAL. 3090 ✉

9 CATS? MORE LIKE 81 LIVES. CAT FAN SEEKING CAT MAN. ONLY SERIOUS INQUIRIES AND PURRRFECT MATCHES. 227, RIGHT MEOW. ✉

19 AND GIVING UP ON LOVE.
OR AM I? OR AREN'T I? OR AM I?

SEEKING RAP COVER BAND

You've taken the leap and opened up shop, but now you need more work. So what do you do? You go hunting. But hunting isn't just chasing down your next meal. It's strategic. It involves setting up traps, staking out the landscape, and striking when the time is right. If you're running around an open field all day chasing a rabbit, you're going to tire out quickly. And if you're chasing two rabbits, they're both going to get away. Good hunters put the right bait out there, wait for the right prize to come along, and then they act. Are you guys hungry?

It's important to note that the theme of this chapter isn't finding work—it's finding clients. The shift in mindset isn't accidental or trivial. Work is a tactical item: a widget, an end-game. Clients are relationships and engagements. Never view clients as a singular, one-time transaction. Clients hire you to do work, and hopefully they hire you over and over again. Clients are grocery stores; work is food. Seriously, are you guys hungry?

In this chapter, we're going to cover building your marketing machine. But first, let's look a little deeper into what a client is and how those relationships form.

Getting Clients

"The biggest lie … would be if I told you I don't worry about where the next client is coming from. I could tell you that once you build up enough of a portfolio, or garner enough experience, or achieve a certain level of notoriety in the industry, this won't be a concern anymore"

Mike Monteiro[1]

You will always have to find new work. Clients that you have for years can go out of business. Your key contact can move on, and her replacement may bring your competitor with her that pushes you out. The market can shift dramatically, and your skills may be outdated. No matter how famous you get or how many clients you lock in, the search for new work never stops.

Whether you plan to offer direct to client services, work for agencies, go through a staffing service, or sell a product directly to users—you need clients. You can call them clients, customers, users, readers, buyers, or mom. The whole purpose of a creative business is to exchange your services or products for income. The people who give you that income are clients.

Never view clients as a singular, one-time transaction.

The constant hustle to find the next client, or get bigger ones, is the toughest part of the job. After over a decade of direct client work myself, it's still exhausting. However, it's also one of the most exciting and fulfilling aspects of the job. The hunt for that perfect client and the joy of working with a household name is thrilling. Some of my fondest memories of my early creative career are closing clients who seemed out of reach. I remember the high from signing the client far more than the actual work we did for them.

When you acquire a client, you are acquiring someone to whom you are responsible for professional advice and direction for their benefit. You develop a relationship with your client so that you can see to their best interests—and be compensated as a professional for doing so.

Fulfilling creative work cannot thrive if it doesn't come from a place of understanding. The best client–creative relationships flourish when you understand your client's business needs first and then find the right solution. The hunt for clients is far closer to dating than it is to traditional sales. You are seeking relationships—some short-term, some long-term—that will sustain your creative business.

The goal isn't always to get direct clients; it's to build an ecosystem of people who trust you enough to talk about you and refer you. Some of them may become clients eventually. But you can't expect to go to networking events or drop a cold email and walk out with a sale most of the time. It's simply not going to happen. And if it is, it's likely not a quality customer that fits your best interests.

Your marketing machine: a systematic series of relationships, points of engagement, and materials that regularly fill your sales pipeline with new client prospects.

Your marketing ecosystem includes referral relationships, an online presence, an offline (local) presence, specialized markets (verticals and horizontals), and third party validation from peers and clients. Over time, the ecosystem will evolve into a marketing machine: a systematic series of relationships, points of engagement, and materials that regularly fill your sales pipeline with new client prospects. These are your traps in the woods, the things that feed you even when you're not actively hunting. So how do we build that?

Two Sides of Marketing

Inbound Marketing

Inbound marketing is when clients come to you directly. It includes referrals, leads from your website or a portfolio showcase like Dribbble, people who find you through social media, search engines, blog posts, and responses to your "available for work" posts on freelance marketplaces and job sites.

Outbound Marketing

Outbound marketing is going out and getting clients whom you've targeted. When we think of sales, we're typically thinking of outbound marketing. It's not as easy for services, but you can increase the likelihood of closing sales by leveraging your referral relationships. It can be hard to find quality clients via outbound marketing unless you spend significant time qualifying who you contact. Outbound marketing works, and it doesn't have to resemble *The Wolf of Wall Street* or *Glengarry Glen Ross*.

They Work Together

A healthy marketing machine includes both inbound and outbound strategies. They feed one another. It's tough to go very far by only focusing on one side of the equation, so they both need regular attention. Eventually, your inbound strategy can bring in the majority of your work. For some creatives, they can be satisfied with saying "yes" or "no" to requests for work and never "sell" again. For others, you may not be getting the clients you want, even though plenty are reaching out to you. Continuing to work on your outbound strategy, even when you're fully booked, allows you to work with the type of clients you want.

Through inbound marketing, you attract your clients. Your website, blog content you post, and search engine presence, are static. Other parts of your inbound strategy require constant attention. That includes tending to your referral network, your social media presence, and your online reputation.

Outbound marketing is the active hunt for clients. It leverages much of your inbound tools to get you in front of client prospects. First, you go to your referral network to ask for business. Then you contact people you want to work with and direct them to your website or content to validate your qualifications. Finally, you meet with prospects while showing them your work and capabilities.

Building the Machine

Getting your machine up and running isn't linear, but some steps require greater focus early on. You may have a niche client type (healthcare) or niche service type (front-end web animation) from day one. If so, that's great, and it will make your life easier. For those of us who start as generalists, such as web designers or branding consultants, we may not be sure who we want to work with and what we're best at doing.

So while there is no conclusive order to getting things going, it's best to focus on building your machine in roughly the following steps for the first year or two:

1. Referral network

2. Sell yourself/personal brand

3. Online presence (website)

4. Social media

5. Portfolio

6. Content and blogging

7. Email marketing

8. Niche and target marketing

9. Specific skills and horizontal marketing

Now, let's break down each of these steps in detail.

Building Valuable Business Relationships

Referrals come from a network of people who know one another, know what one another does, and have enough trust in one another to introduce them and their services to someone else in their network. It may be a friend, family member, loose acquaintance, co-worker, colleague, or current or past client.

Most of your business will come from referrals. They can come in many forms, not just local contacts introducing you to local contacts. They happen online and through social media as well. When we need a medical specialist, dentist, lawyer, or realtor we often ask our friends and family who they would recommend. In the age of social media, posting "can anyone recommend a good massage therapist" on Facebook will result in quick responses with names, contact info, and testimonials. People do the same thing with creative services. They aren't buying illustration or web design all the time, so when the time comes, they turn to their personal network to find a trusted resource. You want to be a part of that network.

As you build your personal network, you'll be called upon to provide quotes for work and may not have to go through the pitch and bid process. The "get to know you" phase of project submissions is much shorter because the client's network has recommended you.

Some of my best referrals have been to the spouse or relative of a past client. When you do good work and develop a trusting relationship with your clients, they are even willing to refer you to their spouse! Think about that for a second. At times, our work was so good that our client was talking about it over Taco Tuesday at home. There is much less effort involved in working with referral clients because many of the barriers to trust have been removed, and you can jump right into the professional relationship.

How to get referrals

Do good work. The first step in getting good referrals is to be someone worth referring. Do what you said you would do, when you said you would do it, and deliver value. You don't have to be fake or make everyone like you, but you have to be fair and reasonable. Be generous (more on that in a bit), and treat the people in your network with respect.

Say thank you. You don't have to give people money or gifts, but you do want to acknowledge them for passing along a referral. A simple thank you is usually just fine. If a particular resource is sending you referrals often, or sends one really big one, take them out to dinner or lunch. Send a handwritten note. You can put a Starbucks gift card in there if you want, or simply place an article clipping you thought they'd find interesting. It's about letting them know they're being thought of and appreciated. Showing your appreciation doesn't have to be transactional.

Tell clients you rely on referrals. Be honest with them, even put it in your proposals or agreements, that you appreciate referrals. It's up to you to do excellent work and be bold enough to promise the client they'll be satisfied and want to refer you. But asking for referrals weeks or months after the project is over is far less efficient than setting the expectation up front that you need them.

Ask. As plain as it sounds, a solid referral base comes from you asking for referrals. It requires you to put systems in place for follow up with past clients, asking for referrals from current clients, and even asking for referrals from potential clients who turn you down.

Ask habitually. Blocking out one reactive day a quarter when you don't know where your next client is coming from to ask your entire contact database for referrals is a disaster waiting to happen. It makes you seem desperate, and you may very well be. Instead, make it routine and keep a log. You don't have to use a Customer Relationship Manager (CRM) like Salesforce or Pipedrive. You can just use a spreadsheet.

Follow up. When you've asked for a referral and haven't heard back, don't give up. Follow up and make it as easy as possible for them to pass it along. You don't have to be a pest, but some people live in their inbox, and your request is not a high priority. Catching them with a follow up when they're in inbox mode might be enough to get it done.

Be specific. Whether you're asking a client, friend, or local connection for a referral, you have to be clear with them. Tell them who you want, what you want to talk about, and what you'd like to do for them. You can craft the referral email for them and ask them to reword it to their liking. The textbox shows an example.

Example Referral Email

Hi John,

Great seeing you last week at the Chamber event. I noticed you're connected with Stephanie Walker at Acme Corp., and I'd like to chat with her. Acme is working on a new mobile strategy, and I know we'd be a perfect fit to redesign their website. I know you're super busy, so I've put together a quick intro below that you can rework if you're uncomfortable with any of it. I'd really appreciate it if you could pass it along to her. If you're okay with it, I added a note "from you" about the fast turnaround on your last project. Feel free to adjust as you see fit, but simply sending this over to her is a huge help.

Thanks John!

Message for Stephanie:

Hi Stephanie,

I'm connecting you with Brad Weaver at Nine Labs. Brad and I just worked together on our new payroll system interface. They turned it around much faster than we expected and helped us get ahead of the curve on some major deadlines. Brad's interested in learning more about your upcoming mobile strategy. They often rework existing websites for mobile, and he says that Acme is one they'd be thrilled to work on. I'll let you two take it from here.

John

What to do with referrals

When someone does refer you, you're now representing that person and their reputation, so honor them by doing your best. Good referral partners are your lifeblood, and it's easy to lose them. Odds are that if you do excellent work for the person referred, they are going to strengthen your referral partner's opinion of you and drive them to be even more fervent in referring you. You are building strand upon strand in your networking web, strengthening it along the way.

I have turned down unsolicited referrals from clients and colleagues. I appreciated them thinking of me, but it didn't fit for some reason. The way that you turn down a referral is critical. I can't tell you how many times I've given an hour of my time away for free to a referral to help them find the right resource. The benefit to me is three-fold: I've shown my referral partner that I can be trusted with their reputation, I've shown the new referral that I'm a nice guy who is willing to help, and I've passed business along to someone else (becoming the referrer) and they are now a part of my network. You're never too busy to build your referral network; it pays tremendous dividends down the road.

Fix bad referrals

You will get some referrals without any effort on your part. If you're nice or fun to be around, people will want to work with you. If they come across someone who needs your services, they'll probably refer you.

Accidental referrals are those that are unqualified. They're landing in your lap. You may get lucky and have an amazing client come your way. If you're only taking what's thrown your way though, it's probably not the clients you want. Also, this is probably not going to result in enough work to sustain your business long-term.

The accidental referral is a product of your network being unclear in what you do. Moreover, quality referrals won't happen if your personal network doesn't know what you do. That doesn't mean that you should lecture your cousin on the nuances of Rails development and provide her with a list of target clients. But you should make sure that friends and family have a general sense of what you do so that if their friend, employer, or colleague mentions needing services similar to yours, they can at least pass along the information. I've received referrals for everything from data recovery to WLAN networking to mural painting—all of which I'm completely unqualified to perform.

Why some people won't give you referrals

Not every client or colleague is going to give you referrals, even if they love your work. They're busy, so taking the time to refer you may be one more thing for which they don't have time. I've had clients tell me that they don't want to refer me to others because they don't want my attention diverted away from them. I take that as a compliment.

There is a fear that if they refer you to someone and it doesn't go well that it will reflect poorly on them. Even if you've done an amazing job for that client or colleague, they may not have enough confidence to refer you. You may never be able to overcome that because some people care too much about their reputation to put their name on referrals.

There are a few things you can do to overcome the resistance, but sometimes it's just not enough. That's why you need a large network with a lot of people referring you. As you work with them frequently, the fear of you making them look bad may subside. You can offer to provide something, such as a discount or free consultation, exclusively to their contact. You can offer referral fees. You can do all of the legwork and craft the referral email, send it to the client and ask them to send it along. Any of those can help, but remember not to take it personally if they still say no.

Building Your Network

"Be nice, the world is a small town." Austin Kleon[2]

You arrive after driving in circles for twenty minutes trying to find the place, check in, and slap on a stick-on name badge with your name in Sharpie. You hope that you know at least one person there, and you quickly turn into James Bond scanning the crowd for the runaway villain, eyes burning as you refuse to blink. You find her, latch on for dear life, and make your way to the bar. Then you spend the next two hours awkwardly holding a tiny plate with cold catering food and try to shake hands with people who've also been shoving food into their mouths. It's terrifying and odd. What is this magical place? It's open networking.

Putting yourself out there is tough for many creatives. Okay, most creatives. For starters, it means putting on pants. You have to talk about your work and explain what a user experience designer or content strategist actually does to people who probably don't care. It means getting stuck with the eleventh insurance salesperson you've met that night droning on about his home brewing setup and all that you want to do is pick out the spinach stuck between his two front teeth.

So let's start by separating networking from networking events. Open networking events are a small part of a robust networking strategy. They're useful for certain purposes, but as I've lovingly described them here, they can be exhausting. Networking is about finding people with whom you can build relationships (clients) rather than attending an event hoping to find your next project (work).

Going into networking events with one straightforward goal removes much of the pressure: **Can I find at least one person here with whom I'd enjoy a second conversation?** That's it. Don't worry about what they do or if they can hire you, that doesn't matter. You are looking for referral partners who can get you to clients. Go in with zero expectations of "selling" anything.

I'm lucky to be close friends with one of Forbes' experts on networking, Darrah Brustein. She and I regularly meet up just to talk about other people we can connect. We've done very little business together over the years, but we've referred countless clients to one another directly and indirectly. Coincidentally, Darrah puts on one hell of a monthly networking event that's not so awkward.

Darrah summarizes what she calls relationship currency as "your actions + what others say about you = your reputation. This small formula is the most powerful leverage you have in business—and in life, for that matter."[3]

Your relationships can turn your creative business into a juggernaut or bury its still beating heart. While you shouldn't live your life constantly worried about what others think of you, and most certainly don't become a doormat, it's important that you maintain a good reputation when it comes to your work and how you deal with others. How you carry yourself in your local network will shape most secondary opinions of you as your name is passed around. The better you are at building valuable relationships, the stronger your business's reputation will be—regardless of your actual creative work.

Lasting Relationships

"Whom you surround yourself with—and how you connect with them—is the single most important factor in unlocking your growth potential." Sunny Bates[4]

View your network as something that extends far beyond your creative business. It follows you for the rest of your professional life for better or worse, whether you go back to a cubicle, move up to a corner office, or keep working as a solo creative for decades. The relationships you build can influence where you live, where you vacation, your children's school, and so much more.

Find others who you believe will get along and connect them, regardless of profession, and find the time to regularly get together as a group. When you meet people, always look for ways you can help them and stay in touch. When you come across a helpful resource, blog post, or referral, send it to them and don't ask for anything else. Think of it as a "thinking of you" message.

Managing Your Relationships

A Customer Relationship Manager (CRM) is a piece of software you use to keep up with your leads, referrals, and clients. They can be expensive and complicated. They also tend to be overkill for most small businesses. Popular solutions include Salesforce, SugarCRM, and InfusionSoft. Unless you're starting with a sales team, you probably won't need one.

There are lighter weight solutions such as Zoho CRM, Pipedrive, Highrise, and OnePage CRM. These can be useful for inputting potential deals (leads) and people who can connect you to target clients. The challenge is that they vary widely in performance and functionality. Some are glorified address books while others are advanced email platforms built for constant communication.

When you're first starting out, you really don't have to jump into software at all. Gmail's custom tagging feature allows you to add tags like "lead" or "referral partner" to people in your address book. You can use LinkedIn and make notes on individual contacts. You can use a spreadsheet or whiteboard with Post-it notes to keep up with relationships and potential business. You could also try a cork board where you pin business cards up with string connecting the relationships. Then you'll feel like you're tracking a serial killer and it'll be awesome.

Following up with Your Connections

The "just checking in" email with your referral network can be tiresome. But you have to find reasons to stay in contact with your referral partners and clients. Out of sight, out of mind has proven itself true in my past experience. I've had a competitor connect with one of my referral resources at just the right time to get a referral that would have come to me if I had been top of mind.

Balancing constant "check-ins" with a healthy relationship is never easy. I keep a "lunch list," "email list," "online list," and "coffee list" in Evernote with reminders attached to it. In that note I have a rotation of individuals with whom I want to regularly connect. They're grouped by type—client, colleague, friend, acquaintance, and random. As I meet with someone or connect with them, I put the date by their name and move them to the bottom of their group. Every month, I go through the note from the top and set up meetings, calls, or compose emails to people I haven't connected with recently. As we reconnect, I make notes accordingly. The lunch and coffee connections are local or in cities I frequently visit, while the online and email list comprises remote or weaker connections.

Generosity

At the heart of a strong network is an attitude of generosity. When your relationships are transactional, you won't get very far. The worst place to be is feeling like you owe someone a favor. Good referrals aren't like that.

In Adam Grant's book *Give and Take*, he says "from a relationship perspective, givers build deeper and broader connections. When a salesperson truly cares about you, trust forms, and you're more likely to buy, come back for repeat business, and refer new customers. From a motivation perspective, helping others enriches the meaning and purpose of our own lives, showing us that our contributions matter and energizing us to work harder, longer, and smarter."[5] Grant attributes the long-term success of givers to relationships, learning, and motivation.

Your Elevator Pitch

When you are networking, it's tough to explain exactly what you do. The "elevator pitch" or Unique Selling Proposition (USP) is what you're expected to share with others. Perfecting the elevator pitch, however, is the holy grail of the entire sales and marketing aisle at your local bookstore. You can adjust your elevator pitch as often as you like and adapt it for different audiences. It's not a sales pitch, so it can't be stiff and formulaic. It has to fit into ordinary conversation. The kind of conversation you'd have with a stranger on the elevator who asks what you do.

When someone asks what you do, your instinct is to give them a job title. If you're networking with other web designers, you can get specific about what you do, such as front-end Wordpress theming. If you're networking with other communication professionals, you can say you're a web designer. If you're meeting with an open networking group, you might say you work with websites. If you're talking to your grandmother, you can just say you work with computers. You get the point.

But stating your job title isn't enough, you need to be specific about what you do and who you'd like to be connected with. That's where the elevator pitch comes in handy. The point of the elevator pitch is to keep the conversation going and get them to ask you questions.

Crafting an elevator pitch can be broken down into a few steps.

Focus on one problem that you solve; this is your benefit. It's not what you do, it's the result of what you do. For web designers, this wouldn't be "I design websites." Instead, it would be "Companies hire us to make custom designs for their websites that attract their ideal customers."

How are you different? This is your USP, your differentiator. This helps them understand why they should go with you over someone else. USPs require understanding your market, so you'll develop it over time. If you're just starting out, you may be casting a wide net. If you have a proprietary technology or rare certification, this can help. Something like "we have our own content management system built for solo realtors." If not, focus on how you work. What you want to avoid is saying you're "award winning" or "best in show" or "number one." For a web designer, a good example is "we work with small businesses in healthcare to get their patient documents online." Another example could be "we specialize in eCommerce websites for luxury clothing brands."

Stop. After these two parts come together, that's your opening pitch. When you use it, people may respond and say that your work is interesting and they might know someone who would want to hear more. Or, they may be the interested party. If so, you'll use this last part. You're motivating them to learn more. This isn't much different than a "learn more" button on a sales website.

What do you need? If they say they "might know someone," ask them if you could get an introduction. If they say they're interested, ask them if you can set up a meeting. Keep the conversation casual; don't try to sell your product right there unless they really want to ask more questions.

Then go. If you're sharing your pitch with someone who says it's interesting, but isn't a direct prospect, add in what you could use help with. You could add, "so I'm looking to connect with healthcare practices that may have out of date websites and want to get their documents online. Do you know anyone like that?"

My Elevator Pitch

"I help technology companies get their heads around a digital-first strategy. That means I help them be more like Netflix and Amazon and less like Blockbuster and Barnes & Noble. I work with them to assess their problems, find solutions they can afford, and then get them built. And I do it fast."

If they say they're interested or know someone I should connect them with, I add:

"Great. Typically we do what's called a Discovery session with you for a day or two, sometimes a week, to dig into your specific challenges. When can I get on your calendar to chat about that next week?"

If they ask more questions about what "digital-first" is, we've got a whole night of conversation and connections ahead of us. Mission accomplished.

Warm Introductions

You've got a network in place, you're sharing your elevator pitch, and now it's time to start seeking out clients on your own. Rather than randomly calling unqualified prospects to see if they'll "buy" your services, it's best to see if you can get a warm introduction. This means you reach out to someone in your network who is connected to your prospect and ask them to introduce you.

Warm introductions differ from referrals because you are initiating the request for a connection. Not all warm introductions are created equal; they can vary from tepid to boiling hot. I've randomly called a shared connection to find out that my target prospect is their half-brother. I've asked a close referral partner for an introduction to someone I've seen in their Facebook profile photo and they send over a half-written "John, meet Brad. Brad, meet John. Hope you guys can connect!" email on a Friday at 6pm.

The best way to ask for a warm introduction is to tell your referral partner what you need. Here's an example warm introduction request:

Example Warm Introduction Email

Hi John,

You're connected to Mark Adams on Twitter and it seems like you guys interact a bit. Would you be up for the three of us getting coffee next week so that you can introduce me? It looks like they're in the market for updates to their mapping application and I'd like to talk to him about it.

How to Sell Creative Services

Whew, that's a bold section title isn't it? I'm promising to tell you how to actually sell creative services. Shouldn't this be its own book? *Creative Truth 2: Sales Boogaloo?*

Outbound marketing, what we'll call "sales" from here on, comes down to the ask. The more that you can qualify the ask, getting it closer to a referral, the more likely you'll get a positive response. Randomly looking up businesses on Google to call isn't the way to start. You'll need to qualify your prospects through research. Rather than simply sending a lone email (that will promptly be deleted) or making an unexpected phone call (that will be cut short with an "I'm not interested"), put these steps together to get the conversation going and a meeting set up.

Get Specific

Get a notebook or open a spreadsheet. Don't spend your entire day trying to find an app to do this, just use what you have. If you're on a team, use something like Google Docs that you can share with others so everyone can add and edit.

List the types of work you want to do, e.g. web design, PHP development, content strategy, icon design, etc. Then list the types of work you don't want to do, such as database development or cat poster illustration. Be specific and detailed. Leave room to add to these lists. This would be one page in your notebook or tab in your spreadsheet.

Next, list types of companies, clients, or brands you want to work with by market and/ or name, e.g. Nike, polka bands, clean water charities, Indian restaurants, etc. Leave room to add to these lists. This would be a separate page in your notebook or tab in your spreadsheet from your skills/work lists.

Now, take the list of skills/work and the list of brands/markets and put them side by side. Get a separate page or tab open. Go through these lists to determine what skills you want to offer that the companies you are interested in would use. You could assign points and rank each prospect, but don't make it too complicated.

Be very descriptive and use actionable language, e.g. "Nike could hire us to create illustrations for a series of posters," or "the Indian restaurant may need us to develop a custom online order and delivery tool for them." The goal is create specific things that link your services to problems these clients may have.

Finally, take the best ones from this worksheet and create a one-page document outlining your specific services. For example, "we create custom illustrations for athletic shoe brands," or "we customize online ordering systems for Indian restaurants." These are your outbound sales pitches. You may have five, you may have fifty.

Connect

Using your networks on LinkedIn, Twitter, Facebook, email, and your address book, look for connections to those brands or types of companies. This is where your warm introductions can help. Hopefully you can find a shared connection that can facilitate an introduction for you. If you do, ask that shared connection for the intro and put your relevant outbound sales pitch in the request. If you don't have a connection, then it's on to the actual cold calling process.

If possible, try to get your prospect's email. There are some hacks out there for finding emails, I won't go into details here because I'm not a fan, but there are ways. Hopefully it's listed on their website or you can get connected with them on LinkedIn instead. If you can't get an email or direct line of contact, then at least follow them on social media and try to connect through conversation. If they post an interesting article on Twitter or share a compelling post on Medium, comment and engage. This is no different from approaching them at an open networking event. You're having a conversation at this point, not asking for business.

If they are local, do your best to work toward connecting with them in person at an event. No, I'm not advising you to stalk the person. This is about getting yourself in a position to eventually speak with him or her directly; your motives are pure. Try to find something they've written about or a mutual interest, something that you can break the ice with by saying you understand their area of expertise. Depending on who it is, it may be easy to find out what events they'll attend that are open to you. If they are in a particular industry, such as healthcare, and there's an important healthcare meetup or conference coming up, it may be worth making a visit.

Cold Emails

If you are able to reach them via email or LinkedIn, keep it short. Your subject needs to be specific to your skill, e.g. "Illustration for Motocross Event Posters" or "User Experience Design for Rails Apps." The key is that you're using something unique to that person's role or area of authority and something that you can actually do for them.

Example Cold Email

Hi Susan,

I love what Nike has been doing with the Chicago Super Cross Event each January. I illustrate posters and digital art for similar events; here's an example of two I recently created for Monster Jam in Phoenix (link to your work). I'd like contribute to this year's event. Are you available next Tuesday or Thursday afternoon for a quick chat about working together?"

Tone and style are important in your initial email. Saying "what's up dude" may actually work in some cases. Cursing or using a joke may work in others. "Hip hip, cheerio!" may be the best way to close out. They key here is to research your subject a bit to find out how to address him or her. Don't go with, "Dear Sir or Madam" but also don't be presumptuous or too familiar.

Make sure links to all of your online connection points—Twitter, email, website, etc. —are in your email along with your phone number.

If no response is received, wait three or four days after sending the email, then call your prospect. If they pick up, here's a script:

Example Call Script

"Hi Susan, This is Brad Weaver from Nine Labs following up from my message last week. Is now a good time to chat?"

Wait. Don't say anything. If your prospect says "no," then respond:

"I understand. When would be a good time to follow up later today or tomorrow?"

From here, it will become evident if your prospect is willing to talk to you. She may say she's not interested. She may be vague and say "I'm not sure." She may actually give you a time. The key is to shut up and listen. Let them feel a bit uncomfortable.

If, however, they say, "yes, now is a good time to talk," the conversation should continue:

Example Call Script Continued

"Great. I'd like to set up a time to chat with you about working on this year's event or, if you have a few minutes, we can do that now."

Do you notice one thing missing? There's no apology for the interruption. You have to be confident and never apologize for the call. You are bringing a solution to them for a challenge they face; you are not an interruption.

What about voicemail?

Example Voicemail Script

"Hi Susan, This is Brad Weaver from Nine Labs following up from my message last week regarding the Chicago Super Cross Event. I've been working with Monster Jam in Phoenix, and I'd like contribute to this year's event. Are you available next Tuesday or Thursday afternoon for a quick chat about working together? You can reach me at 555-555-5555. Thank you!"

What if you still can't get through?

If you can't get a phone number and there's no reply to your email after one week, send the email again. Simply change the suggested days or times for the call. Don't apologize for nagging or say "sorry we missed each other." Don't ask "why haven't you replied yet?" If there's no response to that second email, then send a third email two weeks later and simply add "I'll connect with you online and keep in touch." Keep all of the asks and scheduling requests in there. You're simply making it clear that you aren't giving up, you're going to work toward the relationship.

While all of this is going on, and if you haven't already, be sure to connect on LinkedIn, Twitter, and any other networks. Don't give up on finding a phone number if you haven't yet; keep checking your connections.

What happens if they say yes?

Set up the meeting and read Chapters 4, 5, and 6 before you go.

Your Online Presence

Your Website

Your online presence revolves around your marketing website. You need a home base where people can find you. This doesn't have to be yourbusiness.com. There are a number of reasons that's ideal, but rather than spending six months designing the perfect website, get something up somewhere as fast as you can so that people can find you.

There are more portfolio website tools for designers than there are designers to use them. New website builders seem to pop up daily, so you've got enough free trials and drag and drop builders that even the most technically challenged creative can build a web presence. Communities like Dribbble and Behance have made it easier than ever to show your work online and be found by potential clients. If you're a writer, having a Medium profile can be enough. Check out a current list of site builders and portfolio tools on the book website.

What a basic creative business website should include

Here are a few things to think about including in your website to drive the right kind of prospect connections. You may not be able to do it all when you start, but you should aim to include most of this when you can get the content together.

- **Contact information.** Make it insanely easy for them to get in touch with you from your website. You can use forms, but don't limit any and all contact to forms. Put phone numbers, email addresses, and physical office directions on the site.

- **Work examples.** Keep your work examples limited to the very best. That may be three pieces or twelve, but don't put everything you've ever done on the website. If your work isn't visual, then you'll want to create case studies. Always focus on the solution provided and what it meant to the client, not for you.

- **Solutions or services.** You don't have to create a list of all services you provide, but you should provide some idea of your capabilities.

- **Third-party validation.** As soon as you can get testimonials, post them. Add the names or logos of businesses you've worked with so that prospects can validate your capabilities.

- **Writing.** If at all possible, try to write about your process. You don't have to create new content, you can simply write about what you observe.

Don't spend a year designing the perfect site; it will never be perfect. Get something out there as fast as possible and keep iterating. The more your website does to make it clear what you do, how you do it, and how much you charge, the better qualified your prospects will be.

The Cobbler's Child

And on that note and in full disclosure, I failed to release a fully functioning portfolio site in my first six years of business. Every time I would attempt to build one, I would get bogged down in the quest for the perfect design, and then I'd have it, and then I'd realize that the technology I planned to build it on was no longer cool and I'd look outdated if I used it. So I'd start over, and over, and over. Six years went by before I had a portfolio site, only to find that I no longer offered visual design work directly to clients and didn't need it or want it out there. Oh, the irony.

I got by, but I could have closed several clients that got away if I had a portfolio site when I met with them. I would come up with some long story about why I didn't have one and then I would have to send them an email full of links and Dropbox folders with work examples. It was a mess. I try not to think about the missed opportunities from not having a proper site. So, as hypocritical as it sounds, I'm advising you not to make the same mistake.

Your Portfolio

Do You Like Me? Check Yes or No.

You pass the note in class. It goes from hand to hand to its intended recipient. She unfolds it, reads it, and then makes a mark. It's folded back up and passed your way. Your heart is racing, you're too embarrassed to open it in class, so you wait until the bell rings. You wait till no one is watching, unfold it, and open your eyes.

That feeling of judgement and the need for validation haunts us all from the time we're barely able to handle multiplication tables. Relationships, teammates, parents, and employers all wield power over us as we seek approval. We all want to be liked.

Your body of work follows you everywhere you go; it's yours and yours alone. It's your story, good and bad, and how you tell that story online can be the difference between getting your next client and toiling away at work you won't enjoy.

What should your portfolio look like?

Your portfolio should represent the work you want, not the work you have. If you keep getting hired to do websites for lawyers, but you want to do websites for iPhone apps, you should probably stop posting lawyer websites in your portfolio. If you don't have any clients asking you to build websites for iPhone apps, then go make one up and riff on other people's work. By talking about what you can and will do moving forward, and supporting your capabilities with examples from past work, you get potential clients away from comparative shopping and into a suitor-seeker mindset.

Even if you have lots of visual examples of your work, you still want to provide context. The problem with portfolios, or at least the way that most of us were told to handle them, is that the work is just sitting there on its own, awaiting judgement. There is no context, no story, and no reasoning behind the work.

If your core service is visual, then of course you want to show strong visual examples. But as you work with bigger brands, a split can occur in how creatives are hired. Some creatives have such a strong visual style that they are hired based on their previous work. They get agents and really don't have to sell themselves much anymore. Those creatives really can get by with a simple site that has images from their body of work and how to get in touch with them. Others may not be as unique or well-known, so they're better served by moving the focus away from past work examples and onto their actual skills and services. Most clients hire you for visual solutions, but they also hire you for your creative thinking.

Case studies

If your work isn't as visually appealing, or if you want to be more of a consultant rather than production artist, shape your presentation around your service offering—what you do—as a story and share examples of past work, in context, for each of those offerings and skills. Your portfolio is a brochure for a product that's for sale: you. Focusing on particular pain points, such as poor usability or low registrations, and how you can solve those problems with your skill set, and then describing past instances (with or without visuals) of how you've succeeded will better serve the client in understanding what it is exactly that you do. Tell the story of what you did and what it meant for your client's business.

> Your portfolio is a brochure for a product that's for sale: you.

Unless your visuals stand on their own, your portfolio should focus on the relationship between the challenges faced and the solutions you provided. Good work solves problems, sometimes in an ugly way.

What If I haven't done any client work yet?

We all had to start somewhere, and it's a catch-22 when you need work samples to get clients, but you need clients in order to create work samples. If you don't have a student portfolio, try to rework or riff on other people's work. For a web or UX designer, this may mean adding to the pile of 24,000 other unsolicited Facebook redesigns on Dribbble and Behance. Honestly, go ahead and make the 24,001st redesign of Facebook. You could make variations of classic film posters or book covers in a new style. You could re-tell a classic story from a new perspective, e.g. "Pride and Prejudice and Zombies." That's how most musicians start; they cover popular bands' work so that people will listen as they develop their original work. It's how you learn.

The added benefit of riffing on other creatives' work is that you begin to understand their process. You see the challenges and thinking that were involved in getting to the final solution.

What If my current work sucks?

So, what do you do when your work isn't going to win awards but it paid the bills? Get yourself in a position to regularly present your work, preferably face to face. The more opportunities you can find to get into a room with a client and actually present your work, the more likely you are to get hired. You are an expert, you know your shit, now get up there and show them what you can do. "Be a scientist when you work, and a snake charmer when you present."[6]

Make better work

Try to create better work outside of client assignments. Sometimes you have clients that won't let you create visually appealing deliverables. Then it's up to you to create visually appealing work on your own and share it. Find the time to work on open-source projects or do a little *pro bono* work where the client gives you carte blanche. Make goofy personal projects like posters or stickers. Find reasons to push yourself and learn new skills that will make you better. Hopefully, that stuff is good and you can post it online for others to see with little care for how it's perceived.

Social Media

Social media is a must in any creative line of work. There are countless not-so-great creatives with immense client portfolios mostly won on their clout or "Klout."

Connecting with other creatives online, especially if you work from home, is the most immediate benefit. Through social media, you are able to find out about the industry at large, not just in your niche or your neck of the woods. Additionally, it's an easy path to visibility for potential clients and hiring agencies.

LinkedIn

It reigns supreme for finding direct client work. It's a social contact database that makes it very easy to find people to help you with warm introductions to people of interest. There are groups for skills (illustration, web design), geographic areas (cities, neighborhoods), and associations or causes (non-profit work, social change, environmental, entrepreneurship). These groups are a natural audience for your blog posts and your expertise. Plus, they're great for finding project partners or freelance help. It's the closest thing to a resumé online and it can absolutely bring in business. I have landed several significant clients who have found me on LinkedIn via searching for someone with my skills, then emailing me, and eventually becoming a client.

Facebook

For use as an individual, it still serves a purpose for connecting with the friends you make along the way. It's good for staying in touch with people who can help you get the word out. Having a Facebook page for your creative business gets mixed results. Some creatives actually use advertising to some success, so it could be of value to you. For the minimal effort involved, it's at least worth a casual connection to industry friends so that you've got someone to drink with when you go to conferences.

Twitter

It can make you an absolute rockstar or send you into fits of depression. It's a great place to stay on top of your craft and know what's changing, what's new, and learn from others. It's an easy avenue to get your work in front of others and, well, it's just fun. The drive to be an industry celebrity can be sad to watch at times, and I hope you don't get caught up in it, but it's undeniable that a strong Twitter presence can increase your notoriety in the industry.

Instagram

For visual creatives, it's a great way to share your work and be found. Getting comments and feedback on your work from people who are in a "visual mindset" can be useful. If you sell your work, e.g. prints, apparel, etc., then Instagram can help build your customer base.

Quora, Stack Overflow, and Reddit

Answering questions online can turn you into an expert with little effort. If you have knowledge to share, people will gladly take it. When I search for solutions to problems I'm facing, I often get posts that are three and four years old at the top of my search results. The person who answered that question couldn't buy that kind of blog or website traffic if they tried. Taking the time to interact with people asking questions about your area of expertise could land you potential clients for years to come.

Messaging apps

It's too early to tell if connecting with clients over messaging apps is good or bad. We keep our clients in our Slack channels, but we aren't to a place where we're putting prospects in there just yet. However, Slack has been instrumental in managing our clients once they're on board. I avoid becoming Facebook friends with clients because I prefer to keep some things personal. The wave of messaging apps that seem to pop up every day presents new challenges when a client wants to connect. Is it one more way for them to connect with you when you're already working together that goes outside of the regular business hours boundaries?

Industry networks

Creative sites such as Dribbble, Behance, GitHub, DeviantArt, and discussion forums are also powerful ways to connect with others and show your work. Writing on community platforms like Medium can give you so much more exposure than only posting on your own blog. Writing for industry blogs is going to give you a greater reach than writing on your own site. Hopefully you can re-publish third party work on your own blog, but either way, writing for well-read publications is a sure-fire way to get noticed.

Blogging, Press, and Media Relations

As Chris Brogan says, your website is your home base and other outlets—industry blogs, social media, or portfolio sites—are your outposts.[7] You need both to reach the maximum audience. You need content that you can share with your work being the center of it all. You don't necessarily have to write wholly original ideas at thousands of words, but you should be able to write about your craft and your interpretation of trends, the work of others, and the implications of changing landscapes. Blogging isn't for everyone, but it can be very effective in shaping your online persona.

Sending press releases can also be effective. There is an over-abundance of business publications and they are constantly in need of new content. Getting set up with Marketwired or another reputable press release service is easy, but expensive. Once you're set up, you can create press releases for big clients that you sign, new service offerings, shows or openings, conference talks, and more.

You can also reach out to media outlets to be interviewed. Those business publications desperate for content also need quotes and Subject Matter Experts (SMEs) for articles in progress. By establishing yourself as an SME that writers can call upon, you can be interviewed often. Additionally you can write the articles yourself. Writing for industry blogs such as *Smashing Magazine* or *Creative Bloq* is prestigious, but won't help you much with outside clients. You could get noticed by other agencies or art directors, but not many clients are reading internal industry publications. Rather, seek out *Wired*, *Fast Company*, *Business Insider*, *Forbes*, and other similar publications.

If you've established a vertical market, pitch publications in that vertical. The more niche the vertical, the more likely you can get picked up. Writing for *Business Insurance* magazine is probably easier than getting picked up by *Vanity Fair*.

Testimonials

Testimonials are online word-of-mouth. Getting testimonials from your aunt, childhood babysitter, and pastor is better than waiting until you get that perfect soundbite from Elon Musk. Get people talking about your business and get it in writing. Place testimonials throughout your website and marketing materials. I even include them in my responses to prospects and in my proposals.

Some clients can't refer you, but they can offer third-party validation by providing a testimonial. You can write a case study about your project and include quotes from them on your website. That is still a referral source if people see it. That client is "referring" you by validating your skills.

How to ask for a testimonial

When asking for testimonials, be specific. Instead of asking "can you give me a testimonial?" ask someone to answer specific questions such as "how do you feel about us delivering the project two weeks early?" or "can you tell me how you felt about the final design once you saw it?" Ask them when they are still riding high after completing your project. Don't wait until weeks after you've finished your work.

Email Marketing

If you're providing fresh content that's valuable to your target audience, and it's not a sales pitch, people will read it. If you're sending out a list of your accomplishments and what you offer every month, it's probably not going to do much for your business. An email marketing program should be based on sharing insights in which your potential clients would be interested. It's an excellent opportunity to showcase your expertise. Write about subjects that they understand and, if you have a vertical market, actual industry trends. For example, if you work in healthcare, write email content about web design solutions in healthcare.

For the tool you use for email marketing, I recommend MailChimp. They have built a product for creatives, by creatives, that is priced fairly. Don't make email marketing any harder than it has to be by using an enterprise-level tool. You simply don't need it. Start with a free plan and as you grow, you can build your list and scale accordingly.

Bringing Your Online Presence Together

Social media, testimonials, your online body of work, your network, and so much more all feed into what's called "thought leadership." Being a thought leader in your industry or local geographic area is the long-term goal. This isn't about ego; some of the strongest thought leaders are typically silent and reserved, only speaking up when they truly have something to say. Conversely, some of the biggest charlatans out there are regularly quoted and posted everywhere you look.

Thought leadership is about having something of value to say, to add to the conversation, and leading through innovation. The more you are sharing good work, good ideas, and good connections, the more respected you will be. Respected individuals are mentioned by in-house creatives to their boss who may be looking to hire someone like you. Respected individuals are known by casual observers of your industry who only need to know enough to hire someone. Getting to a status of thought leadership stems from helping others far more than helping yourself, starting with your clients and customers.

The Geometry of Business: Targeted Vertical and Horizontal Marketing

Specialization on your terms is important to your happiness, so don't let your market or clients do it for you. You probably set out to do a specific type of work, such as poster illustrations or animated micro-sites, for a specific type of client such as rock bands or sports teams. You had a specific vision in your head for the exact kind of project you wanted to do. Mine was highly interactive micro-sites for blockbuster films.

You've established your perfect situation and started your business, but the work that came in was coupon brochures for window washing companies and safety guides for plumbers. It paid well and you could get through it, so you kept taking the work and getting referrals to others in the same industry. Now you are the person known for doing safety brochures for plumbers. Maybe you're happy, but are you doing work that you love? Specialization can save the day. It works in two directions—vertical and horizontal.

Vertical markets are industries and jobs such as healthcare or attorneys. They can get very narrow, such as "home healthcare nurses."

Horizontal markets are tasks and skills such as illustration or web design. Horizontals can also get very narrow, such as "editorial illustration for business magazines."

There are risks and rewards when it comes to specialization and it's not for everyone. Some creatives love working with any type of client, but only doing certain types of work. Others may enjoy only certain clients, e.g. sports teams, but be willing to do just about anything creative for them. There are creative businesses that are very specific in both directions. I have a friend who only does landing page websites for home healthcare device companies. I should note that she's doing quite well and loves her job.

It's unlikely you'll establish your vertical or horizontal market early in your creative business unless you are coming from a current creative position in a particular niche. For example, you already work in the healthcare industry and are striking out on your own. Instead, start with developing a few strong connections in one particular market and going hard after them. Streamline your strategy with these individuals and cater your communications to their particular needs—use a spear instead of a fishing net.

Vertical Marketing

Vertical marketing is tough for creatives. Many of us left a corporate job, where we worked on the same type of project repeatedly, so that we could work with varying client industries. Thus, it's to be expected that the last thing you may want to do is work on the same kind of work over and over again. That's understandable, but there is a significant opportunity for variation, even in the same industry.

My colleagues who work only in pharmaceuticals or construction tend to be much more profitable than those who work in scattershot industries with no specific strategy in place. They actually end up doing a lot more exciting work because their clients trust them due to their reputation and expertise in their industry. They often test new technologies and methods, get to branch out into more radical ideas, and are able to command higher prices.

Networking can be easier in a vertical market. You're no longer going to wide open events where business owners and decision makers vary in size and power—you can focus on going to trade shows and events specific to that industry—and it's likely you'll have little to no local competition. Some colleagues are the only service provider for their specific skill, such as packaging design, in their entire industry for clients of their preferred size. They have a virtual monopoly and the work just shows up at their door.

How to establish a vertical market

You may fall into your vertical because you gain traction in a particular market. Through referrals and repeat business, you may end up doing several projects for health food companies and develop strong connections with the industry. If that's the case, then it's your chance to become a Subject Matter Expert (SME) on that particular industry. As you continue to provide well-informed services to clients in that market, you will establish yourself as the thought leader.

You may have a market you want to go after, but no experience or foothold in that space. The first step is to study the industry and work toward becoming an SME. Write about the industry regarding your services, e.g. "10 Website Design Tips for Health Food Companies," and submit it to trade publications and social networks. Build your knowledge, target specific clients, and as you get the work in the industry, you can begin building your brand.

Vertical marketing isn't for everyone

Vertical marketing in a niche can make it easier to establish a steady stream of business, but it's not a perfect solution. If you want to work in various industries throughout the year, it may not be attractive to you. If you want to spend most of your time in general networking rather than industry-specific networking, that's understandable. It's possible that the industries that interest you don't have a need for your services and the industries that do need your services are of little interest.

Working in a vertical market can force you to grow faster than you like. Demand can soar, clients can grow, and you can have a larger business than you're ready for without warning. When my business fell apart in 2009, much of it was due to our ties to the construction and real estate industries. Our three largest clients were in flooring and tile and two of them were bankrupt before the end of 2009. They represented 70 percent of my business, so the vertical market actually took my business down with it.

Would I work in a vertical market again? Yes, but with greater caution. So far, we aren't strict about it. Much of my current work is in academics and non-government organizations (NGOs), but we're still building apps and interfaces for retail and entertainment brands. Sticking with a vertical carries risk but can reap rewards. Take a look at your local landscape to assess the health of your potential vertical and let that be a factor in determining which markets are interesting to you.

Horizontal Marketing

You have certain skills, some you're better at, and those are the ones you offer. I'm a good designer and strategist, I'm a terrible illustrator—hence, the lovely Becky Simpson doing the illustrations for this book instead of me. That's the simple part, but getting deeper is a little like killing your darlings.

You may be a decent branding designer, but a much better layout designer. You love branding, but you're faster, more effective, and get better results designing layouts than you can with a logo or brand. You may need to let go of pushing branding design as a core service offering so that you can focus on what will be better for paying the bills. You can keep making logos, but don't lead with that offering in the work you seek.

It's hard to say no to an individual skill that you enjoy, especially if you're making some revenue. Being specific, however, really is the fast-track to stability and recognition. There are tattoo artists, session musicians, and illustrators who are hired over and over again to recreate the same style of art for varying clients. It may seem boring, but they're also making enough money that they can take the time to work on "outside" pursuits that keep their skills fresh. Moreover, they tend to find their "next big thing" in their side projects as they make money hand over fist being hired repeatedly for their horizontal specialty.

A web designer may be able to perform the following tasks with proficiency:

- Write a website's marketing content
- Perform basic usability research and create wireframes

- Design a layout and create graphics for the website

- Install website software on the client's server

- Configure and develop a database for the client's content management system

- Code the front-end of the website in HTML, CSS, and JavaScript

- Manipulate the CMS to perform advanced tasks using PHP

- Train the client on the website CMS

- Develop social media marketing programs and SEO strategies for the client

This may look familiar because it's the standard stack for many freelance web designers. It's also exhausting. I know, because it's what I did for years. There's nothing wrong with being a generalist and offering a suite of services to your clients. But, focusing on one particular area of expertise can result in even greater proficiency and higher profits.

If this same web designer focused only on coding the front-end of websites in HTML, CSS, and JavaScript, how good do you think she would get at that particular skill? As technology advances and client tastes mature, the demand for higher quality front-end development has risen. Advanced front-end developers can command fees that are double that of most of generalist freelance web designers. That means she can work half of the time for the same money, or make twice as much money in the same amount of time. Both sound great to me.

Maybe money isn't your motivation, but sanity is. As you spread yourself between multiple skills, you're the proverbial "jack of all trades, master of none." It's difficult to stay sharp in all areas and some start to slip. You struggle in most and thrive in none, and this results in frustration. A horizontal market isn't doing the same thing over and over again. We're talking about creative businesses, so every project is different. Over time, becoming known as "the guy" who does micro-sites for motorcycle tire manufacturers can be more attractive than being "some guy" who did that one site for one tire manufacturer that one time.

Horizontal marketing isn't for everyone

Horizontal marketing isn't for everyone either. You may want to work with specific clients on multiple services and deliverables. If you're controlling who you work with, and setting boundaries on what you can realistically do for them, you can thrive financially and creatively with a wide-ranging skill set.

How to establish a horizontal market

Establishing a horizontal market is really up to you. If you're strong in a particular skill, then focus on selling that expertise to your clients. If it's profoundly specialized and can't stand on its own, e.g. JavaScript front-end web development, then partner with other creatives or agencies. Your website and social media content should reflect your area of expertise. Immerse yourself in that particular skill and build your reputation as a thought leader.

You may need to assess your current skills to see what you're actually good at. You may be getting by with everything and enjoying it all. One way to do it is to take a look at your hourly reports and see how much time you're spending on each skill vs. its overall contribution to the project. If you're particularly fast with front-end development but slow with home page design, you may need to focus on increasing your development workload.

Quick Marketing Tips

Never start by telling a prospect what's wrong with their product, service, content, etc.

Even if you see an immediate failure that you truly believe you can fix, don't point it out to your prospect immediately. When you do point out the flaw, be prepared to demonstrate what you would do to fix it. If you point this out in your initial introduction, then take the time to create a demo, sample, or sketch explaining what you would do to fix it. Telling someone "your website sucks, hire me to make it better" may work once or twice, but it can backfire.

Track your sales progress

Consistently track your performance against your goals. What gets measured gets improved. Set deadlines for how many prospects you're going to get and when you're going to get them. You should check in on your prospect goals weekly. Write down your struggles and failures, not just your victories.

Never stop marketing

No matter how much work you have, never stop marketing. Let me stop and repeat that again. No matter how much work you have, never stop marketing. The best time to market is when you're busiest. It forces you to make it part of your routine, it forces you to say "no" to work that doesn't fit, and it will often force you to raise your rates. Those are three huge wins that will add up to a better business.

Geography is of no consequence

It's much easier to network face to face locally, but social media has made it much easier to find clients all over the world. Joining your local Chamber of Commerce and creative associations can help, but there's no reason for you to limit your search for prospects to your local area.

Always Be Marketing

Building lasting relationships to fuel your marketing machine will serve you well for years to come.Establish a strong presence online, leverage your network for qualified connections, and specialize as you see fit. Set goals, deadlines, and keep at it—no matter how busy you are. To quote Alec Baldwin's character in *Glengarry Glen Ross*, "always be closing."

No matter how much work you have, never stop marketing.

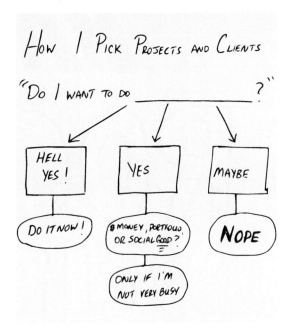

Notes

1. Mike Monteiro, *Design is a Job.*
2. Austin Kleon, *Steal Like An Artist.*
3. http://www.forbes.com/sites/yec/2014/01/28/10-simple-ways-to-improve-your-reputation/.
4. Jocelyn K., Glei, *Maximize Your Potential.*
5. Adam Grant, *Give and Take.*
6. http://muledesign.com/2014/09/13-ways-designers-screw-up-client-presentations.
7. http://chrisbrogan.com/using-outposts-in-your-media-strategy/.

CHAPTER 4

BASIC

ROCKET SCIENCE

PRICING YOUR WORK

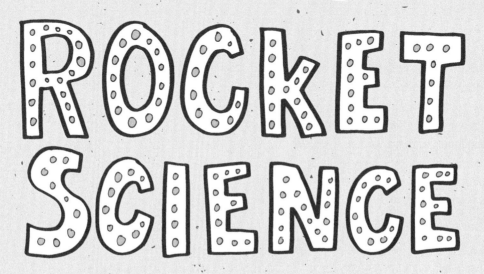

HOURLY   VS.   FLAT FEE   VS.   VALUE-BASED

   VS.   

RETAINER   PACKAGE

"Being good in business is the most fascinating kind of art. Making money is art and working is art and good business is the best art."

Andy Warhol[1]

Building a Pricing Strategy

In this chapter, we're going to cover the math you'll use to build your pricing strategy. We'll then break down several different models and the situations for which they're best suited. The goal is to develop a systematic approach to pricing that will remove much of the emotion and allow you to make sound decisions. You'll then be able to make case-by-case decisions as you work with individual clients and projects to determine the best approach.

Here's what we'll cover:

- Finding your rate and knowing what you need
- Profit and stability
- Shop rates vs. billing rates
- Value and worth
- Market rates
- Applying your rates
- The individual pricing models along with their pros, cons, and use cases
- Moving from task-based pricing to value-based pricing
- Core practices for effective pricing

Money is Uncomfortable

We often hold the money conversation until the end of meetings or wait to "get back" to the client in an email with our quote. Because money makes us uncomfortable, we wait as long as possible, hoping the conversation will somehow come up casually. Holding the financial discussion until everything else has been sorted out doesn't make any damn sense. And yet, we still do it.

Money is the "third tier" of small talk. The first tier is the weather, entertainment, food, hobbies, and sports. The second, topics that are personal and that people feel passionate about such as politics, religion, and relationships and sex. That is what you would discuss with your close friends. The third tier is finance and family. Noelle Howley says that, "Women are more likely to fess up about their weight or their sex lives than about their salaries."[2]

For some of us, we are meeting a client for the first or second time, and often jumping into a conversation that's less comfortable than discussing our sex lives. Okay, maybe that's a stretch, but you get the point. When we disclose our rates and prices to a client, we feel that we're opening up our ledger. You may feel that they're able to deduce how much you make and how you live, which translates to your self-worth. That can make you uncomfortable.

For creatives, it taps into something much deeper—taking what you love and turning it into an asset that you exchange for money. The money conversation can muck up "doing what you love." Maya Angelou famously said, "You can only become truly accomplished at something you love. Don't make money your goal. Instead pursue the things you love doing and then do them so well that people can't take their eyes off of you." I agree that money shouldn't be the goal, but I also agree with Clare Boothe Luce, who said, "Money can't buy happiness, but it can make you awfully comfortable while you're being miserable." You get to choose your attitude toward money; it's up to you to decide if it's important enough to be a priority in your business.

Your Services on a Shelf

When clients are asking us for a price, they are in the market for a solution. Buying a website, photograph, or illustration from you is no different than buying detergent at Target. The client isn't thinking about what it took to formulate, manufacture, package, ship, and display the detergent.

A website is a thing, a widget, or a deliverable. To the client, it's the same thing as the detergent. It has a job to do. The customer has a price they're willing to pay for that solution. If the cost is too high and there's a comparable detergent next to it on the shelf that will get the job done, they'll buy the other one. If the price is too cheap, they question the quality of the detergent and start asking questions. They'll go online and look for reviews of the products and compare them. They'll ask their friends which one they use. They'll look at the packaging, the presentation, and how much is available of each to see which is more popular.

Hundreds of factors and thousands of micro-decisions can go into determining which product they buy. However, it's not always about which solution is the best or cheapest;

it's also about value. As a client's purchasing potential increases, or at least their tastes and desires do, they won't be as likely to compare on price. That, my friend, is the kind of client you want. And that's what we're going to work on in this chapter.

Lost In Translation

When clients ask us for a solutions-based price, we usually respond with services-based pricing. We emphasize the time it will take, with costs by task, to arrive at their solution. We break things down to a level that allows clients to scrutinize every aspect of our process. Unfortunately, we cause confusion with information overload and industry jargon. The result is confused commoditization, and it doesn't help. Clients do not care what it costs to make something, and that includes a website. They're fully aware that there are "hidden" costs to doing business like office space, computers, and employee benefits. All that they care about is the value you're providing—"am I getting what I want at a price I'm happy with?"

Clients may want to know what it's going to take to get the job done. Some may wish to know the steps involved, but we've trained them to expect an unsustainable level of transparency. Moreover, the playing field has significantly changed. In today's landscape, many of our "competitors" are commoditized services. There are website builders that a monkey could use. There are data visualization apps that you dump a spreadsheet into, and it spits out a gorgeous infographic. And we have photography filters by the boatload that can turn a crooked snapshot into an Ansel Adams masterpiece.

We are no longer *only* competing with other creative services shops to sell services. We no longer have the luxury of mystery. In the past, we sat on the shelf like the detergent with a few other service providers. The client took a look at each of us, determined which one they liked the most or was the best value, and made a purchase. Now, we're being compared to solutions that have an entirely different approach. Some clients can't tell the difference between websites built by an $8 a month template tool and a $40,000 custom design.

Teaching an Old Marketplace New Tricks

It takes time to educate clients to compare creatives on value. It also takes significant trust for clients to expect value-based pricing without the task-by-task transparency. You can get there as you grow, but until you do, you have to get control of your pricing strategies and adapt to each client's situation.

Depending on their level of experience in hiring creatives, client expectations will vary, and you won't be able to use a single approach to pricing your work. It's unlikely you'll be able to avoid breaking down your time and costs for everyone you work with, *at least not yet.*

The basis for most pricing strategies is to consider how long it takes us to make the client's solution and calculate that against an hourly rate. For now, we still have to work with that thinking. How we arrive at that hourly rate, and the profit we make, is where we can make the most immediate change.

Read These Books

Rather than try to cover every single angle, I'm also assigning some outside homework. Others have written excellent books on pricing your work, specifically for creatives. Most take a freelancer's perspective, which isn't my only concern, but they're still useful to agency owners.

- *What to Charge: Pricing Strategies for Freelancers and Consultants* by Laurie Lewis
- The *Designer's Guide To Marketing And Pricing: How To Win Clients And What To Charge Them* by Ilise Benun and Peleg Top
- *The Wealthy Freelancer* by Steve Slaunwhite
- *Business Matters: A Freelancer's Guide to Business Success in Any Economy* by Elizabeth Frick
- *Creative, Inc.: The Ultimate Guide to Running a Successful Freelance Business* by Joy Deangdeelert Cho and Meg Mateo Ilasco
- *Double Your Freelancing Rate* by Brennan Dunn

Finding Your Shop Rate and Knowing What You Need

Most people pick an hourly rate out of thin air to start. Maybe they've heard a friend's rate or read it on a blog or in a book. Maybe they've used guidebooks or salary guides that base their results on surveys. But if you're basing your rates on a survey of people who all have bad pricing strategies, are you ending up with a good pricing strategy? The average of bad advice is still bad advice.

Even worse, some creatives determine their prices using their gut, their feelings, or their experience. They look at the cost of past projects that are similar and use that same rate for an entirely different client. That's dangerous. Every client is different, and no two projects are the same. This is money, and money is math. In fact, it's hard math. Financiers, investors, insurance underwriters, and anyone else at the helm of sustainably profitable companies use hard math to determine how much to charge. They know something we're still learning: your gut is not a calculator.

Your gut is not a calculator

We're going to break down the math for determining a creative shop rate. Sometimes this is called a "blended" rate because it's based on your entire business's finances, not any individual creative. We'll cover this again shortly, but for now it's worth noting that this is not your billing rate. If you choose to offer your services to clients at an hourly rate, which you disclose to them, that is a billing rate. Your billing rate can vary from client to client; your "blended" shop rate cannot.

Why You Need a Shop Rate

Your shop rate is the basis for all of your pricing calculations. It's what helps you determine if you're profitable and if the client and their project fit your business needs. It helps you determine if they are of value to you. You are flipping the conversation around and putting yourself in the driver's seat. You can become the shopper instead of the shopped.

Here's why this is different. You only have so many hours in a day. Even if you have a team, you all still collectively have a limited amount of time. You're selling your time to your client for money, and you have a finite amount of hours to sell.

There are already ways to overcome this limitation, but each is fundamentally flawed.

- The first, and most common solution, is to charge more for each of those hours—raising your rates. The flaw is that there is a limit to how high your rates can go. You could price yourself out of the market.

- The second solution is to get people to work for you who make less than your hourly billing rate and to make money on each hour that you sell. The flaw is that your overhead can rise considerably faster and employees may not produce the quality work that your client expects.

- The third solution is to build in profit on a per-project basis. The challenge is that it takes an immense amount of work to calculate costs and profits on a per-project basis. You can spend an entire day just getting a quote back to a client, with no guarantee of winning the work.

So what's the solution? **Find out what it costs to run your business, add in profit, and then determine how much of your time you can give to each client project.**

You can then know, with confidence, how much money you're getting for your time. You can then determine what you need to do to grow your business and where you can take risks. Most importantly, you will be in control of your pricing strategy. You are then capable, if you so choose, to move from a commoditized pricing situation—hours for money—to a value-based system.

Calculating Your Shop Rate

$$(Expenses + Profit) \div Hours = Rate$$

That's it. It's not the theory of relativity, but it can change your thinking. Each component, starting with expenses, includes everything it takes to run your creative shop profitably. You'll use this formula repeatedly to assess the health of your shop and see where to adjust your expenses and staffing. I recalculate my shop rate every quarter. Some people may only do it once a year. It depends on how often your staffing or expenses change. You will want to adjust it whenever you make a full-time hire.

Now, let's break down each part and determine your actual shop rate.

Expenses

Recurring expenses

$$(\text{Recurring Expenses} + \tfrac{1}{12} \text{ of Annual Expenses})$$
$$+$$
$$(\text{Your Salary} + \text{Staff Salaries} + \text{Contractor Fees})$$
$$\times$$
$$1.25 \ [25\% \text{ for Taxes}]$$
$$=$$
$$\text{Expenses}$$

This includes rent for office space, subscriptions to software and services, phone and internet bills, utilities, insurance, legal and accounting fees, meals, transportation, office supplies, and anything else that you regularly purchase. Some numbers are fixed, such as your health and liability insurance premiums, and others may vary, such as office supplies. Setting realistic budgets for each category is the best way to approximate costs. Sticking to those budgets isn't always easy. Be honest with yourself.

If you tend to spend $500 a month on meals or $300 a month on fonts, budget for it rather than trying to make cuts that you may not stick with.

One twelfth of annual expenses

There are purchases and fees that happen occasionally or annually. They tend to be large purchases such as computers, furniture, business licenses, and software updates. It also includes travel to conferences, hotels, and membership dues. Some annual expenses are predictable, and others may be unexpected.

If you plan to buy a new computer every three years and it will cost $3,600, you should allocate $1,200 a year toward it, meaning you should put $100 a month in your operating budget for computer equipment. If you have multiple employees, you'll do this for each person and build a per-person computer line item in your budget.

Keeping up with these annual expenses requires discipline. You can set aside savings accounts to keep the funds separate. Allocate the budgets in your accounting app or keep up with it in a spreadsheet. Breaking up your annual budgets keeps you from having to take on "extra" work or debt to pay for it. You Need a Budget (YNAB) is an effective tool for putting these budgets together for your personal and business expenses.

Your salary

First, allocate a salary to yourself. Even if you don't pay yourself through a payroll service, you need to set a salary. If you're using guidebooks that tell you how much a graphic designer in Chicago should make each year, then that number can go here. This is important. You aren't just taking that salary out of the guidebook and slicing it up to get your hourly rate. Your salary that you make personally should be entirely separate from the costs of doing business.

The easy way to do it is to develop a personal budget for a comfortable living and determine what that would take each month. You can certainly dive deeper into bonuses, margins, and all sorts of complexities, but for simplicity, find out how much you need to make each month, net after taxes, to be comfortable.

Again, be real with yourself. Don't just get by with the minimal amount; that's a recipe for debt and frustration. Give yourself a $300 a month clothing budget if you know you're going to spend it; don't lie to yourself. Find out what you spend using services such as Mint to see how you're spending your money and be honest. Think about birthdays, holidays, vacations, home repairs, and big purchases. It's important to understand what your cost of living is to get this number.

Staff salaries

If you have employees, their gross salaries are expenses. You'll want to use the actual number that your business is paying out through your payroll provider, which may include various taxes and insurance contributions. If your employee is a 1099 contractor and responsible for her own taxes, then you simply calculate her agreed-upon monthly pay.

The important part about salaries is that you include the whole dollar amount for your entire team. You may have revenue generating employees, such as designers and developers, and you may have non-revenue generating employees such as project managers and office assistants. Putting everyone's salary in your budget as an expense is critical to leveraging your hourly calculations in the later part of the formula.

Contractor costs

If you're using contractors, it's difficult to determine how much they'll cost. If they're on a single project, then their cost for that project is factored into its operating cost, not your shop expenses. It's no different from a font or software license you would need to buy for that specific client project. If, however, you have contractors who are a regular part of your team, you may need to consider their costs as part of your operating overhead.

If contractors play a significant role in your shop, you may need to review and adjust your formula more often. That's why we calculate it quarterly at our shop. We may have a contractor for a three- to six-month period to get us through multiple projects, but we also have him working on internal projects. He's more like an employee than doing off-site work on a single client project. We simply add in his cost and his hours to the formula.

Twenty-five percent for taxes

Your taxes actually fall on your gross income, not on your expenses, but that's difficult to predict. What you can predict is your expenditures and that you will have to make enough money to cover your expenditures. This is a safe spot to ensure you're holding enough back to cover your tax liability. Almost all small creative businesses, from solo shops to 100-employee firms, are LLCs, S-Corps, or some sort of partnership. The owner(s) pay taxes on their personal tax returns. The business is typically responsible to pay the owners additional money when filing taxes to cover any taxes owed, but that number can be huge. If you're not storing money away to cover it, it may not be there when it's time to file.

Thus, a general rule that will get you close to storing away enough for taxes is to add up your recurring expenses, annual expenses, salary, staff salary, and contractor costs, then multiply that number by 1.25. For example, if your total operating costs were $10,000 per month, you would multiply that by 1.25 to get $12,500 per month. Yes, you are saving taxes on top of having them in your salary. Trust me, you're going to need it when you're profitable.

You will have deductions and write-offs, especially with your annual expenses and payroll taxes, but this will get you close. The goal is to save more than necessary with this calculation, so you'll have additional funds stored away for unexpected expenses. Your accountant will most likely advise you to make quarterly estimated payments, so you'll be refilling your tax savings every quarter. Having a little extra can protect you in months where you may miss the mark.

It all comes together

Adding all of this up will give you the first part of your shop rate equation. If you've taken any economics courses, you may recognize that you've just calculated your Direct Personal Expense (DPE) and your Overhead. Now, there are much more complicated, and accurate, ways to calculate your DPE and Overhead. If you grow to a point that you can have an accountant perform percentage-based calculations, please do so.

For most of us, our knowledge is limited and we can't accurately forecast where our business will be next week, much less next year. So this number can change often, possibly monthly, quarterly, or annually. It depends on the size of your business and the expenses that pop up. But for most small shops or solo creatives, this will do just fine. Here's an example:

An Example Expense Calculation	
Monthly recurring costs	$4,000
Annual costs ($\frac{1}{12}$ of $9,600)	$800
Your salary	$10,000
Staff salaries	$6,000
Contractor costs	$2,000
	$22,800
$22,800 x 1.25 (25% in taxes)	
Total Monthly Expenses	**$28,500**

Profit

To accurately calculate profit, you have to understand your cost. We've just covered that for your entire shop. To reiterate the shift in thinking, rather than trying to do this for each individual project, you're doing this for your entire shop on an annual basis. The number can and will move, but it should not shift dramatically from month to month unless something big happens.

Item	Cost
Start-Up & Annual Costs	
Office Furniture (Desks, Chairs, Tables)	$0.00
Computer hardware and software	$0.00
Association or Membership Fees	$0.00
Printing - Business Cards, Marketing Materials	$0.00
Office Decoration	$0.00
Software - One time purchase	$0.00
Lease Deposits	$0.00
Legal or Accounting Retainers	$0.00
Business licenses and permits	$0.00
Sponsorships or Marketing	$0.00
Travel, Conferences	$0.00
Other	$0.00
Total	$0.00
Split over 12 months (Divide total among 12 months equally) = COST PER MONTH	$0.00
Ongoing Monthly Expenses	
Salary of owner-manager (amount you need to pay yourself)	$0.00
All other salaries, wages, & commissions	$0.00
Payroll taxes or self-employment tax	$0.00
Rent	$0.00
Equipment lease payments	$0.00
Advertising (print, PPC, Twitter, Facebook)	$0.00
Postage & shipping costs	$0.00
Supplies (inks, toners, labels, paper goods, etc.)	$0.00
Cell Phone	$0.00
IVN or Phone Services	$0.00
Virtual Assistants	$0.00
Utilities	$0.00
Internet	$0.00
Hosting & Servers (AWS	$0.00
SaaS (Dropbox, Creative Cloud, Slack, Basecamp, etc.)	$0.00
General business insurance	$0.00
Other Insurance (business vehicles, etc.)	$0.00
Health insurance	$0.00
Interest & principal on loans & credit cards	$0.00
Misc. Debt	$0.00
Recurring Legal and other professional fees	$0.00
Miscellaneous	$0.00
Total	$0.00
TOTALS	$0.00

Here's where things get interesting for creative shops. Profit is a moving target for almost any business, and most small businesses are able to accurately predict the time and effort involved in meeting client deliverables. Food costs, construction materials, fabrics, etc. Whatever materials are involved can be inventoried. Time, however, isn't as easy to inventory. People get sick, projects take longer than expected, and costs rise considerably.

Moreover, with creative services, approval of our final deliverables is often subjective. We may "complete" a project per our client agreement, only to receive a laundry list of changes and adjustments. We can choose to fight the adjustments, ask for more money, or get to work and start cutting into our profits.

That's why so many creatives choose hourly pricing. They're afraid to give flat-fee quotes because of the risk involved. So we toggle between flat-fee projects, where we hope to make a profit, and hourly billing, where we're scrutinized for the time spent on each line-item. Our only shot at profit is to mark up someone who makes less than us per hour. Moreover, both scenarios make it difficult to make a consistent profit.

Making a consistent profit

To make a consistent profit, build it into the operating costs of your shop. Instead of trying to make a profit on each individual project, you make a profit on your entire business.

We've calculated our expenses:

$$(\text{Recurring Expenses} + \tfrac{1}{12} \text{ of Annual Expenses})$$
$$+$$
$$(\text{Your Salary} + \text{Staff Salaries} + \text{Contractor Fees})$$
$$\times$$
$$1.25 \ [25\% \text{ for taxes}]$$
$$=$$
$$\text{Expenses}$$

and now, we're going to calculate for a profit of 20 percent:

Expenses × 1.20 [Profit] = Total Operating Cost

So you've added up all of your costs and then multiplied that cost by an additional 20 percent. If your operating costs were $10,000 per month, they are now $12,000 per month when you include profit.

Here, we're using cost-plus pricing, which maximizes net gains and avoids arbitrary decision-making. The downside is that it's built for commodities. But for this part of our pricing strategy, we are actually dealing with a commodity: the cost of each hour that you're selling.

A cost-plus pricing calculation looks like this: **Cost + (Cost × % Profit) = Price**

$$\text{Cost} + (\text{Cost} \times \% \text{ Profit}) = \text{Price}$$

Look familiar? It's identical to our profit formula above. The difference is that we're not setting a public price, we're setting a rate. A rate that our clients never see. We're only using it to determine how much we need to charge for each hour we have to sell as a shop, not as individual creatives. There are no junior rates and senior rates here. Remember, shop rates and billing rates are different and we will break that down in a bit.

Clients don't care about your profit

Clients care about their profit, not yours. If you break down your proposals or invoices for them, you can't stick 20 percent on the end of the invoice for "profit." I mean, you could, but I'd like to hear how that works out. Trying to add your profit to your hourly rates or per-project pricing is exhausting. Building it into your operating costs means you don't even have to think about it.

You are still going to have to control hours, expenditures, and client revisions. Trying to control profit margins as well just makes it more difficult. Rather than trying to sort out your profit every time over and over again, know that you have a baseline that's covered. You don't have to explain anything to your clients when it comes to making a baseline profit. Keep in mind that this isn't your only opportunity for a profit. You still have the ability to mark up resources, use value-based pricing, and leverage numerous pricing strategies for even greater profitability.

Profitability matters

If you're not making a profit, is your business worth it? Think about it. If you're dealing with all of the challenges of running your own business to only make your operational costs, why not just get a job and go home at 5pm every day? The purpose of being in business for yourself is freedom. Freedom isn't sustainable without profit. Additional and unexpected expenses will arise, and having money in reserve to deal with the unexpected is critical to enjoying what you do.

Note that 20 percent is a guideline, and you may not feel like that's ideal for you. At a minimum, you should make at least 10 percent of your operating costs in profit. So if your annual operating costs are $180,000 ($15,000 per month for twelve months), then you need to make at the very least an additional $18,000 in profit each year.

Hours

The final piece of our formula is hours. Hours are the billable time you have available to work. If you have employees, this is the sum of everyone's billable time added together. If you can work one hundred billable hours per month and you're on your own, then the hours part of your shop rate formula is 100. It's that simple. If you have employees, you add their billable hours together to get your shop's total bucket of hours. Let's unpack that a bit.

No one works forty billable hours

Unless you work eighty hours, you won't have forty billable hours every week. There are numerous reasons why all of your time won't go to billable work, but a few broad guidelines should help you find a good, realistic number for your average.

Your creative business may still be in the side hustle phase. So it may be easier knowing you have a fixed amount of time, say ten or twenty hours a week, to devote to the side business and still sleep. Administrative tasks might be low because you may only have one client at a time.

If you're in your creative business full-time, it's a bit more difficult. Tracking your time for everything, including operations and meetings, will go a long way in helping you find your available billable hours. When you factor in everything from checking email to filing papers, driving to and from meetings, eating, sleeping, and having a life, you'll find that you only spend about half of your working hours on billable client work.

The unscientific general consensus is that most creatives hit a maximum average of thirty billable hours per week when they're solo. If they're part of a team, but not in charge, they may be able to hit thirty-five in a long week. If they're managing others, it dips into the fifteen to twenty-hour range. Certainly you can work nights, weekends, and overtime to get in far more than that; and at times that will be necessary to make your deadlines. But remember, the goal here is to find a real number that is sustainable long-term for your business—an average for fifty-two weeks a year.

The average knowledge worker receives over one hundred emails per day[3] which will take up to 15 percent of their time to manage. That means if you work fifty hours a week, you're spending fourteen hours on email alone. As you grow into your leadership role, that number often goes up and can be more than a quarter of your time.

For most solo creatives who do direct client work, a reasonable average is about twenty-five hours a week. Since there is an average of four weeks in a month, you will most likely end up with one hundred billable hours available each month.

Non-billable team members

If anyone on your team isn't billable, their costs are covered because their salary is part of your expenses. You don't have to sort out how much time they're spending on a particular project before you provide a quote nor do you have to factor it into your client costs. However, you certainly can if it's outside of your normal overhead.

If you have a dedicated project manager spending a significant portion of her time on a particular project, you may want to set a project management budget and calculate it against your shop rate. That can get messy because your project managers aren't always billable. You could have her contribute ten hours a week to your overall bucket of shop hours, but that's if she is consistently a big part of your billable project costs. I've found it much easier to consider admin and project management as operational overhead, no different from paying for computers or utilities.

In summary, it's difficult to estimate how much work there is for project management, operations, and other nebulous project contributions. At the very least, track billable and non-billable time during a project so that you can determine how it went.

What about teams?

Junior designers or developers may be able to contribute thirty-five billable hours a week consistently. They get assigned work and they sit down and do it. Other than a few meetings here and there, they may not have distractions. But, what about vacations, sick time, emergencies, and inevitable hiccups? That's why it's best to find a more reasonable number for your team members, such as twenty-five or thirty, rather than trying to push for more hours.

Remember that the shop rate isn't your billing rate, so you're not trying to make it lower than is necessary to be competitive. You want it to be accurate so that you're confident you're charging the right amount for your work.

Item	Cost
Expenses	$94,000
Profit (20%)	$18,800
Total Operating Cost	**$112,800**
Billable Hours per week	
Owner	10
Creative Director	18
Designer	22
Developer	25
Project Manager	0
Designer	28
Developer	28
Account Executive	0
Writer	25
Project Manager	0
Designer	30
Apprentice	20
Intern	5
TOTAL BILLABLE HOURS PER WEEK	211
TOTAL MONTHLY HOURS (Weekly total multiplied by 4)	844
Rate (Total Operating Cost divided by Total Monthly Hours)	$134

You've taken the red pill

You've just pulled the wool off your eyes and you now know what it really costs to run a creative business. You have a hard number that is a fact, not a guess, that you can use to determine what to charge. You can get better at time estimates, and we're going to work on that soon, but you won't go anywhere if the rate you use to calculate your projects is based on emotions or guesswork.

Shop Rate vs. Billing Rate

The difference between your shop rate and your billing rate is simple. Your shop rate is private: it's only for you and your business partners. Your billing rate is public: you disclose it to your clients whom you charge hourly. Determining a billing rate, however, is anything but simple.

Some creative businesses have no use for a billing rate. Writers, editorial illustrators, fine art photographers, and many other creative skills don't effectively translate to time for money. But there is still a market that determines what prices are reasonable.

That's where the guidebooks, surveys, and conversations with your colleagues come in handy. The value of your services to your market determines your rate. If you're in an extremely competitive market, such as web design, it's hard to compete with hourly prices. If you're in a more specialized market, such as editorial illustration, the going rate for a finished illustration may come in a whole dollar amount.

Why not use my shop rate as my billing rate?

The honest answer is that you can. If your shop rate is something your client market will bear, it's perfectly fine to use it as your billing rate. The problem, however, is that not every client is going to accept your billing rate. If they ask you to come down, and you want the work, you're coming down from your shop rate and cutting into your necessary revenue. Another issue is that it's difficult to explain why the same rate applies to junior employees and senior employees. Clients that are paying top dollar expect top-level talent to do all of the work.

So a billing rate is a guess?

Yep, more or less. A shop rate is based on solid math. A billing rate is something that you feel your market will bear, covers your income needs, and sounds "about right" in light of what you know. It should never be less than your shop rate, and it's ideal if it's at least 15% greater. Where you go from there is really guesswork and gut feelings.

This is where it gets messy

The "blended" shop rate that we've covered isn't anything new or revolutionary. It's what Don Draper probably used, so it's retro. The prevailing wisdom for the last ten or fifteen years, since design has become more common with freelancers and small agencies, has been to use varying rates for each team member, task, or role. For example, you charge $100 an hour for senior designers, $75 an hour for junior designers, and $50 an hour for interns. Another example would be $100 an hour for design work but only $50 an hour for meetings.

That's how we priced our work in my first business, and it was a nightmare. It allowed our clients to determine who got the majority of the workload instead of us determining who was best suited to do the job. It commoditized our services. But hourly billing may be unavoidable for you, so you have to have a billing rate.

What if my shop rate is significantly more than my billing rate?

If you've been in business for a while and you've determined that your shop rate is significantly more than what you've been billing, you have to raise your rates. We'll go into detail in just a bit on how to do that. Until you can get your billing rates in line with your shop rate, you'll have to make adjustments. You may have to outsource some of your work to a cheaper resource. You may have to cut costs. You may have to forego profit while you work toward a higher billing rate.

If your shop rate is $200 an hour and your market won't bear any more than $125 an hour, you've got some tough decisions to make. If the limitation is geographic, then start marketing outside of your local area where clients are willing to pay higher rates. The easiest thing to do is cut overhead. If cutting overhead isn't an option, then you may have to hire junior creatives at lower rates that you can make a profit on for every hour that they work. Their lower salaries will lower your shop rate since they generate more billable hours with a lower salary to overhead contribution.

What if I'm not experienced or talented enough to justify my shop rate?

Well, then you're going to make less money. There's just no other way to put it. If you can't make enough money in your creative business with the rate that your market will bear, then you probably should start out as a side hustle until you are skilled and experienced enough to charge more. Keep in mind that value is relative, and you may find clients who are more than happy to pay full market rates for your work right now.

My shop rate is insane, I can't sleep at night if I charge this!

You've been realistic in your estimates; this is what you need to live. Your responsibilities may be greater than others, or you may live somewhere expensive. I'm the main breadwinner of my household and my wife only works part-time. We live in a very expensive zip code and invest heavily in our children's education. Could we move somewhere cheaper, use one car, and not invest in additional outlets for our children? Sure. Should I give that up because I feel bad about my shop rate? Of course not.

For example, $120 an hour may sound like a lot, but for most of us $12,000 a month to run a business isn't that high. In fact, it's low. When you consider taxes, expenses, and overhead, you'll probably keep about $8,000 of that $12,000, or 75 percent, for your pay. That's roughly a $96,000 a year salary. For most of us, that isn't far-fetched for being a creative professional. When we say $96,000 a year, that number sounds normal. But when we say $120 an hour, it may sound high. And that's why knowing your shop rate can change your attitude, and knowing is half the battle.

The whole point of being in business for yourself is to have the power to create the lifestyle you want. That may mean a big house in the suburbs and expensive cars. It could mean a vagabond lifestyle living out of a backpack in a different country every season. The freedom that comes with creative life doesn't mean rich or poor, it means creating the life you want on your terms. If the life you want calls for a large salary, then it's justified. You don't owe anyone an apology.

Now, with that said, maybe you have to scale up to that lifestyle. Can you make cuts right now and slowly increase your salary and costs? Can you work somewhere cheaper or reduce your meal expenses? There are things that can't move such as your mortgage and insurance, and things that can such as expendable income and non-critical overhead. So if your shop rate seems very high, take a look at your expenses and make adjustments where you know you'll actually make lifestyle changes, but don't apologize for making a comfortable living.

My shop rate still seems astronomical, what could be wrong?

Something may be wrong with your costs. But now you know where to look. Here are some things you can look for:

- Are your employees' skills commensurate with their pay? Are you overpaying them?

- Are you top-heavy, meaning you have partners or multiple owners and your salaries are your biggest expense?

- Are you paying yourself too much?

- Is your rent or lease too high?

- Do you have excessive services or fees? Can you do without some of them?

- Can you reduce your profit goals and still be comfortable?

Raising Your Rates

Whether it's with an existing client or all new clients going forward, raising your rates and prices is ripe for self-deprecation, unnecessary apology, and squeamishness. The idea of simply charging more for the same services makes some people uneasy. The first couple of times you do it, it's going to give you a slight panic attack. Once you get used to it, you'll do it all the time!

It's easy to tie your experience level, and your self-worth, to your rates. When raising them, you run the risk of losing a client. But do you want to keep clients around who can't see your value as you work with them? Keep in mind that if you're charging more money per client or hour, you need fewer clients to make the same amount of money. So losing a cheap client may not be so unfortunate.

For some, a rate increase can improve your perceived value to the client. It becomes clear that you're in demand when you're confident enough to command higher rates. That means you're increasing in professionalism and skill. Sometimes people just like the more expensive option. So you may, in fact, attract even more clients with a higher rate.

Making more money is important to your craft. The more freedom you have to take time between clients and projects, the more time you have to learn and improve. It will increase your enjoyment of your job if you're making more money for the same amount of work. Raising your rates is something you'll never regret. What you will regret is six years into your career, you're still charging the same rate as when you've started, and you're wondering why you work eighteen hours a day.

How to Raise Your Rates

- Set an effective date and stick to it.

- For all new clients going forward from that date, use the new rate.

- For existing clients, give yourself at least 1 quarter before implementing the new rate. At or before the 90 day/1 quarter mark before your effective date, communicate the rate change to your client.

- For your larger or longer-term clients who you can meet with face to face, it's best to communicate the rate change in person.

- Put the rate change in writing per any contract terms you have. If you have a retainer, you'll need an updated retainer agreement. Another reason for the lead time is so that the updated contract can be processed.

- Keep it short; you don't need to give them one hundred reasons why. If it's an email, it can simply be, "as of March 1, we are increasing our rate from $100 per hour to $150 per hour. Invoices will reflect the new rate. Attached is an updated agreement with the new rate. Please sign and return it as soon as you can and let me know if you have any questions."

- For the phone call, a basic script could be, "Hi Jim, thanks for taking my call. We're getting things in order for the upcoming quarter, and one change is our billing rate. It's that time of year that we take a look at everything and we're raising it. It's not for 90 days, so there's plenty of time to get invoicing lined up. I'll need to get an updated agreement over to you with the new rate in place, and when you get a chance, I'd appreciate it if you could sign it and send it back over. Nothing you need to do, it'll be business as usual. Any questions for me?"

- Do not apologize.

What if the client asks why you're raising your rate?

- Discuss the value of your work with your clients. That means speaking with them, without mentioning the possible rate increase, about how you're doing and the value it provides. Ask specific questions such as "am I making your job easier?", "do you feel that we're exceeding expectations?", and "are we providing value to the company?" Once you have these answers, use them in your rebuttal if they resist your rate increase.

- It's important to quantify your value, so try to find specific cases where you've made a difference. For example, a campaign you wrote was their most well-received of the year, your most recent design was their all-time best seller, or call hold times are down 10 percent thanks to the new FAQ page on the website. Try to find stats for everything that you can think of that you've done with them.

- You should know their goals for the year; if not, find out what they are before discussing the rate increase. Consider your increased role in these objectives. Demonstrate how your increased focus can help.

- Tell them you have to be selective with your clients. Your business is growing, and it's important that you give your clients your best work every time. You are receiving more and more requests for work, and people are willing to pay higher rates. You want to keep this client, so you're offering them the first right of refusal on staying with you as a client. You are willing to work with them on your rate increase timeline, but you can't do the same work for different clients for less money.

- The client will ask about a loyalty discount or "what about the fact that we worked with you when others wouldn't." Yes, that's true, they may have taken a chance on you when you were first starting out or when your work wasn't as good. That time has passed; you are now in demand and your work has improved. Your value has increased, and others are seeing that value. You can show them loyalty by offering a longer timeline to increase the rate. However, make it clear that the greatest way you can show loyalty is by sticking with them and already knowing the ins and outs of their business.

Rate compromises to consider

For an existing client, you may not make a big jump. If your daily rate is going from $1,000 to $2,000 or your hourly rate from $50 to $100, it may be hard to make that much of a leap in one quarter. Offer a graduated scale. For the day rate, go to $1,500 on your new rate effective date and then to the full $2,000 a full quarter later. For hourly, you could work in percentages, such as breaking the increase up in thirds. On the effective date, go up to $65, and then three months later go up to $85, then to the full

$100 a full six months after your effective date. Sometimes it's best just to rip off the band-aid and make the jump, but if it means losing a client altogether that you can't afford to lose, this is an option.

If they aren't willing to budge on the rate increase, offer to refer them to someone else who is at that rate. Be willing to walk away and compromise on the count of clients over the cost of your services.

Now What?

You've got your shop rate and maybe a billing rate. You're equipped to raise your rates. So what's next? Now, you work with different approaches to pricing to determine what works best for your clients and services.

There is no one size fits all solution. It's unlikely that you'll ever land on a single pricing model for every client and project unless you stick to hourly pricing exclusively. There are seven pricing models that work well for creative businesses:

- Hourly billing
- Project-based pricing/fixed fee
- Value-based pricing
- Time and value-based retainers
- Package pricing
- Performance-based pricing
- Equity/ownership pricing

Throughout the rest of this chapter, we'll break down each model including pros and cons, use cases, and how to implement them.

PRICING MODELS

Pricing Model 1: Hourly Billing

Providing services at an hourly rate isn't something that warrants an explanation, but being successful as a billed-hourly creative does. It's much more than just sharing an hourly rate, keeping up with the hours worked, and sending an invoice.

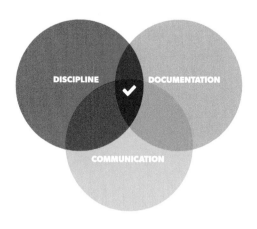

Hourly billing can be an excellent way to start, and some larger shops even go back to hourly rates after years of project-based pricing success. But it requires much more scrutiny than most are willing to endure if you want to be profitable, which often doesn't foster client trust. The key to hourly success comes down to discipline, documentation, and communication.

Discipline

To be successful with hourly billing, you have to be consistently "on the clock" when you're working. Even the most minor part of a project, such as answering an email, has to be treated as project work and tracked. Failing to track the "little things" can chip away at any profit margins built into your hourly rate.

Clients have no way of knowing if their requests are simple or can take hours to complete. Rather than guessing at whether to track something, you have to track everything, even five-minute tasks. Otherwise, you can turn any innocent client into a "bad one." This constant need to validate everything you do can be exhausting, but it also means you're getting paid for what you work. That's fair and honest, and it's the lowest-risk way to bill.

You also have to keep up with your non-billable hours for operations, personal projects, and business development. If you're going to work as an hourly-only creative, then you have to treat your own business as your most important client. That means "billing" yourself hourly for each part of your business. For example, if you're working on business development, you have to set budgets for how much time you can allot to emails, online research, and networking. Track those hours as well. The same goes for bookkeeping, continuing education, and general administration. Every hour you spend on a proposal or responding to incoming work requests should be tracked.

If you're using the shop rate formula, you've allotted yourself non-billable time by only counting a fraction of your working hours for billable work. For example, you've based your shop rate on twenty-five billable hours a week, so you should then have fifteen hours a week left over for non-billable work. So why is it such a big deal to track everything?

For one, you are probably spending far more than fifteen hours on non-billable work. By tracking your time spent, you may be able to determine where you can outsource services to increase efficiency. If you're spending three hours a week on accounting and you're charging $100 an hour, can you get someone to manage your books for less than $300 a week? You probably can, and you'll "save" money in the process.

Having a detailed understanding of the time you're spending helps you know where you need help, where you can be profitable, and what you can stop doing.

Documentation

For all of this to come together, you have to track your time. As basic as it sounds, it's one of the most common challenges creatives face. I struggle with time tracking. If you also struggle with documentation, hourly billing may not be best for you.

There are, however, creatives with whom I work who are wonderful at documentation and are far happier on an hourly schedule. In fact, a few of the most successful and profitable creatives I know are hourly-only operators. The key to their success is finding a time-tracking solution that is near-impossible to ignore. For some, it's a stopwatch and paper ledger. For others, it's a suite of time-tracking services that integrate. For most, myself included, it's finding an integrated time-tracking and invoicing solution with multiple points of entry.

Practically, this means having a trigger. Something like an app on your phone or computer, a stopwatch, an egg timer, or a paper ledger that you set out on your desk. That trigger indicates "I am tracking the time that I am spending on this task." Ideally you should work in limited bursts of time and have a definitive start and stop time for working on this particular task.

In your tracking tool be overly descriptive of what you're doing and provide notes. Don't write "coding" or "researching" for the task. Use descriptive, actionable terms such as "sketched the home page lower feature area" or "coded the color variables for the internal pages." If you're using an electronic tool, try using tags or other taxonomies that you can later search to tie time spent to particular descriptive words. The more data you have, the more informed you are about the health of your business. Time-tracking data, regardless of whether you bill hourly, is useful data.

Documentation also keeps you honest when it comes to billing your clients. It helps you understand just how much work was needed to accomplish projects in part or as a whole. You may find that you're spending far too much time on setting up your design grid or your structural markup. That can lead you to invest in learning a framework or taking an extra couple of days to build re-usable base grids that can cut start time down.

One practical example that I found was the amount of time wasted on many of our micro-site projects seeking quality stock photography. Many of our clients insisted on finding unique and beautiful photos that enhanced the design instead of creating unnecessary noise. I would spend entire days looking at and documenting photography options on multiple sites and organizing them into lightboxes. Only by looking at time-tracking data did it become apparent that it was worth investing the time and money in a higher-grade service that we could hire to source our photography for us. In the end, we can charge the client for the service, at a markup, and use that time on more important parts of the project while a real photography sourcing professional does the work.

Documentation is important as you move into bringing in freelance help or outside vendors. If you're billing your client hourly at one rate and having someone else perform work at a lower hourly rate, you have to hold yourself, and everyone involved, accountable for tracking their time. Far too often this is where creatives end up losing money on hourly projects. That helps you understand if you have the right people helping you at the right rates. It also ensures that there aren't gaping holes in your explanation to a client when it comes to an overage, delay, or increase in the requested allotment of hours for the next project.

Communication

Hourly billing can increase the risk of miscommunication and client dissatisfaction. To avoid frustration and financial loss, regularly communicate with your clients the time spent on their project. Many creatives are afraid to report periodically to their clients because they aren't spending the time they've said they would on the work.

If you're struggling with working the amount of time you said you would, or you've found that something you quoted at ten hours is only taking two, then it's time for you to move onto project-based pricing or raise your rates.

The worst hourly billing scenario is feeling like you have to hide what you're doing to justify over-charging. If it's something easy that you can knock out in half an hour, then you need to do the right thing and charge that client for a half an hour. Next time, make it clear to the client that you've done the base work and establish a flat fee for similar work going forward.

A practical example might be a brochure that the client updates quarterly. You may have found a way to update that information quickly and all formatting stays intact. In the past, it may have taken hours to get everything looking right, but now it's fast. So you feel that you should charge the client that same $500 you charged in the past even though it only took you about $100 worth of time to do it. In this scenario, rather than lying about it on your hourly report, just tell the client what's going on. That is an opportunity to make it clear that you are more advanced than when you started with them, and you can raise your hourly rate. You can then use that rate to charge more for other work that's of greater value to you and your client.

At a minimum, you should be sending your client hourly reports at the 50 percent mark of your billing period. If you bill your client monthly, they should be receiving an hourly report no less than every two weeks. If you bill weekly, then your client should get a report halfway through the week. It can be informal, a plain email stating how many hours you've logged this week and what was accomplished that takes mere minutes to compile and send.

Clients appreciate hourly billing for cost controls but also fear it for the unknown. The more you keep a client in the dark when it comes to progress, time spent, and budget remaining, the more nervous they will become. When clients are nervous, they tend to make demands rather than requests and be less forgiving with delays. Being in constant communication with your clients about what you've done and how long it's taken—which equates to how much it costs—will keep things much more civil and productive.

Hourly billing can be restrictive. It makes the relationship feel transactional. The more often you are in communication with your client, the less it seems like a commodity exchange vs. a collaborative relationship. For most of us, we're doing custom work and the client wants to feel like they are getting a unique solution to their problem from a craftsman. Personalized attention-to-detail goes a long way in managing clients who always want more and change their minds constantly. It fosters the ideals of hand-crafted work that makes the recipient more likely to accept it as a work of art rather than a purchased product. You can mitigate the challenges of hourly billing by putting communication and collaboration at the forefront.

Hourly Billing in Summary

Hourly billing is not my favorite way to price your work, but it has merit. I tend to avoid it because I believe that creative isn't a commodity and, therefore, shouldn't equate to hours in/hours out. Many clients ask for hourly billing, but they often hate it; they just don't know of any other way to work.

Hourly billing is unpredictable for you and your client. As you gain experience, you can improve the accuracy of hourly estimates, but far too often projects take at least 1.5x the amount of time they should. Asking for more hours is rarely enjoyable.

As you get further along in your career, hourly billing can penalize you if you're fast or find more efficient ways of working. Raising your rates can help, but for longer-term clients, it can be harder to raise rates over and over again as you improve. Hourly billing can make it difficult for you to predict your income, which increases stress levels and the likelihood of taking on bad clients and sub-par work.

Hourly billing isn't complicated, but it can be messy. For many creatives, the biggest draw is that you are getting paid for the time that you work; this feels stable and sure-footed. Hourly pricing is best for nebulous, undefined deliverables because it keeps you from under-pricing or over-committing to something that's unclear. One of the greatest wins for hourly billing is how much easier it is to say no to change requests. When it's clear to a client that the change will cost more money, it forces them to take the time to decide if it's worth it.

Key advantages

- Clients love it
- You're paid for your time
- Easy to sell
- Easy to calculate
- You're in control of change requests

Key risks

- Unpredictable

- Commoditizes your work

- Limited opportunity for profit

- Requires higher rates or markup to make significant margins

When to Use Hourly Billing

Hourly billing is ideal for freelance workers who are consistently working one level away from the client, e.g. for an ad agency or larger creative firm. It's unlikely you will find anyone who will hire you on a value or retainer basis at an agency or staffing firm. It's also ideal for any work involving sophisticated technology such as a website or app development.

Hourly billing isn't a long-term solution for most creatives unless you choose to remain freelance. You will only become profitable by raising your rates, which has a ceiling. It's ideal for starting out or when you're having difficulty closing larger clients.

For non-freelancers, such as small shops or agencies, hourly should only be used for maintenance or initial work with a new client. It's not a long-term strategy for growth without a retainer due to unpredictability. While some shops thrive on hourly billing programs, they also have to scale their staffing significantly to keep up with demand. There is an opportunity for profit, but it's not the easiest way to go about it.

Tasks well-suited for hourly billing

- Complex programming and development

- Agency or subcontracted work

- Repairs or maintenance work

- Small strategy consulting or single features

- Production-only creative with established brand assets and creative

- Creative or technical writing

- Social media strategy

- Animation

Pricing Model 2:
Project-based and Flat-fee Pricing

Project-based or "flat-fee" pricing is the most common model for creative businesses. Someone asks you how much a website costs, you tell them $4,000, you work on that website, and you charge them $4,000 no matter how long it takes. Most likely you'll charge half of the project cost ($2,000) upfront and the other half in the end when you deliver the final product.

The price is static and can't be moved. You and your client have agreed upon a fixed price for the deliverables in your contract, and you will deliver those items for that price, regardless of the cost involved. Only if there are excessive changes outside of the scope of work would you then ask for more money. That conversation, however, can be awkward and difficult.

Many creatives try to avoid asking for more hours to complete the work, which can lead to losing money. The hesitation to bill for overages relates to how the project is billed, how it's structured, or how you communicate with the client. Moving to more flexible pricing models is the best solution, but if you're sticking with project-based pricing, there are ways to improve these areas of concern.

Ways To Improve Your Margins With Project-Based Pricing

Don't tie your payment schedule to deliverables in the project, such as start and end. We'll dive deeper into this in Chapter 5. By breaking the project down into smaller and more frequent payments, which are on a time-based schedule, you remove the client's leverage to withhold payment while requesting changes. It ensures that you're not making excessive changes just to get the client to sign off on the next payment milestone.

Make your subcontracted resources project-based as well. Instead of having subcontractors or freelancers work for you on an hourly basis, get them to give you a fixed-fee quote for any work that they do on project-based work. That way if their contributions to the project go over budget, you can quantify those costs for your client and have more predictable line-item budgets from the start.

Break your projects into smaller "projects." Don't try to create a single statement of work for all of the work involved for months at a time. If your projects are of any substantial size, try to break it up into smaller components that you can complete and bill for with higher frequency. The risk lies in not having a guarantee of the later parts of the project, but if you're doing quality work and establishing a strong relationship with the client, that shouldn't be an issue.

Safe Yet Risky

When I first started out, my project prices were just a shot in the dark. I often went with what felt right in my gut, what my friends were charging, or what I had been charging for similar work. I learned to use my hourly billing rate to calculate the project cost by taking into account all of the moving parts of the project—time to design, meetings, coding, software, content entry, layout, outlines—plus how long I thought each one would take, and then multiplying that by my rate in order to come up with a rough project cost.

That model worked okay, but I was still losing money on most of my projects. Even as my time estimates improved, something wasn't right. That's when I learned that this model can work, but only if you're using your shop rate. If your billing rate is less than your shop rate, then using your billing rate means that you're not considering your operational costs and profit goals when calculating your project totals. Even if you're making "enough" with your billing rate, you aren't working with concrete numbers based on your entire shop needs. Only by using your shop rate, which covers all of your needs, can you then price flat-fee projects with confidence.

In addition to calculating your time estimate by your shop rate, add 20 percent worth of hours for overages. If you count up 100 hours for the entire project by going through each piece, you'll budget for 120 hours multiplied by your shop rate.

Example Project Calculation for a Basic Website

Meetings	18 hours	Development Polish	10 hours
Wireframes	8 hours	Training & Documentation	8 hours
Design Concepts	12 hours	Quality Assurance	10 hours
Design Review	4 hours	Handoff to Client & Launch	4 hours
Design Refinement	20 hours		
Initial Development	30 hours	**Project Total**	154 hours
Front-end Development	20 hours	**20% Padding**	31 hours
Design Refinement	10 hours	**Total Hours**	185 hours

Shop Rate: $150 per hour   185 x $150 = $27,750

Easy To Sell, Not Quite As Easy To Manage

Project-based pricing is very attractive for clients. It allows them to be in complete control of what they're spending and what they're getting. Clients can give you a list of what they want, you agree to a price for that list, and then you go build it. It sounds fair and easy because it's very similar to commoditized transactions. It's as close to buying the detergent at Target as your client is going to get. The client doesn't care what you have to do to produce their solution; they just want to know they're getting a price they can afford and the final product that they want.

It would be lovely if every project went that way, but project-based pricing is where many creative businesses fail, go bankrupt, or just fall apart against the grind of continuous client work. There's nothing to limit the number of changes or the level of subjectivity the client brings to what is "final" and triggers final payment. Being as detailed as possible in your agreements can mitigate some risk, but not all. It takes strong contracts, communication, and process management to keep project-based pricing profitable. We'll dive deep into that in the next chapter.

By using your shop rate to calculate the time involved and its cost, you are at least covering your overhead and profit goals as long as you end up completing the work in the amount of time estimated. But many of us, myself included, suck at estimating. There are just too many gray areas or complete unknowns when it comes to client work. Asking as many questions as possible can help, but often we just need to get the proposal submitted to win the work. So that's where project pricing can cause many of the problems it promises to fix. Now, let's look at some ways to improve our time estimates.

Improving Your Time Estimates

The best way to improve your time estimates is to get away from writing proposals. This can be remedied with Discovery sessions, which we'll cover in detail in the next chapter. If, however, your client isn't interested in Discovery, there are ways to get more information up front for higher accuracy in your time estimates.

Don't give them what they want. Your clients are writing their requests for proposals, yet they aren't creatives. So why would you give them what they're asking for when they don't know what to ask for? Yet, that's how most of us write our statements of work: we list a price or estimate the time it will take for each line item the client is requesting. The first, and most important, step in getting your time estimates right is to stop and ask detailed questions about the client's goals and their desired solutions rather than what they think they need.

Track your time on every project and keep it categorized. The more data you have to determine how long it takes you and your team to complete similar work on past projects, the more accurate you'll be with future estimates.

Get outside help. If you're working with new technology or something you're unfamiliar with, hire an experienced vendor to help you write your proposal and create your estimates. If you're going to have to hire help anyway, try to get them to help you with the estimate for "free" in the hope that you'll win the work together.

Be as detailed as possible. There's a fine line between spending too much time on an estimate and getting it right. Try to break bigger phases into smaller deliverables that use action words. So instead of calling a phase "research" and allocating ten hours to it, break it down into two points for "Search for Inspiration: 4 hours" and "Analyze Competitors: 6 hours." That way you're tying the hours to active processes rather than generic titles.

Always break down your projects consistently. Use proposal software with templates or create your own in your document editor of choice. Set restrictions for yourself on the buckets you place your time and resources in so that you're sure to cover every phase. For most shops, you'll be doing a few different types of project "types" that can serve as general templates for phases and deliverables.

Review projects immediately for estimate accuracy. As soon as you complete a phase of a project, take the time to compare your actual hours to your original estimates and notate the reason for any notable differences. Don't wait until you complete the entire project; do this at the end of each phase or at least weekly. Use this data to determine where you continue to experience overages and can improve your process.

Cover Your Assets

Freelance or solo workers should be careful any time you bring in outside resources to flat-free projects. If they aren't agreeing to a flat fee as well and plan to stick to it, you could actually end up spending more money than you make to get the work done. Get accurate quotes and contracts with anyone you hire. Agencies should consider all factors in the project price including the operational overhead that surrounds the work.

The Bigger They Are, The Harder They Fall

As you grow, you'll hopefully take on larger projects for larger clients. As budgets increase, so does risk. You'll likely take on projects that involve new technology or multiple team members, which increases the complexity of your time estimates. I, along with several colleagues, have gone into projects counting on a subcontractor that we've estimated a healthy $10,000 for only to end up spending $30,000 on two or three different contractors to get the work done. I've had contractors charge me for increases in scope beyond my control, be unqualified despite their assurances and work samples, or simply not do the work.

Even without subcontractors, there are countless unknowns in creative projects. The more complex the project, the more opportunities for things to go wrong. If your projects involve technology, such as websites and apps, then you're at a much higher risk for losing money.

Project-based Pricing in Summary

Project-based pricing is the first step away from commoditized transactions for your work. By keeping the time involved in creating your client's solution irrelevant, at least to the client, you're on the right track to providing value rather than an itemized receipt that they can scrutinize. As you become more efficient, hire help that costs less than your shop rate, and work on projects similar to past work, you can maximize profits without worrying about spending unnecessary time on client work just to get in enough hours.

Developing relationships directly with clients, rather than working through agencies and staffing firms, means that you're in a position to charge more for your work than just the hours involved. You can begin to see profit above and beyond your basic forecasts and experience significant growth. The key is to be as accurate as possible in your time estimates and learn from past mistakes to improve your accuracy.

Key advantages

- Clients love it
- Very predictable
- Common and expected by clients
- Opportunity for profit is high

Key risks

- Tendency to undercharge

- Risk of going over budget and losing money

- Tough to cover unexpected challenges

- Commonality can lead to limited understanding of value

When To Use Project-based Pricing

Project-based pricing is ideal for small shops or anyone new to creative business. It's the first step toward value-based pricing and higher profit margins. It's great for people who do similar work for similar clients on a repeat basis, e.g. Wordpress websites for restaurants.

Project-based pricing can be your long-term solution if you're good at time estimates. You can become profitable through hiring staff or freelancers or by charging more per project. There is no limit to the size client you can work with using this model. Never use this model for ongoing support unless you are doing the same thing each month without the possibility of technical complications.

Tasks well-suited for project-based pricing

- Strategy and consulting

- Design

- Front-end web development (HTML, CSS, JS)

- Template projects

- One-off components of larger ongoing projects

Project and Hourly, like Peanut Butter and Jelly

You don't have to pick a single pricing strategy. A combination can work in both the long and short term. Project-based pricing and hourly billing are the two simplest models to both sell and manage. For anyone new to creative business, these two models are where you're likely to land, and both are acceptable.

If you are a designer who works on technology projects, you may take a blended approach to your work. You could charge hourly rates for the technology development, but project-based pricing for your design work. The gist is that these two models aren't in conflict, they can work together or be used on a client to client basis. Here are a few guidelines to help you determine which is best in certain situations.

Working with the same client on similar work regularly

Hourly

Rather than trying to come up with project budgets over and over again, if you're doing repetitive work for the same client it's best to run a clock and invoice often. This relationship should transition into a retainer down the road, but for the time being hourly works great. You should have enough rapport with the client to be open about how long things will take, and they should have you situated well enough in their accounting system for frequent and on-time payment.

A project's deliverables are unclear

Hourly

Clarity is the ultimate weapon for accurate time estimates. If the client's desired outcomes, or the actual solutions they're asking to be completed, aren't clear, then pricing hourly is the best way to protect yourself. Clients may push you to give them a fixed cost for something they can't even define, and that is the worst situation to be in as a creative. Unless you can clearly state what will be delivered, how it will be formatted, when it is needed, and what it's supposed to accomplish, you really can't offer a fixed fee.

The client asks about money a lot up front

Project

If clients come to you with a dollar amount from the start, or are consistently asking for a "ballpark price", then hourly is going to be difficult. Giving price-conscious customers itemized receipts often results in them nitpicking the outcome. Since they're leading with price, they have concerns about overages and what they can afford. Sending them into a project without complete clarity on what will be delivered for a set cost is a recipe for frustration.

The scope of the project changed several times when meeting with the client

Hourly

Before you write that project-based proposal, stop and think about how the client is going to handle the scope of work. Indecision and unclear deliverables are clear signs that the client doesn't know what they want. If you're unable to get them to compensate you to write a detailed proposal after extensive interviews, then you're likely to lose money with a project-based price. If you have already committed to providing a fixed fee to the client, you can either decide to walk away from the project or significantly increase your time estimate. You should also take the extra time to write an extremely detailed deliverables section in your contract.

It's clear you can get it done faster than it should be

Project

If you've done similar work in the past that you can repurpose, or if you're providing something simple that makes a huge difference for the client, you should be compensated for your expertise and effort rather than your time. In addition, pricing by project means that if you can get it done faster, your profit is even higher, so you're motivated to get it done. This is the initial seed for value-based pricing, and a step in the right direction.

You're doing very complex technology work

Hourly

Project-based pricing can be wrecked by unknowns and technological hurdles. As you do more complex work for clients, it becomes increasingly difficult to estimate how long a project will take. In this case, some agencies with hundreds of employees and millions of dollars in revenue stick to an hourly-only billing policy. That's perfectly fine. Often their hourly rate is $250 per hour or more, and no employee is making that much money, so the owners are making a profit due to the economy of scale.

Pricing Model 3:
Value-based Pricing

"Price is what you pay. Value is what you get." Warren Buffet[4]

The Old Engineer

A small riverside community was poised to grow and thrive thanks to the opening of a much-needed dam with the Army Corps of Engineers. On the afternoon before the dam was to open to the public, tests were run, and the spillway doors wouldn't open. Executives from the local power company had flown in for the next morning's grand festivities. The mayor, local senator, and everyone involved in the project were desperately scrambling to get the dam working, but to no avail.

One of the senior engineers on the project dug out his phone and called his long-retired former boss. The old man made the evening drive over in his beat-up truck. After hearing everyone's ideas about what could be wrong, he slowly climbed his way up to the spillway doors. He crawled into a small space behind a service door with only a flashlight. A few minutes later, he crawled back out and told a young mechanic that he needed two particular wrenches. He said, I'll be right back, and got back in his truck. He drove to the local hardware store and bought two screws and a valve at a cost $6.32. Then, he made his way back to the job site. With the newly-purchased parts and the two wrenches in hand, he crawled back in through the service door. Several minutes later he yelled out "try it now" and everyone reached for their radios. The control center technician pressed a button. With a smooth and calculated motion, the spillway doors slowly opened.

Cheers erupted throughout the team as everyone watched the water run over the spillway ramp and into what would become the hydroelectric basin. The old engineer was a hero. He slowly made his way over to his truck and came back with a thick metal clipboard. He pulled out a pen and filled out a carbon-copy form, tore off the top sheet, and handed it to the project manager. It was an invoice for $10,006.32. The manager looked at the old engineer, then the invoice, then back at him again. "That's $10,000 for me knowing how to fix this, and $6.32 for the parts. A check will do just fine," said the old engineer. The project manager paused, tried to speak, then thought better of it. Then, he made his way to his truck to dig out his check book as the old engineer stood and smiled.

Thanks to my good friend and business partner, J. Cornelius, for this story.

What is Value-based Pricing?

Value-based pricing is driven by customer demand and their willingness to pay. It's based on three components:

- **What your market will bear.** This may be your local market, e.g. Atlanta, Georgia, or your horizontal market, e.g. web design. You can get granular and define your market as "custom logo designs for consumer brands in the United States." This also means understanding your competition and what they are charging for similar work with clients of similar size.

- **Your track record and past experience.** If you have extensive experience with a particular type of client, technology, or style of design, then you fall into the "expert" category. Experts can charge more for their services. As you've been successful with past clients, gathering data and feedback that you can share with future clients allows them to see that hiring you means that they're more likely to get desirable results.

- **The perceived value to the client.** This doesn't apply in every case, but often you'll be called upon to detail how your work is "worth more" to the client than the work of others. You may have to quantify it by agreeing to certain performance metrics, such as increases in sales, or describing how your work can improve the client's business and clearly defining "improve" in the context of your work. This can evolve into performance-based pricing, which we'll cover later.

You may offer a different price to two separate clients for the same work. Clients aren't paying you for your time; they're paying you for solutions. Thus, those solutions are worth more to some clients than others.

The lynchpin of value-based pricing is a client who's satisfied with what she paid for what she received. She may not be *happy* about spending more money, but she understands that by spending more money, she's getting exceptional results. It's your job, however, to deliver the expected and exceptional results.

"The value of what I do," Karen said, "is based on the impact I can have on my client's business. Impact is how they value my services. So I look at pricing from their point of view. They don't hire me to design a website for the sake of designing a website. They hire me to design a website that's going to help them grow their business. I find when I look at it like that— from their perspective—it's clear I'm not selling time. Instead, I'm selling a solution that is going to make an impact for my client and achieve some business objective."

Mike McDerment[5]

Value Is in the eye of the beholder

A Hermes bag may only cost a thousand dollars to make, but customers are willing to pay tens of thousands to own it. Demand and quality are two of the biggest factors in value-based pricing, but there is much more to it when it comes to creative services. In all likelihood, your services will allow your customers to gain a competitive advantage and that alone is worth far more than the simple cost of your time and resources. The tens of thousands of dollars most people would spend on the Hermes bag isn't hindered by competition; they are deciding to spend that much money on *the* bag they truly want, not just *any* bag. In the same way, your clients can hire someone to create an illustration for them for $500 vs. your $5,000 fee. But is that illustration the one they want? Is that illustration the one that's going to get the attention they desire?

Your business isn't your client's business

No matter how good you are or your perceived market value, some clients simply won't care. Even clients who do care about your reputation and past experience can still be turned off by value-based pricing. The goal isn't to convince them how awesome you are and that you deserve higher fees because of your experience. The goal is to help them see that you can provide better results with a more substantial impact in a more reasonable time-frame. If you can't do better, stronger, faster, then you're not ready for value-based pricing.

"Better" doesn't mean that your work is necessarily more appealing than someone else's. It means that it's the best solution for the client based on your past experience and their goals. It doesn't mean that it looks more expensive, or is even more expensive to create, than something made by an hourly creative. It simply means that you're providing the ideal solution for their business needs.

"Stronger" doesn't mean that your work is bigger in scope than someone else's. It means that it significantly moves the needle in the right direction for your client. It means that you've done something that most creatives couldn't do for this client due to your expertise and skill. By working with your client to define their vision for success, and exceeding those expectations and metrics, you're providing tremendous value.

"Faster" doesn't mean quick; it means faster than it would take someone with far less experience. It means that you can quickly arrive at decisions in meetings without having to validate every idea. It means you can quickly create mockups or outlines on the fly without having to do extensive research because you've had similar experiences in the past. The client may get their work at a later time from you than a cheaper resource, but not at the same quality. By delivering exceptional quality with efficiency, you're creating additional value for your client.

A client's perceived value won't always align with yours

At times it may help to quantify the value of your work. This means trying to find a number, such as increasing revenue by $X or increasing visitors by X%. We'll break this down a bit more shortly. Sometimes, however, you can't quantify the value of your work. So the client will develop their own perception of the value your work provides. At times, their vision and yours may not line up. Let's go back to the Hermes bag. I know how much they cost, but I'm not as impressed as my wife when I see one. This doesn't change the perceived value of the bag to its target audience, but it means that some people won't be impressed. And let's keep in mind that 99 percent of the population couldn't tell a knock-off from the real thing, much like clients who can't tell the difference between a template logo design and something custom.

Overcoming the gap in perception means finding ways to help clients understand the overall impact your work will have on their business. The owner of the Hermes bag can't stop me in the street to tell me how nice the bag is unless I engage her in a conversation. But simply listing off the features of the bag only gets me to see it being worth $1,000. So by listing how great you are and all of the things you've done, you're only getting your client to be okay with a commoditized price, something suited for project-based pricing. To get them over the river to value-based pricing, you have to inspire them and get them away from commodities.

Comparison is key

Here's where value-based pricing falls apart for many creatives. Value refers to the value of the creative individual—you—not what the client actually values. To further explain, you're moving away from a commodity to a relationship. "Value" refers to the value of the individual designer, not what the client values. There is no way to fully know what a client values. If you try to compare what you're offering to something else the client could do with the funds, you're getting back into commodities. You are not a new coffee maker or additional headcount. You are an expert in your field bringing valuable advice and deliverables to your client.

There are ways to quantify value to make it easier for a client to swallow, but the mentality has to change from what the client values to the client valuing you and your expertise. This isn't easy.

The key is that you have to know your competition enough to be confident with your pricing. You have to broaden your view to the entire field which includes knowing what others are charging for similar work. It's a balancing act. If you are significantly higher than everyone else, you may price yourself out of the market. If you're too cheap, you'll be considered inexperienced or the client may be concerned that you're not understanding the scope of work. Value-based pricing only works when you can confidently price based on what your market will bear.

How do you find out what others are charging?

- **Ask.** Yep, ask other creatives what they're charging. Look at a project and ask them what they charged. You'll be shocked at how many people will tell you. Or, call the client and ask them what they paid. What's the worst that could happen? Being told no.

- **Go where the clients are.** Instead of networking with other creatives, go to client events and trade shows and ask them what they paid for their website or logo, whatever creative work you're doing. People will tell you this stuff; it's nuts, but they will.

- **Get involved.** Go to conferences, join trade associations, and sit in roundtables with your peers and talk about pricing. Join online groups of other creative owners; many are discussing pricing.

- **Monitor.** Setup Google alerts for freelance pricing guides and pricing surveys. They're constantly being done and published on blogs and by associations.

- **Use guidebooks, but with caution.** You can find out what salaries and rates of others are through some professional guidebooks on sites like Coroloft, Robert Half Group, the Graphic Artists Guild, or the annual Artist's & Graphic Designer's Market. These can help, but they're mostly for freelancers. Staffing companies also publish annual reports on salaries and other metrics, but they're still based on freelance rates.

- **Read the recommended books.** With this book, I wanted to include as much as I could on pricing based on my experience and expertise. There are others who've taken deeper dives in the books recommended at the start of this chapter. I'll continue to add to that list on the website.

How To Use Value-Based Pricing

Actually using a value-based price is no different than providing a quote using a flat-fee price. The difference is the actual dollar amount. I know that's confusing, it's why this subject is difficult. How you get to the value-based price is almost entirely subjective. This is where your gut, your emotions, and your perception come back into play for pricing. You have your shop rate and you know what you need to make. That removed the gut, that was calculated. You're now looking at a project, and you have a rough idea of how long it will take to do it and what resources are involved. Hopefully you have some data behind that from past work. By taking the time involved and multiplying it by your shop rate, you're ending up with a standard flat-fee project price. The jump to value is like playing a hand of cards. How high in price can you go, and how confident are you in what you're holding, and still win the business? That's what knowing your market, your clients, and your capabilities will get you.

Competing with value-based pricing is difficult, and dangerous, when you are first starting out. You can actually lose money on value-based pricing, even if it seems like much more than you'll need to complete the work. Clients are paying more so they expect more; so you have to be able to deliver. Here are some additional considerations when implementing value-based pricing:

- **Value-based pricing is still about perceived value.** If you have a strong body of work, impressive client list, or powerful testimonials, it's going to make it easier to sell on value. In addition, the stronger the referral to the prospect, the more likely they are to trust you are worth your price.

- **Your Unique Selling Proposition (USP) is a factor.** If you're offering the exact same services and solutions as others, then you're going to be compared with them. If you have something unique to offer, however, it becomes less about competing with others over cost and more about the client getting the exact services they want.

- **Clients expect results that can be measured.** I don't recommend tying your pay to metrics that you can't control, but your client will want some data or analytics to help them see the success of your work. Performance-based pricing calls for your pay to scale with results, but this is different. Your client is agreeing to your full value-based price, but their satisfaction is likely to require some measurable results. This means you need to set expectations up front for what what your work can accomplish. If it's going to result in more press or more sales, you have to establish baseline numbers before you start to then measure against after you're done.

Pseudo-calculating Value-based Prices

You are no longer using your shop rate to determine value-based pricing. It's reasonable, and common, for a project that may cost $20,000 to complete to be priced at $100,000. That's not built upon setting a 500 percent markup, it comes from setting a price that captures the value your customer receives. To reiterate Warren Buffet's quote, "price is what you pay, value is what you get."

There is no calculation model to follow. You should come up with rough estimates of the time involved and multiply it by your shop rate just to be sure you're covering your bases. It's doubtful, however, that if you're in a position to offer value-based pricing that you can't glance at most projects and know that you'll be covered. We're not talking about going from a $4,000 quote to a $6,000 quote. We're talking about going from a $4,000 quote to a $26,000 quote.

Asking the client some direct questions can tell you all that you need to know.

- Does this allow you to increase what you charge your customers? By how much more?

- How much is a new customer worth to you?

- How many new customers could this change get you?

- What does success look like from this project?

- What would make this project a smashing success in your view?

From this discussion, you will have an idea of what the client believes the financial impact will be. You can then determine the internal "market" for your work and your price. If a client expects the overall value of the increased business to be worth $100,000 and you're asking for $100,000 for the project, they're not likely to agree. If, however, the increased business is worth $100,000 and your project is $20,000, they will be more receptive.

Is Your client ready?

You'll get a feeling for whether a client is focused on growth instead of a hard return on investment. If the conversation keeps going back to metrics and measurement, you may be headed for performance-based pricing. If you're not ready for that model, then it means that the client needs help understanding the value.

You still need metrics

As shared when discussing hourly pricing, you will always need to track your hours and costs, even with value-based pricing. You should never arrive at a point in your practice where you don't know how profitable a project is. Even if it's 99 percent profitable, you still need to know. Above all, you want to understand how efficient you and your team have been with the project. Just because you're at a higher profit margin with value-based pricing (and that's not always true), doesn't mean that there isn't an opportunity for more profit. You may find that putting senior employees on a particular task instead of junior staff can increase efficiency by much more than the difference in salary. You may find that purchasing a particular piece of software at a premium will make a process much faster and cheaper over the course of several projects, something you couldn't calculate without metrics across all of your work.

You Matter And You Are Valuable

Your customers aren't you; they can afford things that you can't. So don't ever think that your work is "too much" for them. You have no idea how much is too much for them. How many times have you bought something you couldn't really afford because you wanted or needed it? Your clients will do the same thing. If you project value, worth, and exclusivity, they will want you beyond standard reason. They'll buy you, even if they can't afford you.

Especially Female Creatives

One thing I've noticed in my research is that women tend to struggle with value-based pricing. I want that to change. Some of the best creatives in the world are women, many of them far better than I am at the exact same task. They deserve to be paid just as much, if not more, than any man. I'm not a psychologist, so I'm not sure if this stems from the idea of hard negotiation being "unladylike" or if women are being taken advantage of in pricing negotiations. I'm not sure that women are being underpriced by male clients any more than female clients, so I'm not calling this a gender equality issue. What I have seen is women who are making less per hour, less on per-project work, and missing out on value-based pricing more often than their male counterparts. On our website, we want to continue the dialogue and get everyone on a level playing field. I can't fix the issue myself, I'm one guy. What I can do is call it out so that we can fix it together.

Sometimes It Just Won't Happen

Many clients will pay a very high hourly fee, such as $400 an hour, based on perceived value, but they still need hourly reports and itemization. They're fine with paying a lot of money for a solution, but they're still concerned with what it takes to get there. They simply aren't going to go for value-based pricing. You can decide if you want to work with them.

You Don't Have To Actually Say "Value"

This is essentially project-based or flat-fee pricing in the eye of the client. You're not disclosing your hourly breakdowns with your shop rate on your project-based quotes, so you're really not giving clients anything new when it comes to value-based pricing. Your simply charging clients more because you can and they can afford it.

What's The Difference Between Value-based Pricing and Project-based Pricing?

What the market will bear. It's really that simple. If your prospects and clients can pay the prices you're asking, then you can use value-based pricing. If they can't, then you either have to choose a new market or go down on your prices.

Value-based Pricing in Summary

Value-based pricing isn't for the fearful; it takes guts. Pricing by value puts you in a higher income bracket, but it also puts in a higher accountability spectrum. You are tying your services to an outcome: marketing, revenue, process improvement, traffic, retention, etc. It's imperative that you never tie value-based pricing to actual numbers or metrics such as increase by X amount of dollars or customers. You have no control over your client's sales and marketing abilities and you can never know everything that's going on. If you must commit to metrics as part of the agreement, make sure it's numbers you can heavily influence such as leads or traffic, never actual dollars and profit. If the client wants this level of metrics, then you should look into a Performance-based pricing model that can yield higher pay for stronger results.

You don't have to wait for your next big project to work on value-based pricing. Take a current, or past, client project and go through this process. Try to be objective. Or you could take a proposal that you didn't win and do the same thing. You may not be able to find out the value from the client, but it could be a great opportunity to call them back up and ask a few questions. They may hire you the next time. Going through some of your lost proposals could also help you spot patterns and missed opportunities. Would pricing for value have won the job?

In the end, when you only price by cost your client is paying for your efficiency. As you improve your processes, your income potential goes down. That's the complete opposite of growing a business. Clients don't actually care how long it takes you to do any particular task, they just want the task done right and for the work to accomplish their goals.

Value-based pricing for repeat clients can be difficult to sustain over a long period of time. Working with clients to discount your work, without calling it a discount and devaluing it, can pay big dividends. Depending on how much work you are doing for them and how often it occurs, you can consider providing lower prices as long as the client retains you for your services up front rather than on a per-project basis. We'll cover that next.

Key advantages

- Unlimited income potential

- You're paid for your experience and expertise

- Freedom to think and create

Key risks

- Higher prices mean longer sales cycles and a bigger pool of prospects

- You can still lose money if you aren't setting proper expectations

- Clients tend to expect the moon; you have to be prepared to give it to them

When To Use Value-based Pricing

Value-based pricing is the best pricing model if you can make it work. Getting paid for the impact your work has on your client's business is where you can find true profit and true freedom. It's also the hardest pricing model to implement. It's likely you will always have to fall back on another model, such as retainers or project/flat fee, to complement your value-based pricing strategy. Some clients will always be commodity-based and expect a dollar for hour type setup. However, any size business, from solo to large agency, can work with value-based pricing.

Tasks well-suited for value-based pricing

- Marketing strategy

- Information Architecture

- User Experience design

- Branding

- Editorial and advertising design and illustration

- Naming and writing for products

- App design and development

- Art/illustration/photography (especially if it's part of a product line or will be sold)

- Copyrighted material creation

- Software or technology development for resale

Pricing Model 4: Retainer Pricing

Retainers, or ongoing engagements, can bring stability and predictability to your business. It's the closest thing to a regular paycheck you can get. A retainer is a pre-set and pre-billed amount of money a client pays for a time period or volume of work. For example, the client agrees to pay you $10,000 per month to deliver a particular amount of work. This can be based on time, as in the client agrees to buy 100 hours per month at $100 per hour, or it can be value-based, as in $10,000 per month to deliver certain features or deliverables.

The majority of creative retainers are time-based retainers and there are two types: rolling vs. use it or lose it. In a rolling retainer, the client buys 100 hours and you track your time. If the client only uses 90 hours of your time in a given month, you roll over 10 hours to the next month, giving them 110 hours. In a use it or lose it retainer, the client buys 100 hours and you track your time but if there is any time left, it's unused and the client simply gets a fresh 100 hours the next month.

Rollover retainers are not a good idea, and I don't recommend them. You can end up owing your client significantly more work than you can handle in a given month. You could end up doing meaningless work just so your client can "burn through" the hours you owe them. Use it or lose it retainers are what most ad agencies and large creative shops use, and so should you.

Getting Retainer Clients

Acquiring retainer clients is typically skills-based more than relationship-based. A particular skill or service you provide may be of ongoing value to a client, such as writing their monthly newsletter or designing their quarterly brochure. Instead of starting and stopping a new project every time for similar work, you agree to a pre-set fee to complete the work on a regular basis.

Moving existing clients to retainers can lead you to additional work and revenue streams. You can virtually become the agency of record for small business clients through retainer relationships. It may be that you've commonly done the same work for them over and over or that you work well together, and they want you to take on additional work for them. Either way, return clients are good clients.

- **Most retainers happen after an initial project.** Getting a client on retainer requires trust. A client you've never worked with before isn't likely to agree to a long-term retainer out of the gate.

- **A workshop or Discovery session is a fast way to start.** If a client's needs are ongoing, but you haven't worked together yet, a great way to foster trust is to spend a few days in a workshop or Discovery session. We'll break those down a bit more in the next chapter.

- **Try a day rate.** Instead of booking hours, you could also charge a daily or weekly rate for work rather than hourly. You can have the client book you for entire days to work on whatever they need at a set rate. It allows you to audit their processes and see how they work, ensuring that they're a good fit for a retainer. You may decide you don't want to work with the client after this session, so it can keep you from getting into a bad retainer relationship.

- **Look for the tired people.** Ideal clients for retainers often have in-house teams that are either overwhelmed or lack your particular skills. Others are clients who have enough ongoing work that they need your skills regularly, but they aren't in a position to make a full-time hire. In both scenarios, you may work yourself out of a job by increasing their revenue enough to hire your eventual replacement. Transitioning out of the retainer will happen at some point. Hopefully you've established rapport, and they see you as indispensable, so they'll retain you for consulting instead of production going forward.

Hourly retainers mean more work, and that's not always a good thing

As you acquire more clients on hourly retainers, you may have to scale your business. You can only work so many hours, and once you sell all of your time, you're out of inventory. You can increase the cost of your hours, which you should do periodically, but you will eventually price yourself out of that client's acceptable range for hourly work. If your goal is to hire employees and scale your business, time-based retainers are perfect. You essentially have a contract with a client to pay for your new hire. Each time you add a retainer, it is hours that you can assign to employees. On the flip side, if you lose that client, you have to find something else for that employee to work on, or you'll have to let them go.

Value-based Retainers: Scale Your Skills Instead of Your Time

If, however, you aren't interested in hiring additional staff, value-based retainers are ideal. You will hit a ceiling with the hourly rate a client is willing to pay. Moving away from time and into deliverables for your retained work allows you to increase your revenue (and profit) while taking on additional clients.

If you can find a process to reduce the time it takes to layout a brochure or produce a chunk of code, you are no longer penalized for the increased efficiency by decreasing your billable hours—**you are paid the same amount of money regardless of how long it takes.**

Clients are coming to you for solutions, just like value-based pricing, but they need solutions on a repeat basis. That may mean you're working with them on an ongoing project for months or years, and they need your skills or expertise at certain points. Your work is too valuable for them to pay you for your time, so they pay you a set fee each week, month, or quarter to be a part of the process.

Value-based retainers are risky if you don't have strong project management skills. It's not for the novice pricing strategist. You will still need to calculate how long it takes and base your estimates with your client on the time allotted. You're not tracking your time on any client reports, but you still need to know if you're making money.

Your Contract Is Critical

A strong retainer agreement is crucial in setting expectations for all parties involved. Thursday Bram provided an excellent list of the key details that should always make it into the contract:[6]

- The amount you're to receive each month

- The date you're to be paid by

- Any invoicing procedures you're expected to follow

- Exactly how much work and what type of work you expect to do

- When your client needs to let you know about the month's work by

- What notification you need before the retainer relationship can be ended

- Anything else that is relevant for ensuring that work is completed in a timely fashion

- You may also want to set a date for the contract to expire, if only so that you have a scheduled point when you can raise your rates with your client. You can, of course, just announce a rate hike whenever you need to, but give your client plenty of notice about it.

Retainer Pricing in Summary

Stability and predictability come easiest with retainers, but they're still not a guarantee. They will require scale unless you're okay with one client owning a substantial portion of your business. Retainers are the closest thing to a steady paycheck and make it easier to hire help and make major decisions such as office space, equipment purchases, or pursuing products.

Freelancers should be careful to not let a retainer consume all of their time and always diversify their revenue. Small shops and agencies should move to use it or lose it models quickly and soon after move to value-based retainers as they build trust with clients. Make sure you're tracking everything and invoicing consistently.

Key advantages

- Steady, predictable income

- One less client you have to replace each month

- Fosters stronger client relationships, meaning less time spent re-learning new businesses over and over

- Help with vertical marketing. As you learn from a client in an ongoing relationship, you become an expert in their industry and build a body of work for which others will hire you.

Key risks

- Clients can think that you work for them as an employee and treat you as such

- It can make you lazy if you slack off on pursuing additional work

- If you allow rollovers, it can give you a stack of unfilled hours for which you've spent the money but haven't done the work

- The temptation to pad hours when you're close to using up the retainer. It's stealing.

When to Use Retainer Pricing

Retainers are the next logical step for your regular hourly and project-based clients. Rather than starting new projects over and over again, and dealing with the paperwork, it's best for both parties to simplify billing and communications with an ongoing relationship.

Retainers aren't ideal for new clients unless it's a situation built for long-term engagement from the start. Even in that scenario, it's best to do a short project to test out the relationship before diving head-first into a retainer.

Value-based retainers are the closest thing to perfect when it comes to pricing your services. Having a client pay you a set amount of money for your thinking and skills can give you the support you need to build your ideal business day, week, month and year. It should provide maximum flexibility as long as your agreements and communications are reliable.

Tasks well-suited for Retainer Pricing

Specific tasks suited to hourly retainers:

- Repetitive/cyclical graphic or web design
- Websites that require routine maintenance
- Creative or technical writing
- Web development
- Application or mobile development
- Illustration

Specific tasks suited to value-based retainers:

- Information Architecture and content strategy
- User Experience design
- Brand strategy
- Marketing strategy
- Social media strategy

Pricing Model 5: Package Pricing

Publishing pricing directly on your website or in print materials is standard in some creative industries while taboo in others. For illustrators, it's common to publish pricing by size or publication circulation. The same is true for photographers who take commission work. Some industries expect to compare assets on price or to place talent in individual "tiers" based on their experience, location, and price.

For consulting services such as design, development, and strategy, package pricing can be an excellent way to get a business up and running. However, long-term use of package pricing can commoditize your services. Above all, putting your prices out front before you've analyzed the client's problem puts your needs (money) above theirs (solutions). You've removed the ability to find the pain points and address them directly because you have fit their problem into your process. If your package pricing includes Discovery and analysis of client problems, that won't be an issue.

Some creatives, however, have found a sweet spot with package pricing and have built exceptional businesses. We'll break down some best practices rather than pros and cons. If you're happy with the work you're getting, then it's not a bad way to go. Let's see if it's right for you or whether we can help you improve.

Package Pricing Examples

- **Brand package.** A logo, website, brochure, and business cards for a new business at a fixed price. We offer a basic word mark logo plus a pitch deck (Powerpoint style presentation for startups) at a fixed cost for price-conscious startups.

- **Template customization.** Theme customization for websites using tools like Wordpress or Squarespace or brochure templates from design marketplaces. Maybe you have a set of pre-made templates from which clients can choose.

- **Consulting workshops and day-rates.** At our agency, we offer a full-day and weekly User Experience workshop and publicly post the price for all to see. The client can quickly determine if they can afford our services by testing the waters with our consulting package.

- **Analysis or reviews.** Offer to analyze someone's existing materials or program at a fixed cost and provide a report. It also allows clients to test you out.

- **Photoshoots and videos.** Photographers and videographers can do well with pre-priced packages for a certain number of shots or amount of time.

You get commodity clients and sometimes they're just what you need

By providing a public, up-front price some business can be won by price-conscious customers looking for the best deal from a reputable resource. Those customers may be price-conscious today, but they may be very well-off tomorrow and still want to work with you. They're not all window shoppers and tire kickers.

State Your Range, Not Your Price

There's also the option to offer price ranges. Many design firms offer ranges that certain services may fall within on their websites. For example, "CMS-based websites range from $5,000 to $20,000". You can provide bulleted lists of what's offered in certain ranges and weed out unqualified buyers quickly with these price ranges. Setting a minimum project cost is another common practice. For example, "projects with our agency start at $10,000" says that we do not accept projects that are less than $10,000.

For those who avoid the awkward

A big win for package pricing is the elimination of negotiations. If you aren't a fan of negotiating cost or deliverables, this makes it much easier for a client to decide if they can afford you. It's useful for repeat clients such as agencies who may need the same work over and over again, and it can create a predictable revenue stream. For clients with various business units, such as locations or events, package pricing makes it easy for them to build your services into their budget and guarantee future business for you. If you are into template-oriented graphic or web design, it's easy to say no to big changes when using packages.

Clients take the wheel

Clients can feel in control when package pricing is in use, and for some that's ideal. Additionally, it's great for recurring services such as SEO, social media, and other easily repeated tasks. It can, at times, feel like a lightweight retainer by having a client repeatedly buy the same service over and over again.

Profit isn't as evident

It's likely that profit won't be as high with packaging unless you create very efficient processes or subcontract the labor to cheaper resources. As higher volume comes from package priced work, your timelines tighten and operational responsibilities increase. It's hard to do high-quality work, and it can feel quite lifeless if you're selling production work, such as design or writing, as a package. There is little room for error or miscommunication unless your packages include revisions and consulting time.

Package pricing, however, is fulfilling for some creatives who love the production side of work more than the actual thinking and ideation. For those that just love to turn out designs or code, it's an excellent way to constantly work on something new. It is also useful for minimizing risk since it means you'll have leverage with clients when it comes to change orders.

Package Pricing in Summary

Package pricing puts choice in the customer's hand and can reduce the time taken to close business. It's great for production-oriented shops or consulting-oriented businesses who want to be paid to sort out the client's needs. Packages are good for photographers because their services are typically shopped based on price due to consumers viewing creative as a commodity. Quick actions such as designing product logos and marks or icons in mass are another typical avenue for package pricing. Overall, it's a stable business model for freelancers and small shops.

Key advantages

- Makes it difficult for clients to "bargain you down"
- Good for repeat clients and agency relationships
- Good for clients with multiple businesses or business units
- Good for template-oriented designers
- Client feels in control
- If you like avoiding confrontation, this is good
- If you feel like you're feeding your soul with commodity-based work, or that packages allow you to do other work that is fulfilling, this is a great approach

Key risks

- Minimal opportunity for profit without high volume
- High volume means tight timelines
- Difficult to do high-quality work
- Little room for error

When to Use Package Pricing

Packages are a safe way to start out; it's predictable for you and your clients. For the creative jack of all trades who can handle just about anything a marketing client needs, it's an excellent way to diversify your offering. Generalists can thrive with package pricing because they may not be good enough for any single task, such as writing or graphic design, to sell that only against other specialists, but they can quickly sell packages.

It requires you to establish a taste for the word "no" when it comes to clients who want to deviate from the package offerings. Profit is limited but possible, but you're much better off moving to a different model as you grow. You can develop packages with offerings such as day rates or workshops into something more profitable, so don't write off this pricing strategy regardless of where you are in your career.

Tasks well-suited for package pricing

- Photography sessions

- Consulting (branding, User Experience, content strategy)

- Branding and design

- Small websites

- Testing and research

- Micro design such as icons or illustration systems with limited concepts and rounds of revision

- Full brand packages such as a logo, identity materials, website, brochures all in one

- Theme/template-based projects such as Wordpress websites, fliers, or brochures

- Startups and launch sites using a framework

Pricing Model 6:
Performance-based Pricing

Performance-based pricing is a serious risk with the chance for a serious payout. You base your fee on the performance of your work. Your work has to be able to affect a measurable outcome for your client, such as higher revenue or increased efficiency. Most often performance-based pricing is tied to analytics, so it's more common with web or application design projects. It is an increasingly common model with advertising agencies where media purchases had been the conventional model for decades. Now, agencies are being compensated for their direct involvement in their clients' success, and seeing record profits in the process.[7]

This model relies on a bulletproof contract with clear metrics and clear terms. If you don't have the money to have an attorney help you create the contract and terms, you shouldn't be messing with this model. If you do want to get involved in performance-based pricing, it's also best to work with a client who's used this model with other creatives. Someone has to go first with every client, but I wouldn't recommend being the guinea pig for something this complicated.

So if this model is risky and only for specific types of work, why bother? Performance-based pricing can result in powerful working relationships that closely align the buyer's goals and the seller's goals. It can create the ultimate bond between creative and client because you are now heavily invested in the outcome of the work. Also, it's insurance for both you and your client; there is no way to underprice performance-based work as long as your metrics line up. If your work makes your client rich, it makes you rich. If your work turns out okay for your client, it turns out okay for you.

> Performance-based pricing can result in powerful working relationships that closely align the buyer's goals and the seller's goals.

Another benefit of this model is the deep level of engagement you'll have with your client. There are constant discussions both before, during, and after the work is completed. This type of engagement can result in a long-term relationship that can be of tremendous value.

Using Performance-based Pricing

- **Use value-based pricing first.** Unless you've handled the type of client that expects big results without knowing everything you've done to get them there, you're probably not ready for this model.

- **Be willing to lose.** If your work is good and the metrics are right, you shouldn't be afraid of this model. But your business should not be in a position that failure would put you under or in severe financial distress.

- **No rush.** This isn't the kind of agreement or plan you can rush. If the client is calling for a quick turnaround or a fast start, it isn't a good fit for performance-based pricing.

- **The formula is the lynchpin.** Whatever the calculation is for your pay for performance agreement, make sure it is extraordinarily clear. Don't leave anything to chance or assumption.

- **Don't use SEO as the metric.** If your creative work stands on its own, but the client wants to set up a performance model based on Search Engine Optimization (SEO) performance, run in the other direction. It's becoming common to base "bonuses" on SEO rankings, such as being #1 for the client's preferred search term, but you can't control SEO rankings, so you can't control your pay. You never want to be in a pricing situation where you aren't in control of your pay. SEO-based pay is for SEO consultants.

Pricing Model 7: Equity Pricing

If you're joining a startup or building a product, you may be offered partial ownership of the business. It may be in lieu of any cash payment, or it may be a mix of equity and a reduced cash payment. I've been down this road before personally and had a bad experience, but I've had close colleagues take the risk and come out quite well. In my situation, I had little control over the day-to-day operations. Others have either been lucky to land with a hit company or had some influence on the outcome.

This approach isn't for everyone and certainly not for someone who needs the money now. It's a great approach for side projects, small engagements, or something that you'd be willing to do for free if your schedule allows. It's not a good approach if you're giving up a large number of cash bookings or dropping clients to accommodate this project.

If you're in the market for a job or thinking about backing off of your creative business for a while to join with others, then it may make more sense. Just keep in mind that taking equity all depends on where the company is at the time you get involved. If the company has not received any outside funding, your ownership will be significantly diluted once it does. If it has taken on funding, you're going to be offered a tiny amount of equity, less than 5 percent, which isn't much unless the company is on the way toward making millions.

You'll still need to keep up with the cash value of your time involved for several reasons, most notably for tax purposes. In addition to keeping up with your time, ask yourself these questions:

- **Are you getting only equity or being paid cash as well?** If your ownership is a mix of cash and equity, then you may be able to stomach the risk. Your cash payment for your services will need clear separation from your equity and you'll need extensive documentation denoting the separation between your fee (a payout) and your equity (stock).

- **Are you investing any cash?** If you're bringing cash into the business, then you're in an entirely different situation. You'll need the advice of an attorney who specializes in startups or mergers and acquisitions. Do not ever attempt to put cash into a business without involving a serious professional.

- **Will you stick around?** If you plan to stay involved either as a partner, consultant, or employee, then you'll have to determine how it affects the rest of your business. It could be a huge decision that limits your ability to serve other clients; don't let it catch you off-guard.

- **Will your work be re-used or re-sold?** Intellectual property and copyright can be critical in equity pricing. If you're creating the brand or the core technology or design for the product, you should be compensated accordingly. If they use the brand for merchandising or resell items, your agreements should include provisions for royalties and future dividends. Again, get an attorney involved.

What is a realistic expectation?

No less than 25 percent. If a client is offering you 5 percent equity for creating important assets for the business, then they don't value your work. That isn't the kind of client you want. You want to work with businesses that value creative and design as much as utilities or office space. If a client is offering you a small percentage, they may be past their initial funding. If they've received funding, they have money to pay you. If you still want to take equity, that's your choice, but you should consider a cash and equity mix at that point.

How to say no but still get the work

You don't have to lose the client if they're only offering equity at first. You can offer to help them raise the money to pay you by advising them or connecting them with investors. You could offer to create a presentation or other small work for them to help them along in their quest for the cash they'll need to pay you. It's technically working for free, but it may be worth it to you. If they simply can't come up with the cash and the situation doesn't look promising, it may just be a client you have to let get away.

Additional Pricing Factors

There's more than just your time involved in creative work; you also have to consider overhead and costs. While calculating your hourly rate with all of your expenses included covers most of it, it isn't necessarily enough for some larger tasks. From meals purchased during all-day work sessions to user research gifts, there are a lot of "little things" that can add up over time. Any equipment or software you purchase specifically for a project should be charged to the client at a markup. Your time and expertise to acquire the tools to perform the job should not be free.

If you're in countries that require VAT, keep in mind that when providing B2B services you'll likely owe VAT. There are even certain creative services in the U.S. that should have sales taxes charged and collected. Unless you're handing over a physical deliverable, such as a print, it shouldn't be an issue. But you'll still need to check with your accountant. It's best to find out now so that you're not caught off-guard at year-end.

Sometimes you can't break down a project by deliverables

When you look at a project, you may not be able to estimate the amount of hours it will take, but your experience will most likely tell you how many weeks it will take. For example, a project may take six weeks to complete. It is about half of your time each week, and you have thirty billable hours, so you'll allocate fifteen per week. Multiply fifteen hours by six weeks, and you'll get ninety hours. If you then multiply ninety hours by a $150 an hour Shop Rate, you'll get a $13,500 project budget. That's your minimum project budget to "break even." You'll want to work up from that number to determine the fit for your client, but that will give you the absolute basement price that you can afford to consider. If you can build in additional profit and increase the budget closer to $15,000, that will provide the room you need to deal with any overages or unexpected challenges. Then you can go from there into value-based pricing.

Rush rates

If a client is asking for hourly work but has an extremely tight timeline, you have every right to charge them a higher hourly billing rate. The general rule is that rush rates should be double your standard hourly billing rate. It isn't necessarily to punish the client for bad planning. It can, however, keep clients who don't value your schedule from "forgetting" to tell you about a deadline. It's the cost of getting something sooner than everyone else would. If it works for FedEx, it's good enough for you.

Pricing for consulting

What do you do when there's no end product to deliver, but you don't want to offer hourly? Offer day rates or weekly rates at a fixed cost, e.g. $5,000 per day. Not everything has to be a project or an hour; you can sell your engagement for a fixed amount of time with no particular outcome in mind.

Rules for Effective Pricing

Work with your Service Army. Manage your money and stay in contact with your accountant, banker, and attorney. Review your cash flow and billing at least quarterly to see how you can improve.

Get a contract. The next chapter goes into greater detail on the pitfalls of not having a contract, but every project, whether it's $50 or $50,000, must have a contract. Never ever ever work without a contract. Things can and will go wrong.

Define the scope in writing. Always get the scope of work in your contract and log any changes to that scope in writing either in your project management tool or an email archive that you store offline.

Invoice on time. More on this in the next chapter, but invoice when you say you will and do it the same way at the same time. The accounts payable person with your client is your best friend: send him or her donuts.

Tie your payments to deliverables instead of time. Never bill when work is done: bill by date and time and get it in writing. More on this in the next chapter as well.

Track your time. Everyone on your team, even administrative employees, should track all time spent on client projects. Even if you're flat rate, you still have to know how long your work takes and if you're profitable. Knowing the time involved helps you more accurately quote future work. Use a time-tracking tool that produces reports so that you can compare projects, time periods, and employees.

Log communications. Anything a client requests should be in writing. Any files or assets a client provides should live in one place, and you should have a record of who submitted it and when. Use a project management tool instead of email for all client communications, both between you and the client and between you and any employees or freelancers. This is your project documentation. More on this in Chapter 6.

Set boundaries. Define what an overage is and what costs it will incur. You can be flexible with good clients, but you must keep track of scope changes, change orders, revisions, or changes to the project. When they occur, they trigger billing changes.

Conduct post-mortems. Build a review, retrospective, or post-mortem into your project plan. As soon as you finish a project, review it to see how things went and take notes. Review the time spent, the client satisfaction, and what went well and what didn't. More on this in Chapter 6.

The Key Is Control

Money is messy, but it doesn't have to be. The key is control. The hardest lesson I had to learn as a creative was to avoid emotional pricing. No two projects or clients are the same, and there has to be a method to the madness. The sooner you get control of your pricing strategy, the sooner you will be able to enjoy your work.

Notes

1. http://www.amazon.com/Philosophy-Andy-Warhol-From-Again/dp/0156717204.
2. Noelle Howey, http://www.damemagazine.com/2015/02/11/why-are-we-so-uncomfortable-talking-about-money#sthash.aStlQ5QM.dpuf.
3. http://www.radicati.com/wp/wp-content/uploads/2011/05/Email-Statistics-Report-2011-2015-Executive-Summary.pdf.
4. http://fortune.com/2014/02/24/buffetts-annual-letter-what-you-can-learn-from-my-real-estate-investments/.
5. Mike McDerment, *Breaking the Time Barrier.*
6. http://business.tutsplus.com/articles/how-to-offer-ongoing-freelance-services-on-retainer--fsw-33797.
7. http://hbswk.hbs.edu/item/3021.html.

CHAPTER 5

HOME ECONOMICS

GETTING PAID- CONTRACTS, OPERATIONS AND BILLING

HERE 2
COLLECT
ALL THE
MONEY.
K thx,

"If the restaurant can't be bothered to replace the puck in the urinal or keep the toilets and floors clean, then just imagine what their refrigeration and work spaces look like."

Anthony Bourdain[1]

For your business to survive long-term, it's important to have your operations in order. Think of your creative work and client deliverables as the "front of the house," e.g. the dining room. Then think of the gritty details of running the business—invoicing, cash flow, contracts, and proposals—as the "back of the house", e.g. your kitchen.

As you work more closely with repeat clients, your operations will be visible. They'll become the sort of customers who walk into the kitchen and get to know the chef. Clients can quickly lose confidence in your creative abilities if you appear naive or disorganized when it comes to operations. A transition to value-based or retainer pricing surprisingly increases transparency with your clients as well. They may not see the breakdown of their invoice, but they do see more of you and how you work.

We know we need paperwork and invoices, but this isn't exactly fun. What I've learned is that the more structured your operations, the greater freedom you'll have with your work. The positive change is most visible when it comes to contracts and proposals. You may spend up to half of your time finding clients, but the steps required to get them to sign and spend with you can be made far less painful.

Here's what we'll cover:

- Proposals, requests for proposals (RFPs), and Discovery
- Project questionnaires
- Contracts
- Negotiation and defining scope
- Retainer agreements
- Dealing with client-created contracts
- Working for free
- Non-disclosure agreements, work for hire, and subcontracting
- Invoicing, billing, and late fees
- What to do when clients won't pay
- Taxes
- Cash flow and money management

Proposals

Since none of us can read minds, proposals can be hard. Taking all of the requests, requirements, and restrictions that clients provide and trying to guess how much is too much or too little is exhausting. The proposal in all of its sadistic glory is the key to winning new business. They take forever; they are unpaid, and there is no guarantee they'll result in winning the work.

The ideal proposal is short, direct, and confident. You only need a summary of the project to outline the general scope, your proposed costs, the payment schedule, and your legal provisions. Cut the fluff and pomp and make it about the client. Rather than focusing on what tasks you'll complete, focus on what the client will receive.

How proposals happen

There are a few ways you may end up writing proposals. A client may call you and ask for a ballpark price for a project. You may receive a request for proposal (RFP). You may consult with a client who then wants you to complete a project for them, but needs a formal proposal. We'll look at these paths to proposals first, and then break down the anatomy of an effective proposal.

Requests for Proposals (RFPs)

"We don't respond to RFPs," says the holier than thou creative business owner. Well, keep on ignoring them, because I'll gladly take the business. You should, too.

Requests for proposals (RFPs) typically get one of two responses from creatives: the delete button or a robotic reply with nothing more or less than exactly what the sender requested. In both cases, you're not likely to get much further with the prospect. The RFP process is broken. You, however, can make it work for your business.

The sender may not exactly know what they want or need, but they have to get the request out there. In the past, I assumed everyone sending RFPs was an asshole looking to pit creatives against one another to get the cheapest price. Then I thought it was being written by one creative firm who was in cahoots with the client and was sent only to get additional required bids. They never had any intention of hiring anyone but the firm who helped them write the RFP.

RFPs weren't created by Satan

The truth, however, is that most RFPs are written by people who "are as irritated that they have to write it as you are that you have to reply to it."[2] So the first step is getting in touch with the human being who wrote it. You may find out that they're asking for help rather than putting in an order. With a little conversation and fact-finding, you can put yourself in a much better situation.

An RFP Story

We received an open RFP request from a large non-profit in New York. The RFP itself was pages and pages, with specific technical requirements that not only restricted the technology and creative tools to be used, but the method in which to use them. There was no budget, no timeline, and nebulous levels of engagement expected. The RFP had a single contact and a date that responses were due. It also included strict guidelines for submitting the proposal.

My business partner pinged me on our in-house messaging app, Slack, and asked me to take a look at the RFP, "do we want to talk to them about this?" he said. I skimmed the introduction letter and RFP, then quickly replied, "that proposal would take, at the minimum, forty hours to build when you factor in discussions between the three of us plus our admin. The likelihood of us getting the work is slim to none in that scenario with no examples of (the requested technology) work. I would be interested in a well-crafted reply for us to come in and do a workshop with them for Discovery, but I can't see the effort being worth it to respond blindly to the RFP."

So we crafted a response outlining our Discovery process, which we call a short-term engagement, and how we can take their RFP and our expertise to get the project on the right track. Rather than sit down and power through the proposal with no guarantee of winning the work, we reached out directly to the contact. Within an hour, he had a replied and asked to learn more. Over the next few days, the prospect determined that they couldn't engage us for a Discovery engagement due to their requirements to receive bids, but they could provide greater detail for the RFP.

Within a week, we knew the actual budget, the actual timeline, the full set of requirements, and we had built significant rapport with the final decision maker. Now we knew if the project was worth it and we had project details competing agencies didn't. Beyond the knowledge gained, we were also able to find out where the seemingly strict technology requirements could change and where they were rigid. We even found out what the ongoing support budget would be for subsequent years, thus helping us see the potential lifetime value of the client.

Our prospect had serious concerns about the feasibility of his project, but he had to get it done and time was ticking. Our willingness to engage with him instead of throwing a number out, which meant putting his needs ahead of our own, endeared us to him as a trusted partner. That trust has continued for quite some time as we've worked with them.

Pick up the phone

When RFPs have strict requirements that seem almost ridiculous, that means that the client is grasping at straws. I know that sounds crazy; you would think that screams "client who has their act together," but it doesn't. The client doesn't need another reply to a badly-formed RFP, they need help. Picking up the phone and calling them is the best thing you can do because most creatives won't. Not every RFP comes from an organization that is large or has a required bidding process. They may have asked a friend how to buy a website, and they were told to send out an RFP. They may have no clue what they're doing.[3]

Ask why you received the RFP

Sometimes prospects find you through a search firm or their manual Google search, but most often someone has given them your name, so the RFP was referred to you most likely. It's important also to find out how they got your information and to follow up with the resource that pointed them to you. That resource likes you enough to refer you, so that's a relationship worth nurturing. It may even get you past the RFP phase altogether.

Discovery

The best way to respond to an RFP, however, is with a contract. Rather than giving your time away for free find a way to work with them provisionally to discover the right solution, and price, for their challenge. I present: Discovery.

Discovery is essentially a paid workshop with the client to determine the right response to each of their needs or project requirements. Consider it a first date before getting married. The goal of Discovery is to go deeper and find out why the client needs the particular service they're requesting. Clients tend to focus on the actual work—the widgets and features—rather than the business reasons for them. They've been trained to get a new logo or update their marketing campaign at set times or seasons. Discovery helps you find out what the client actually needs, which may be a new set of brand standards or updated copy rather than the requested deliverable.

With Discovery, you're getting paid to respond to an RFP. The RFP may not contain all of the details you need. For most clients, hiring a service provider without having them do Discovery is like hiring a contractor without blueprints. Moreover, it's like a homeowner designing a house on their own, with little to no knowledge of construction or architecture, and the builder taking the plans and going with it.

> With Discovery, you're getting paid to respond to an RFP.

Discovery isn't just a way to get paid for proposals or avoid free work. It's an important part of getting things right. Discovery ensures that you're using the client's time and resources wisely to do the right things.

How Discovery meetings work

There are four key parts to any Discovery meeting, regardless of your creative skill set:

- **Listening.** You have the client front and center, so now is the time to listen intently to their needs and goals. The more you get from them in this setting, the better off you'll be. Ask open-ended questions that get them to tell you what they need and where they're going. Get data, facts, problems, challenges, and wants all out on the table.

- **Taking notes.** Don't make the client repeat herself later. Get all of the information you can in the meeting and keep it. If you can, have someone on your team take detailed notes like a courtroom stenographer. You can hire a temp to do this as well. Record the meeting audio or even video the meeting. Put your notes in a Google Doc, Basecamp, or another communication tool.

- **Building trust.** It's your chance to show the client who you are and why you're the best. Set the stage with snacks and drinks, a courteous demeanor, and make sure everyone is comfortable sharing. If it's an all-day meeting, go out to lunch and buy. Conversation over food is always more casual and makes us all more human. Don't sit on opposite sides of the table from your client. If you're a team, mix yourselves up with the client throughout the room.

- **Establishing outcomes.** No matter the intended deliverable from your meeting, you need to get very specific about what will happen next. If the goal is to produce a detailed proposal or contract, then define when the client will have it and what's included.

Discovery meetings don't have to result in a proposal. You can start work immediately or write the contract from the meeting. The meeting could be the "interview" process the client wants. Even if the initial plan is to come out with a proposal, ask them if they'd rather move forward with a contract at the end. You've built trust; don't be afraid to ask.

Other possible outcomes of a Discovery meeting could be:

- A full proposal
- A full contract
- A requirements document
- A prototype
- Sketches or wireframes

- A brand name or logo sketches
- A roadmap or Information Architecture schematic
- User Experience goals
- A design or development direction
- Content tone or framework

Knock Out the Ballpark

If a prospect is asking you to give them a ballpark price for a complicated project, you can't do that. What you can say is your minimum cost. You can also reply with the cost of similar projects you've done before. What you shouldn't say is, "well, I need to do a bunch of research and get back to you." You've now pushed the money conversation away, and you're back to blindly creating a proposal. If it's going to take a Discovery meeting, then you have to sell it right then.

If you never give ballpark prices, I think you're losing business. Some clients give you enough information in your initial chat that you do have a general sense of what it should cost. You're not giving them a quote or signing anything; it can change significantly. If you have to go up 5x on the price, that's okay.

Just like a formal proposal, the ballpark is a phone or email proposal. So respond with price bracketing. Give them a few ranges based on what you know, and they could be very wide. You could say "under $10,000, under $50,000, and under $100,000". That's fine. What you can't do is lose the opportunity to speak to the client again. If it's clear that they do need to know what your price range is, be confident and say so. You can say, "we don't take projects for under $25,000" and that may be all they need to know to see that you're either too expensive or right up their alley.

The Anatomy of a Proposal

A simple way to break down proposals is to answer this question: "what, when, and how much?" Remember, clients are buying a commodity, like the detergent on the shelf, not creative services. They need to know what they are getting, when they can have it, and how much it's going to cost. That's what your proposal is supposed to answer. We, however, love to make things complicated.

Pricing expert Brennan Dunn advises that you shouldn't leave the proposal to the client's interpretation and imagination; you have to help them see the work being done. It's the difference between touring a house with empty rooms vs. one that is fully decorated—the buyer must be able to easily see themselves in that home (your proposal) without having to strain their imagination. So when writing proposals, ask yourself: Am I proposing a house or home?

Dunn goes on to break down his proposals like so:

- "Why You're Here"—What problem lies at the root of this project?

- "Where You Want To Be"—What does it mean to solve this problem?

- "What We Want To Do"—What paths are we proposing, and how do these options align with solving the problems of the client?

- "What We'll Be Preparing For"—What can cause this project to fail, and how do we plan on overcoming these risks?

- "Why We're Best For The Project"—What specific domain or business expertise do we have, ideally in the form of a case study, that demonstrates that we understand this problem and how to fix it?

- "How We Can Do This For You"—From the different paths we've propose, how do each of these satisfy the solution we're aiming for, and what kind of ROI can the client expect from each option?

Download a sample proposal kit from the website and find even more proposal resources.

Price Bracketing

In your proposals, clients jump right to the price. It's the part that gives us the most grief if we're offering a fixed fee, whether that's project-based or value-based. So, when presenting a price, it's best to have options.

"If you give a client a single price, you're asking them to accept or not accept your price. The discussion becomes a simple 'yes/no' ordeal."[4] Rather than trying to find the perfect price with every feature the client has requested included, break down the cost into three tiers. The level of detail will vary depending on your work, but at the very least have a short paragraph or summary outlining what's included in each pricing tier. This method, called "price bracketing," was popularized by Dr. Alan Weiss. If you haven't read Dr. Weiss's work on proposals for consulting, it's worth its weight in gold. It's geared toward traditional sales consulting, but you'll still get far more than the cost of the book and your time out of it.

How price bracketing works

Price bracketing, sometimes called price anchoring, means to actually bracket the price you want the client to choose—the middle one—between two others, i.e. bracket it on the left and right. Price anchoring typically uses only one higher price to pull the customer's interest to the lower price. Price bracketing, thus far, has been more effective for services-based pricing whereas price anchoring has been more effective for retail and commodity pricing. Price bracketing and price anchoring are common in retail showrooms and are a bit of a Jedi mind trick. By placing an item that's reasonable in the middle, it helps people avoid extremes—the cheap and the expensive. We don't like extremes. For the most part we like safe. The middle is safe and makes the most sense. It's your job to make the middle safe for your client in your proposals.

Always bracket up. Don't put the minimum cost of the project in the middle and make up some cheaper option with requirements cut out to put on the low end and add frivolous features on the high end. That can actually cause the buyer to walk away or choose the lower tier. You've got to be willing to live with them picking the lower tier if they so choose, so their requirements must be met in the lower tier. What you can do is look at templates or frameworks or stock images instead of custom work in the lower tier. You can cut the amount of time on certain tasks or offer lower-cost printing. There are lots of ways to get the job done without doing it exactly as it should be. Sometimes, that's all the client wants.

Hopefully, though, you're hitting the sweet spot and giving them everything they want and need at the right place in the middle. Meet all of the client's demands in the middle tier, but cover all of their requested features or services in the higher tier. There is a huge difference between demands and requests. Demands are what they expect, requests are what they're asking for. When shopping for a TV, I may request 4K or 3D, but I may not demand it. If I get it, great. But I'm not going to go up in price to get it. You want the same from your clients.

Sample Price Bracketing Page from Proposal

Timing: Time is of the essence. Knowing this, the timelines below are an approximation based on what we feel is a conservative timeline. We have not attached dates to these timelines as we understand people's schedules may change and we intend to remain flexible to accommodate them.

- Project Kickoff - 1 week
- Research Sessions - 6-7 weeks
- Research Findings Review - 1 week
- Database Architecture - 6-8 weeks
- Prototype - 3-6 weeks
- Architecture & Technology Implementation - 12-16 weeks
- Beta Review - 1 week
- User Testing - 2-4 weeks
- Adjustments & QA - 4-6 weeks
- Deployment - 3-4 weeks

Total time to completion: 38-54 Weeks
(depending on option selected and availability of key team members)

Budget: These budgets as ranges. These ranges represent getting you to final delivery of the option you choose. As we work with you to define scope for various tasks we will be able to narrow these ranges to more accurate numbers and will do our best to keep all budgets as low as possible.

There are no hourly or daily fees since you should not have to make an investment decision every time our assistance may be needed, nor should your team have to seek permission to spend money if they need our help. This is inclusive of all meetings and expenses, so long as all work required is in the general Atlanta area. All administrative, logistical, and communication expenses are included, so there is no further amount due for any option. Travel to Acme, Inc. offices for project kick-off and occasional meetings is expected, however travel costs are not included in these budgets.

- Option 1: $148,600 to $164,200
- Option 2: $177,400 to $191,200
- Option 3: $186,200 to $219,600

Should you accept this proposal, payment terms are as follows:

- An initial deposit equal to 20% of the projected project cost
- Bi-weekly invoices for the remaining 80% balance divided by the projected timeline.
- For example, if Option 1 is chosen at $154,000 with a timeline of 40 weeks, a deposit of $30,800 will be due upon agreement and bi-weekly invoices in the amount of $6,160 will be sent.

We offer a discount of 10% when the full fee is paid upon execution of the agreement.
This project, once approved, is non-cancelable for any reason, although it may be delayed, rescheduled, and otherwise postponed without any penalty whatsoever.

Terms:

- This proposal is good for 30 days from date of preparation.
- Material changes to the nature and/or scope of work you ask us to perform will void this proposal and require a new one be prepared by us.
- Repeated changes to nature and/or scope requiring us prepare new proposals may require you pay a preparation fee per instance.
- Should parties agree to perform the work described herein, this proposal shall serve as an exhibit of the subsequent Master Services Agreement executed between the parties.

This is a form of loss aversion, or the tendency to strongly prefer avoiding losses over acquiring gains. If they need every single feature in their RFP, they have no choice but to go with the higher tier. If they can remove things that have been added purely for the sake of seeing how much it will cost, you could end up with what they really need in the middle tier. This goes back to the problem with most RFPs— they're written by people who don't actually know what they want. If you can get them in a Discovery meeting to find out what they need, and put all of that in your middle tier, then add all of the fluff they don't actually need back in the higher tier, you're doing the valuable work at the right cost and it looks like a "bargain" to them.

The lowest tier should always be what you can live with and the middle tier, the target, should be the right balance of profit and feasibility. Present the highest tier as a premium option. Studies have shown that 10 percent of buyers always go with the premium option as long as it's within 20 percent of the cost of the middle option. So one out of ten proposals that you do this way should result in the prospect going with the price that's significantly more than your target. So be prepared to deliver on that higher cost option as well.

Bracketing in your proposals

Some advise to start with the higher price and go down, others to start with the lowest. At our agency, we list them side by side in three columns. We're not afraid of sticker shock; we'd rather the client move along if money is going to keep them from working with us.

Never negotiate on price. Make it clear that the pricing options are what they are and if the client wants to pay less, they will have to give up the features or options that make up the higher price. You must stand your ground on pricing; it's essential for establishing your authority with the client. Getting your prices right is crucial to providing margin for growth and allowing you to spend the right amount of time on the work, resulting in the high quality your client expects.

Presenting the price

- **Don't use round numbers.** People assume that round prices like $500 are artificially higher.[5] Instead, use more precise numbers such as $512. A rational decision tends to require rational solutions. Part of those solutions is a price that feels "exact" to your prospect.
- **Present your payments up front instead of the whole price.** If the prospect is very cost-conscious, present the price as "three payments of $1000 due on the 10th of each month" rather than "$3000." You're still going to have to break down the price in your payment terms, why not put them front and center?

- **Don't bold the price.** When formatting your proposal, keep the price in line with other text. In fact, make it smaller if you can. A smaller font can communicate a smaller price.
- **Remove the comma.** Use $1700 instead of $1,700. The comma makes a price seem larger as well.

Closing sales and getting the job

We've covered marketing and sales, but you still have to get the client to sign their contract and pay your deposit. Before we dig into the nuts and bolts of contracts, let's talk about what it takes to get the client from proposal to signature.

- **Present your proposal.** Don't send your proposal out on its own like some puppy into the wilderness. Try to set up a time to go over it with your client face to face, over video, or via phone. Present your proposal just like you would your work. Go through the details and offer to explain anything that the client doesn't understand. It allows you to ask the client to sign right then and there. You aren't wondering whether they've seen it and reviewed it; you've done that with them.

- **Print your proposal.** Paper is heavy. If you've ever received a subpoena or bought a home, you know how much paperwork can change your perspective of a situation. You can make an impact by printing out your proposal on quality paper and having it delivered to your client. If you're meeting with them face to face, having multiple copies printed and bound for everyone in the meeting makes things much more formal.

- **Include the invoice.** You need a separate invoice for your deposit, and you should attach it to the proposal. Make it clear that you're ready to receive a check right now.

Contracts

Starting work without a contract is no different than jumping into bed with a complete stranger and not protecting yourself. I know that's crass, but that's the level of insanity and danger that working without a contract evokes.

Andrew Clarke created his "Contract Killer" in 2008, and it's still going strong.[6] Clarke's open-source contract is readily available and free to use on Github. For those unfamiliar with Github, it means you can "fork" or copy Clarke's contract and edit it to your liking. You can then merge your version with updates he makes down the road. His contract was written in plain language that anyone can understand, and it covers all of the bases. It's for web design, but you can easily adapt it for most creative work.

Regardless of your creative business type, every contract must include:

- The scope of work

- Ownership and distribution rights for the work

- Revisions

- Timeline

- Payment schedule, including late fees

- Legal jurisdiction

- Expenses and overages

- Kill Clause or termination statutes

Clarke has done a wonderful job of capturing the fundamental anatomy of a firm contract. Where things get interesting is if you have intellectual property rights, redistribution, copyright, royalties, and other complications to consider. It's worth the investment to have an attorney that specializes in creative contracts prepare your actual terms once you start billing over $100,000 projects. It's a good idea to do it at any time, but once you break six figures, it's a necessity. If you haven't heard of Gabe Levine in San Francisco, please reach out to him. Gabe is an expert on legal matters for creative businesses, and his blog at mylawyergabe.com is a treasure trove of advice.

Focus on money

The purpose of contracts is to ensure that you get paid and that your client gets the work. It's a financial transaction. Thus, the contract should be focused on the financial transaction. Clearly state the "who, how, what, when, where, and why" for payment terms. Don't forget to cover late fees, delays, cancelation, and revisions.

Master Services Agreement (MSA)

Rather than writing contracts over and over again, using master services agreements (MSAs), will save you time and headaches. For clients with a legal department, each contract they sign will have to be reviewed by an attorney or legal counsel.

Instead of creating a new contract with the identical legalese in it as the last five before it, use an MSA. An MSA has all of the legal agreements such as copyright, revisions, and jurisdiction. Both parties agree to it, it goes on file, and you then amend it with a statement of work for each project. So the MSA looks just like what many would call a contract: you just strip out the scope of work, timeline, payment schedule, and any additional non-standard information that will change with each project.

The MSA defines the relationship and how you will work together. It should never be for more than one year. Always renew your MSAs, putting an end date on them, so that you can change processes if they aren't working.

An MSA should include:

- The services you will be providing. It should outline your business capabilities, protecting you from being asked to do things that aren't in your expertise

- How work will be handled and delivered including file management, release of ownership, and approval processes

- How you'll be paid including methods of payment, terms and due dates, and taxes or service fees

- Methods of communication

- Warranties or ongoing support of work once it's delivered

- Legal jurisdiction in the event that there is a dispute

- Copyright, reproduction, resell, and other terms regarding ownership of the work

- At will engagement and how work can be terminated, including how to communicate termination, what fees are required, and how much warning is required

Download a sample MSA on the website.

Statement of Work (SOW)

The SOW and MSA work together to build your contract. Once you have an MSA in place with your client, you create a new SOW for each project or deliverable. The SOW includes the scope of work, the costs, the timeline, the payment schedule, and anything else not normally in your MSA such as royalties or additional liabilities. The SOW is much faster to create and build and usually flies through legal departments for quicker approval. The SOW should not overlap with or override the MSA. If it's important enough to include in more than one or two SOWs, it should probably be in your MSA. If it's a one-off issue such as copyright or release that varies from your norm, it will be in your SOW. The SOW will typically override the MSA in a legal dispute.

Cover yourself in your SOW, but don't try to cram in every single detail and line item about the project. For one, it would take you longer than the actual work. More importantly, you need the flexibility to change how you work as you go along. Unless you predicate the project on a particular method or course of action, don't put it in the SOW. If you need to list a method but are unsure which will be best, list them all and state that you will use which one works best.

Sample Contract Page with Prices

Phase 1 Timing and Budget: 4-6 Weeks / $11,700
Phase 2 Timing and Budget: 6-10 weeks Weeks / $24,400
Phase 3 Timing and Budget: 5-8 Weeks / $22,800

Estimated Completion: August 17th, 2015

Total Budget: $56,900 (± 10%)

Payment

Each phase will be invoiced separately as follows:

- 50% due at the beginning of the Phase
- 20% due 2 weeks after beginning of the Phase
- 20% due 4 weeks after the beginning of the Phase
- 10% due at phase completion

Terms

- This Statement of Work is good for 30 days from date of preparation.
- Material changes to the nature and/or scope of work you ask us to perform will void this proposal and require a new one be prepared by us.
- Repeated changes to nature and/or scope requiring us prepare new proposals may require you to pay a preparation fee per instance.
- Should parties agree to perform the work described herein, this proposal shall serve as an exhibit of the Master Services Agreement executed between the parties.

An SOW should include:

- The timeline for this particular deliverable. When you'll start and stop, what the phases are and what parts or features to deliver in each phase

- The definition of the specific deliverable and the scope of work to detail. Base it on requirements and specifications that you've gathered in Discovery or the proposal process

- The cost of the deliverable including the payment timeline

- The people involved in this particular deliverable

Download a sample SOW from the website.

Retainer Agreement

Your MSA can cover retainers as well, and even if you don't use an MSA, you should still set the same legal standards for retainers. You'll just want to add terms and conditions around terminating the retainer. The general rule is that retainers can be terminated with thirty days' notice in writing, what's known as "at will." If your client turns in their notice at twenty-eight days, you can decide whether you want to charge them for another month. If they turn it in with ten days' notice, they'll still need to pay the bill whether they want you to keep working or not. This lead-time protects you from the sudden drop in cash-flow and prevents the client from frivolously canceling the agreement on a whim.

Retainer agreements should include:

- Strict language around what services you will and won't provide

- Your time of response, e.g. 24 hours, one week, etc.

- What happens if the client goes over their budget or leaves hours on the table

- Termination rules and notice

The Client's Contract

At times, the client may want you to sign their contract instead of one you create. It's often the case if you're working for another creative firm or agency. You're not a lawyer, and unless you've set up a legal retainer, it may not be feasible to hire an attorney to review the contract for you. I have never worked under a client's contract. In fact, I've walked away from hundreds of thousands of dollars' worth of work because of this exact issue. As someone with a legal background, and having seen friends litigate with clients, it's just not worth it. If, however, you do choose to work under a client's contract, get legal help.

Veronica Picciafuoco shared these key phrases to watch out for in a client's contract in her article[7] on "A List Apart:"

- **Parties, particularly when companies are involved.** Make sure the people you're dealing with have the power to bind their companies.

- **IP provisions.** Who owns copyright and when, and what the licensing limitations are.

- **Your representation and warranties.** The fewer, the better. Under-promise and over-deliver!

- **Termination.** What happens if someone wants to get out of the deal early?

- **Dispute resolution.** The clause no lawyer ever wants to give up. Watch this one, because you don't want to let a client drag you to a court a thousand miles away. If you can agree to arbitration or mediation, even better.

The Pause Clause

My friends at nGen Works implemented what they call "The Pause Clause" to overcome the repeated issue of clients delaying projects indefinitely. It states, "If a client deliverable—such as input, approvals, or payment—is late more than 10 business days the project will be considered 'on hold.' Once the deliverable is received and the project is re-activated it will be rescheduled based on nGen Works' current workload and availability. Just to say it loud and clear, it could be weeks to get you back in the system if the project is put on hold."[8]

They stick to it, they never take it out of their contracts, and they use it. Believe it or not, it works, and they've seen significant improvements when it comes to clients sticking to the timeline.

What to Do if the Client Wants You to Alter Your MSA or Standard SOW

Clients often ask us to change a single phrase or term in our agreement. If it's one of the terms we've had our attorney prepare in our MSA that we use with all clients, we refuse. We may offer a "rider" or amendment to the agreement that allows an exception for a particular use case, typically around copyright or royalties, but that's it.

If a client is asking you to alter terms regarding ownership of work or assets, that's reasonable and can be handled with separate agreements. If, however, a client is asking you to alter your terms around revisions or deliverables or legal protection, you have to be willing to walk away. We can't afford to undermine hundreds of other contracts we have with other clients by altering one for one client.

If you do decide to alter your terms, you must denote the change from your standard agreement. It's to protect you in the event that you work with the client again or that your terms change at a later time. Never physically alter your contract terms and fail to denote the change.

Working For Free

Doing work for free, whether it's an internship or just when you're starting out, is considered a rite of passage for creatives. You start out cleaning toilets, getting coffee, and sorting mail—or at least the creative equivalent. Anyone who has written for a magazine as a freelancer or done a logo for a "friend" can tell you that it's astonishing how little some people will pay for creative services.

The idea of doing a new creative a "favor" by allowing them the privilege of doing their work for "exposure" is so prevalent that it's actually recommended to many entrepreneurs in guidebooks and startup culture blogs. Conversely, there are fervent "no spec" movements that scream every time a creative does work for free. Websites like 99 Designs have damaged the integrity of creative work by having people work for free in the hope of getting paid for it. The infamous "logo contest" is one of the worst outcomes of the crowdfunding and startup movements.

Spec and Pro Bono Work

Speculative work, better known as spec work, is work done without an agreement of compensation. The AIGA shares these textbook examples[9]:

- Speculative or "spec" work: work done for free, in hopes of getting paid for it

- Competitions: work done in the hopes of winning a prize—in whatever form that might take

- Volunteer work: work done as a favor or for the experience, without the expectation of being paid

- Internships: a form of volunteer work that involves educational gain

- Pro bono work: volunteer work done "for the public good"

The AIGA's official position is right in line with my own: "Clients risk compromised quality. Little time, energy and thought can go into speculative work, which precludes the most important element of most design projects—the research, thoughtful consideration of alternatives, and development and testing of prototype designs. Designers risk being taken advantage of. Some clients may see this as a way to get free work; it also diminishes the true economic value of the contribution designers make toward client's objectives. There are legal risks for both parties should aspects of intellectual property, trademark and trade-dress infringements become a factor."[10] The AIGA and most organizations do not have an explicit "no spec" policy. They do, however, strongly advise you to consider the circumstances beyond "getting exposure" before deciding to work without direct payment.

Working for free can be useful

Jessica Hische's flow map at shouldiworkforfree.com is spot on. She breaks down scenarios where you could consider working for free. The key question when it comes to free work is "will it move you forward as an individual more than as a business?" Your business can't afford to work for free unless there are tax benefits. But you may be able to work for free as an individual.

There are some creative firms that have worked out a way to work for free and remain profitable. Our Atlanta neighbors Matchstic have their "On The House" program in which they serve one local non-profit each year with a large project free of charge.[11] They build this into their cost of doing business and make it easier to give this project the same focus and attention as clients paying full price.

Seth Godin recommended asking these questions before deciding whether to work for free:[12]

- Do they pay other people who do this work? Do their competitors?

- Am I learning enough from this interaction to call this part of my education?

- Is this public work with my name on it, or am I just saving them cash to do a job they should pay for?

- If I get paid, is it more likely the organization will pay closer attention, promote it better and treat it more seriously?

- Do I care about their mission? Can they afford to do this professionally?

- Will I get noticed by the right people, people who will help me spread the word to the point where I can get hired to do this professionally?

- What's the risk to me, my internal monologue and my reputation if I do this work?

"The more generous you are with your ideas, and the more they spread, the more likely it is your perceived value goes up... (but) if you're busy doing free work because it's a good way to hide from the difficult job of getting paid for your work, stop. When you confuse busy for productive, you're sabotaging your ability to do important work in the future. On the other hand, if you're turning down free gigs because the exposure frightens you, the same is true ... you're ducking behind the need to get paid as a way to hide your art."

Seth Godin[13]

You can change your mind

Your position on working for free may oscillate over the course of your creative career. That's normal. When you have lots of work, lots of money, and no time, it's easy to scoff at spec work. When you have little work, little money, and lots of time, it's easy to scoff at spec work. When you have enough work, enough money, and enough time, it can feel right to work on exciting things without money being involved. If it's moving you forward and you can afford to do it, give it a shot. If it's a client asking you to work for free because they're too cheap to pay for quality creative, walk away.

Documents

Non-disclosure Agreement (NDA)

The NDA is the prenup of business. A non-disclosure agreement is an agreement intended to protect confidential materials or ideas. Your prospective client's goal with an NDA is to restrict access to their information by third parties. You are agreeing not to disclose information covered by the agreement. An NDA is designed to create a confidential relationship between you and your client to protect any type of confidential and proprietary information or trade secrets.[14]

By asking someone to sign an NDA before you will tell them anything, your client is starting out in mistrust. Creative work is predicated on trust. Working with paranoid individuals rarely ends well.

On several occasions, our agency has lost work or turned down a prospect over non-disclosure agreements. Until we are under contract using our MSA, we won't sign anything. Even when we're under contract, we never sign NDAs that include non-compete agreements, i.e. we're not allowed to work with other clients in the same industry.

Most clients create NDAs out of fear that someone will steal their idea. It's an absolute waste of time. Without patents, copyrights, and armies of attorneys, it's virtually impossible to enforce an NDA. By signing an NDA, you agree that the client can, however, sue you for just about anything that doesn't sit with them. If a client refuses to tell you anything about their project until you sign an NDA, just move along. Try your best to explain your MSA handily covers the protection of private information and data, but blindly signing an NDA isn't in the cards.

It's perfectly fine to sign an NDA once you are engaged with the client under your terms, but you should have your attorney check the NDA first.

Download a sample NDA from the website.

Work for Hire (WFH)

Work made for hire (WFH) is work created by you or your employees for a client in which you agree that the client retains full authorship of the work. What this means is that the client legally created the work, you didn't. The WFH document creates the exception to the rule that the person who actually creates a work is the legally recognized author of that work.[15] By signing a WFH, you are attributing the authorship and ownership of that work to your client.

When you hire contractors or freelancers to create work for your clients, it's imperative that you get WFH agreements from them before allowing them to perform client work. Any employees you hire should sign a WFH agreement as well. If a client asks you to sign a WFH agreement, it's best to consider value-based pricing. You are forfeiting any rights to stop reproduction and resale of your work. The client could use your work in a clothing line or downloadable materials and continue to make money without compensating you. Thus, you should be compensated considerably more for any WFH deliverables.

Download a sample WFH agreement from the website.

A Very Short List of Very Important Documents

To recap, these are the minimum documents you need to run a stable creative business:

- Proposal template
- Master services agreement
- Statement of work (contract)
- Retainer agreement
- Non-disclosure agreement (NDA)
- Work for hire agreement (WFH)

Getting Paid—Invoicing, Billing, and Collections

The low-hanging fruit when it comes to improving operations is your billing practices. If you've got multiple wounds, the one bleeding money should be plugged first.

A quick note about Ilise Benun's *The Creative Professional's Guide to Money*, which I reference several times in this section. Her book was one of the most important parts of my restructuring, and I'm truly grateful for her contributions. I hope that my book will do the same for others. To be honest, I could have just put "read her book" in bold letters instead of writing this section. I do have some additional insights from my experience, and that's why that didn't happen. Trying to write something better than Ilise on certain topics is futile, so I quoted her.

I first met Ilise in 2008 at the Creative Freelancer Conference. She's been a source of wisdom ever since. She was kind enough to provide technical editing for this book after I reached out to her. Since this book is about transparency, I want to be abundantly clear that no one quoted in this book, including Ilise, is getting a kick-back from me for suggesting their materials. She just wrote a damn good book and it helped get me out of the hole. I think you'll benefit from it. I want you to get the best advice out there and, at times, it's already written by someone else.

Money Up Front

Never start work for any client without a cleared payment for deposit. When you work without a deposit, you are telling your client that they can pay you when they're ready and that you don't take your business seriously. That isn't hyperbole; it's been proven time and again by countless colleagues who've made this grave mistake. No matter who it is and how often you've worked with them, never start work without a deposit on the work. If the client has slow billing practices and is in a rush, then offer them credit card payments or escrow. If they truly need the work done, they'll find a way to get you paid. Any client that refuses to make a down payment on the work, no matter how tempting it may be to work with them, is a client you shouldn't have.

Don't be afraid to ask for it all up front

Ideally you should bill 100 percent of the cost upfront for any work that has no physical deliverables such as consulting, coaching, or content that will live on the client's server from the start. Your ability to receive delayed payment directly correlates to your leverage. If you have all of the work and the client has nothing, you have all of the leverage. If the client has half of the work and you have half of the payment, you're even. If the client has all of the work and you have none of the payment, you have no leverage.

What if the client can't pay up front?

Then you can't work for them. If you're in a financial position that makes you feel desperate for the work, then fix your financial situation. Doing work without pay is probably going to make it worse. If they can't give you a deposit, then what assurance do you have that they can pay future invoices on time? I wish I could give you a list of exceptions and circumstances for working around this, but there are none. Don't work without a deposit.

Money up front means money up front

I do want to be clear that when I say get a deposit before you work, I mean have the deposit in your bank account before you do any work. That doesn't mean that the client has put the check in the mail or sent it in for processing. You have the actual money in your bank account and can use it, and then you start working.

Invoicing

Invoices are the lifeblood of your business. Treat them with the utmost care. They're how you get paid. They're the documentation for the transactional agreement between you and your client. No matter how much or how often, all invoices should follow three simple rules:

- Send an invoice immediately upon agreement and send them the same way every time. Don't mix messages.

- Find out who handles processing your invoice and get their email; send it directly to them. Don't rely on your contact or project manager to turn the invoice into accounts payable for you.

- Use invoicing services or software or let your accountant do it. Keep it somewhere that's built for invoicing and can be tied to your accounting systems. Don't throw it in a word processor document. Don't be informal.

Never tie invoicing to deliverables, only to time

How often have you been 90 percent done with a project but only hold half of the payment as the client continues to delay finishing the project? While 50/50 billing at start and finish is fine, tying it to an arbitrary deadline such as "when the project is complete" is a recipe for disaster. Establish two dates at the outset, one of which is the start of work. Regardless of how complete the project is, the remaining payment is due on the agreed upon date. You can split this into smaller amounts and more frequent dates, such as thirds or quarters or even weekly billing.

However you do it, **never tie payment to deliverables**. An example is one-third up front, middle third at thirty days, and final payment at sixty days. If, at the sixty-day date, *you* are the one who's behind and the client has delivered all requirements on time, you can then choose not to bill for the final payment yet. Just never be in a position where you've done the work and are ready to be paid, but the client has to "sign off" before you can collect.

Bill on a schedule

You could bill monthly or weekly and invoice all of your clients at the same time, the same way. You could send invoices every Friday or the first Tuesday of every month, and they're all due on the same day. It can increase predictability and reduce some operational overhead since you can deal with all invoicing in one sitting.

The anatomy of an invoice

The ideal invoice should include:

- Your tax ID or EIN number

- Your mailing address, phone number, and a contact email

- Issue date and due date

- A list of the services or products provided, with line-item pricing

- A total

- The agreed-upon terms, such as net thirty days or due upon receipt

Download a sample invoice from the website.

Collections

You will have at least one deadbeat client in your career, hopefully not many more. It's just a part of a services-based business. Threatening to burn down their house or break their knees isn't going to get you very far, so you simply need to take all of the steps to protect you and your business. One of the many reasons not to have a single client take up more than 25 percent of your annual business is that they could be the one who doesn't pay. Getting a deposit, and establishing milestone payments, can reduce the risk of getting stiffed. You can go to a collections service, send your attorney after them, or show up at their door. At times, these tactics work and, sometimes, the client simply isn't going to pay.

Other than being a complete jerk, there are other reasons why a client may not pay:

- They're unhappy with the work

- They don't have the money

- Your project is caught in the middle of internal politics

- They're big, and they pay whenever they want, often seeing if they can get away with never paying small businesses

- They have slow internal processes, and you aren't a priority

- Your contact doesn't pay the bills and hasn't turned in the invoice or did so without following protocol

- They consider the work incomplete yet you've delivered everything in scope

What to do when a client doesn't pay

In *The Creative Professional's Guide to Money,* business coach and marketing consultant Ilise Benun outlines the steps you should take in the event that a client doesn't pay :[16]

- Remain professional and don't stress

- Stop work immediately

- Be squeaky

- Offer other payment options

- Offer a payment plan

- Charge late fees

- Send a personal letter

- Get a letter from your lawyer

- Show up in person

- Advise next steps but don't make empty threats

- Take them to small claims court

Ilise is spot on with her steps. I'm a bit more heavy-handed when it comes to collections due to my legal background, so here's the "Brad-flavored" spin on her explanations.

- **You may be angry, but don't react in anger.** Only start communication with a clear head and be careful what you put in writing.

- **Stop work and make it clear you're keeping any completed work.** Clients will push back on this, asking for you to continue, but it's important that you're not any further in the hole in the event that the money never arrives.

- **Call and email every week or every day.** Remain professional, but be a pest.

- **Give them the name of loan sharks.** Ok, maybe not, but allow them to use a credit card or wire transfer to pay you. Don't give them the excuse of check processing once they are late.

- **Agree to a payment plan, but only with a promissory note.** If it's excessively past due, you can give them the option to get you some money instead of demanding it all right now. But do not restart work once the payment plan is in place; you're adding more debt while in collections. Only restart work when it's all paid back.

- **Your late fees should compound, not be a single fee.** Do not ever waive them. They should be in your contract, and you need to use them. We charge 5 percent per month, and it compounds, meaning we add 10 percent in the second month, 15 percent in the third and so on. Communicate that they are being added; the additional fees may be enough to get the client to pay.

- **Send a letter or have your attorney send one.** Use certified mail to make sure it's delivered. The letter should be strongly worded but not full of threats. Make it clear what will happen if they don't pay.

- **Knock on their door if they're local.** I've done this myself. I've shown up unannounced and asked for payment on the spot. It's much harder to avoid and lie to someone face to face.

- **Stand your ground and take action.** If you say you're going to go into collections, do it. Report them to the Better Business Bureau and notify your local Chamber of Commerce.

- **Go to Court.** Small claims court is a hassle, but may be necessary. Even if you break even, the message you send by litigating is an important one.

- **Write it off.** The time, effort, and expense involved in chasing down some clients is more than the value of the work. Involve your accountant in helping you decide whether to write off an invoice and what the implications may be.

- **Take it away.** Web designers and developers could take the recourse of removing the client's website or taking out the features they've built. It's risky, and ill-advised unless your attorney advises you to do so. I've seen it result in the designer being sued for damages and lost business.

What to do with unpaid work

If it's custom work, such as writing or illustration, which you can't re-use for another project, then you may just be out of luck. If you can find a way to repurpose the work for another client or turn it into stock or a product, try to get some money out of it.

If you're in the unfortunate situation where you owe others money, such as subcontractors or equipment rentals, you may have to get them to join you in a lawsuit. You may also have to take out a loan to pay your vendor. Any time you hire vendors as part of a project, pay them first out of your deposit and pay yourself last. That way, if you are stiffed, at least you're only out your own money instead of still having to pay someone else plus miss out on the expected income.

A bit more on collections

- Put a due date on your agreement, not fifteen days or net thirty. Put an actual date such as February 12. There should also be an issue date on the invoice.
- If you aren't sending the invoice with ample processing time, you can't hold the client to a late fee. Find out how long it takes them to process and send your invoice ahead of time if it's more than your agreed-upon net terms. For example, if it takes them an average of thirty days to process payments and your terms are net fifteen, you can't expect them to pay you on time. Send the invoice at least thirty days ahead of when it's due.
- Send a separate invoice with the late fee as an actual line item on it once it's past due, don't just change the amount due without detailing the fee.

Taxes

Taxes were a big problem for me starting out. If you're coming from the standard employment world where your employer has always filed your taxes for you, the small business world of tax management can be a rude awakening. In the United States, you're responsible for paying some varying taxes to local and national government from each paycheck in addition to taxes on your actual income per dollar earned. It's important to ensure that you're considering the taxes you'll be paying into your salary calculation and treat it as an expense on a monthly basis.

Make payments

You're supposed to pay quarterly because it is considered avoiding interest when you don't. You don't *have* to make the payments, but if your averages are off when the year is broken up, you can be charged backed interest for any quarters that were above average. There are fines and fees for not making estimated quarterly payments. Your estimated payments don't have to be exact, no one can predict the future, but you should pay roughly 25 percent of your net billings each quarter in taxes.

It requires discipline to leave the tax allocated money alone when you're struggling from month to month. Sending in that money on a quarterly basis rather than annually can help remove some of the temptation to dip into your tax allocations. But with the freedom of self-reporting taxable income when you are your own business comes the risk of never saving your tax money and being sent a large tax bill at the end of each year.

What to do when you can't pay your taxes

Don't hide. The worst thing you can do is fail to report your actual income. Turn it in and work with your accountant to find out where you stand. Tax authorities are more than willing to work with you on payment plans as long as you're filing on time.

Don't let it happen again. If you can't afford to pay your taxes with what you're bringing in, then you have to raise your rates or lower your expenses. Tax debt is far worse than any other debt because the interest is heavy and the debt can never be written off.

Cash Flow

Money Management on an Irregular Income

If your income isn't predictable, you're not in control. When you're not in control, you're stressed. It's your business, your income, and your schedule. There is no reason for it to be out of your hands or "unpredictable." You have everything you need to predict what you'll make each week or month. You got into business for yourself to get more control, so get control of your finances.

Save, budget, and be smart with your money

There are countless books on money management and budgeting. Financial experts including Dave Ramsey have done an excellent job breaking down step-by-step programs for managing your money on an irregular income. These resources are on the website. Rather than repeat their advice, what I will say is that you don't have to have an irregular income. If you're billing correctly and using your shop rate, you should have control of your cash flow, and it shouldn't feel much different from a regular paycheck.

Don't rob Peter to pay Paul

Don't spend your deposits before you're working. If you're 20 percent of the way into a project but you've already spent 50 percent of the money, you're not managing your cash flow. Never use money from one project to pay for work or resources in another. Learn to allocate your payments from each project into budgeted buckets over the course of the work.

- When you receive your deposit and then start a project, earmark any funds for materials or freelancers in your accounting software. If possible, put it in a separate account.

- Pay your freelancers' deposits out of the deposit first.

- If it's time to pay bills, but you haven't closed any new work or received final payments on projects, you may have to use your deposit to get by. In that event, make note of how much you've taken from the deposit and pay it back as soon as additional funds come in. Only until all resources and contractors on a project have been paid in full for the entire project should you use funds to operate your business.

- After everyone is paid, and the project is complete, then you can calculate your profit and savings contributions.

Tie it to your work

For your shop rate, you have to know your expenses and how much you need to make in salary. That same math can be used to calculate how much work you need. Break down your monthly goals into projects, weeks, or clients—depending on your pricing strategy. If you use project-based pricing and your goal is $5,000 per month, then a simple formula is to say you need two projects at $2,500 each per month. Or five projects at $1,000 each per month.

If you use retainers or value-based pricing, it's best to break it down by clients and/ or weeks. If your goal is $10,000 per month, then you need $2,500 per week or two clients retained at $5,000 per month each. Of course, one client at $6,000 and one client at $4,000 is the same; it's not about everything being the same size. In fact, a mix is best. For that same $10,000 goal, something like one client at $4,000 per month, three clients at $1,500 per month each, and two small clients at $750 per month each is what you'll be more likely to end up with. In Ilise Benun's *The Creative Professionals Guide to Money,* she provides a series of exercises to determine your actual goals and how to manage them. It's worth the time to go through her exercises to determine what works for you.

Close the right business at the right time

Filling your pipeline with prospects and assigning a predictable dollar value to them helps you focus on closing the right business at the right time. If you're not staffed to handle three $4,000 per month clients at the same time, closing all three of them in the same month is going to be a problem. It's just like meals; you don't eat breakfast, lunch, and dinner at the same time at 7am. You eat throughout the day as your body burns calories and needs to be replenished. Your cash flow is just the same. Having reliable prospects lined up weeks or months down the road will remove a tremendous amount of stress from your life.

No more than 33 percent from one client

Never let a single client be more than a third of your annual billings. It's simply too dangerous to have that much of your business relying on one relationship. That client has far too much leverage over you and your workflow. If you're staffing up to accommodate a client as they grow, then make sure you're growing other clients or subcontracting some of the work to outside sources. It protects your cash flow and allows you to cut contractors off if the client drops you. If you're solo and a client is trying to take up more than a third of your time in a given year, then they need to compensate you much more. Otherwise, you'll need to hire help and then bring on additional clients.

Running Out of Money is Normal, and to be Expected

At some point, you will get an unwanted email from your bank. There won't be enough money, and you may not have any idea when, or where from, the next check is coming. It doesn't matter if you have loans or lines of credit or safety nets in place. It's a rite of passage for most business owners. If you've ever had a fireside chat over drinks with other creative business owners, almost every person will have a story or two about the time they ran out of money.

For me, there've been countless times where we've been a week away from missing payroll. I'd like to say that will never happen again, but I've been there too many times. There are ways to prepare for it and mitigate the damage, such as having savings or a line of credit.

It's embarrassing, it's humbling, it's scary, and it will take your breath away. But being on the other side of it, and realizing you survived, is one of the coolest scars you'll ever bear. What you can do is always trust that work will arrive, and money will come in if you're sticking to the process. Just like quicksand, the worst thing you can do is flail about and fight it. Be methodical, stick to the plan, and work yourself out of it step by step.

An Orderly House Is a Happy House

Getting your house in order, and keeping it that way, requires systems and documentation. The benefit is far more freedom to create and grow. As you build your methods of operation, you can repurpose your effort and use templates and frameworks to become much more efficient. Having strong operations empowers you to handle proposals, contracts, and invoices with confidence. Plus, you won't have to dig through piles of disorganized papers when a client is late or doesn't pay.

Less time spent on repetitive and tedious operational tasks doesn't just mean more time to create. It also means less stress, more time to relax, and an improved ability to deal with the unexpected. It helps the overwhelming seem more manageable and can have a lasting impact on your bottom line.

Notes

1. Anthony Bourdain, *Kitchen Confidential*, p. 68.
2. Mike Monteriro, *Design is a Job*.
3. Ibid.
4. Mike McDerment, *Breaking the Time Barrier*.
5. http://web.missouri.edu/~segerti/capstone/anchorprecision.pdf.
6. http://stuffandnonsense.co.uk/projects/contract-killer/.
7. http://alistapart.com/article/designing-contracts-for-the-xxi-century.
8. http://ngenworks.com/business/the-pause-clause/.
9. http://www.aiga.org/position-spec-work/.
10. http://www.aiga.org/position-spec-work/.
11. http://matchstic.com/about/on-the-house.
12. http://sethgodin.typepad.com/seths _ blog/2013/02/should-you-work-for-free.html.
13. Ibid.
14. http://en.wikipedia.org/wiki/Non-disclosure _ agreement.
15. http://en.wikipedia.org/wiki/Work _ for _ hire.
16. Ilise Benun, T*he Creative Professional's Guide to Money*, pp. 148–150.

CHAPTER 6

A Very DELICATE Matter

Managing Client Expectations

"I've never had a problem with a dumb client. There is no such thing as a bad client. Part of our job is to do good work and get the client to accept it."

Bob Gill[1]

Imagine yourself in the Bill Murray classic *Groundhog Day*, but instead of being asked to do the weather report every day for eternity, it's going to the same job interview. That's what it feels like at times as you move from client to client in creative business. You are asked, over and over, to explain who you are and what you do, why you're the best choice, what it will cost, and then you review the same rules and stipulations. It's not necessarily a negative; it's just something that you have to get used to.

Every time you start with a new client, or even a new project with the same client, you're establishing trust and rapport. It's up to you to set the tone for the working relationship. It means sticking to your guns when it comes to pricing and choosing who you work with and putting systems in place. You have to stand your ground, but you also have to work with other humans. By setting proper expectations and communicating with empathy, you can build better client relationships.

Yes, clients will walk all over you if you allow it. You are your own individual, as is the business, and you will always have needs to which you must attend. The balancing act between standing your ground while making concessions is tough, but it's the key to building lasting relationships that follow you throughout your career.

Here's what we'll cover:

- Setting client expectations
- Communication and project management
- Showing your work
- Feedback and critique
- Revisions and scope creep
- Client reviews
- Copyright and protecting your work
- Getting more work out of existing clients
- Fixing or ending a client relationship

Setting Client Expectations

Get to know your clients, they're not all the same. Some have worked with creatives before, and some have no idea how any of this works. Some clients are more controlling, and some are uninvolved. While you shouldn't jump into Facebook friend requests and pajama parties, it's a good idea to get to know your clients as people. In your initial meetings or calls, a little "get to know you" ice breaker can help. Knowing simple things like whether a client is married or has children or what part of town they live in can help you understand why a deadline or meeting may be at a particular time.

Lay the Foundation

Agree up front on how you will work together. If there is a problem, how will you handle it? Who handles approving revisions and changes? When will you regularly talk and check in for progress reports? The scope of work in your contract isn't always enough. Break the scope down as much as possible so that the client understands what's going to be done, and when.

Set budget expectations up front. No one likes a flat tire or busted pipe; the same goes for your clients. Unexpected expenses are the fastest way to mistrust and frustration. If you expect the client to buy materials or pay for certain travel expenses, spell it out. Don't just tack it on an invoice. The same goes for what overages look like and how to bill meetings. If a client sees that she's being charged per employee in a meeting, and two of your people are just sitting there on their laptops the whole time, she's going to wonder why they're there.

Get it in writing. Set expectations in writing so that you both know how things should work. Don't leave it up to interpretation. Write down what you will and won't do as far as skills and services. Set working hours. Set communication parameters. Anything left up to chance, it's on you if the client expects it to be done.

Define the relationship (DTR). We always ask our clients two questions at the end of our kick-off meeting: "What would make this project an absolute home run?" and "what can we do in this project to make you want to work with us again?" We make no qualms about our intention to have this client for the long haul. By setting the tone up front that this isn't a transaction or a one-night-stand, we're letting the client know we expect a relationship. We have the DTR conversation up front.

Communications and Project Management

Don't hide your process from your clients as if it's a magic trick. Clients won't be shocked that you use stock images, read tutorials, or copy styles from your inspiration research. Clients are hiring you for solutions, not what it took to get there. They aren't as interested in your process as you might think.

What clients *are* interested in is what they'll get, when they'll get it, and whether it's what they intended. The less mystery around those three questions, the better your working relationship will be. Yes, I hear the concern about open design processes regarding micro-management. I'm not saying that you should pull up a chair beside your client while you're designing or writing and letting them see every step. It means sharing with them on a frequent basis so that they know what's going on. It may be screenshots, wireframes, photos of work in progress, snippets of features, outlines, and so much more. Depending on your work and your process, you can find ways to involve your clients.

Showing Your Work in Progress

Show your work early and often; don't wait to get feedback from the client. The more "big reveals" you have, the more likely the client is to have strong feelings about the direction you're going. The more open you are with the client on a regular basis, even daily, about your creative direction, the better the feedback will be.

Use a Project Management Tool

Email isn't a good system for communicating with clients. Even if you have powerful filters and search, it makes it difficult for everyone to know what's going on. As more people get involved, they can be left out of important conversations happening in someone else's inbox. Use a tool such as Basecamp, Trello, Asana, or other project management tools to house client communications.

You don't have to get a project management certification or start using Scrum or Agile processes; you just need to get all of your chatter and files in one spot. At Nine Labs, we use Asana. It has pros and cons, but it does an excellent job of keeping everyone involved and letting them see what happened. You can go back and find out what transpired while you were out, pull any shared files, and create to-do lists with accountability.

Use a Chat Tool

In the past year, we've been using chat systems with our clients, not just our team. The trust and rapport we have with our clients on chat are noticeably stronger. The fear of having a chat channel with your clients is that they'll bug you all day for little things. That's not been the case for us so far.

Using Slack, we now have an archive of every public conversation surrounding a project. Anyone on the client team who is out of the office or busy can catch up on what's transpired and get into the conversation. Everyone is less likely to miss out on details or instructions. Our work has improved, and so have our margins. By involving clients in conversations on the fly, we've reduced the amount of meetings we schedule by half. We can rip through quick chat sessions to get a host of questions answered and make progress that same day.

I've also found that we get interrupted less since we're on chat. Email takes so long to work through and making a request for a file or review via email can mean leaving your inbox open while you're in "revision limbo". With chat, we know when they're available, and we can have a quick discussion. With the file in view, we can take action and move forward immediately.

The benefits of having open chat communications with our clients and team heavily outweigh the risks and we plan to get every client in chat eventually. I'd recommend you consider it as well.

Be Consistent With How You Intake Client Communication

Set expectations for where and how the client is to communicate and stick to it. If you use a project management system such as Basecamp or Asana to manage files and client feedback, make sure that you're getting your clients to handle all communications in that system. Mixed channels—email, project management software, instant messaging, and text—are part of the job, but ensure that formal requests and documents are all in one place. It's the fastest way for things to be forgotten and miscommunication to occur.

If a client isn't willing to go through your onboarding process and log into Basecamp, they're presumably going to be a difficult client. You can soften the blow by having someone on your team ensure that you move all communications into your project management tool, but I'm not willing to do that. Most of the tools on the market integrate with email, so the client can just reply to your message, and it will show up in the project management system. If they're not willing to reply to an email, they're probably not a client you want to keep.

Presenting Your Work and Receiving Feedback

Just like your proposals, you don't want clients looking at your work without context. Any time that you present work to a client for review, do it with confidence and explain your thinking. Here are a few tips on what to do when presenting the work:

- **Don't apologize**. If the work isn't up to par, let the client make that decision. Don't start off by saying anything about it not being what you had hoped or that it could have been better or anything else that devalues your effort.

- **Tell them what to do**. Be specific about what you want the client to do with the work. Do you need feedback? If so, on what do you need feedback? When do you need the feedback? If you need them to provide additional information, point out how that information is part of the work and where it applies.

- **Don't list**. Present the work as a whole, don't point out the obvious. If what they asked for is there, they will see it. If you did something different or made a change, point that out. Only spend your time focusing on points of contention or interest, don't point out the obvious.

- **Let it breathe**. Don't over-explain the work. Let the client digest it. Simply set the tone and provide enough context for your thinking so that the client knows what they're looking at.

- **Don't be offended**. If the client is unhappy with the work and tears it apart, that's their right. They've bought it and if they don't like it, they can say so. As long as they aren't calling you names or tearing you apart, you can't take it personally.

- **"Like" is your worst enemy**. Don't ask the client if they like it, ask them to provide feedback. Clients should never like or dislike your work. The outcome should work or not work. "Like" is a subjective word, as are love and hate. The more you find yourself asking clients if they "like it" or "love it," the more you'll get subjective feedback. We can fall in and out of like, but things that work continue to work. Your solution is for a specific place and time, a particular problem that your client is facing that you've been asked to solve. It's your job to find a solution for them that works, that does the job, not something that they like. At times, I've given clients solutions that they didn't like, but it worked.

Post-mortems and Client Reviews

As soon as you complete a project, get feedback from the client. It's where your testimonials will come from, but it's also the best time to learn about what worked and what didn't. It's best to have this meeting internally first. If you're solo, then you can still ask yourself tough questions and write down honest answers. After you have your internal meeting (post-mortem), you can then have a client review with these same four questions.

- **What went well?** Always lead with the wins and successes from the project. List anything that went according to plan or exceeded expectations.

- **What didn't go well?** It isn't necessarily a time to gripe. It's a time to take an honest look at what didn't go well, not who didn't perform or anything else personal.

- **What did we learn?** Recap the good and the bad lessons learned that you can use for future work.

- **What can we do better next time?** No project is perfect, so take note of what you can do in the future to improve. It may not even be unique to the work, it could just be better communications or delivery practices.

As soon as you conduct these meetings, get everything together and act. Don't wait to review projects until weeks or months after they're complete. Make this a part of your project delivery process so that everyone is fresh and still has a clear picture of this particular project.

- **Take detailed notes.** During the meetings, take detailed notes or record them. Keep them on file for future use.

- **Write case studies or blog posts.** If you're going to create a case study or blog post outlining this project, do it now. Even if you need to wait for analytics or additional data before knowing how it truly went, start the narrative now.

- **Ask for testimonials.** Hopefully the client is happy with the work. If so, this is the time to ask for testimonials when everyone is still engaged.

- **Update your portfolio.** If there are visuals or samples from the project that should go in your portfolio, on your website, or on any showcase sites, do that work now as well.

- **Organize your assets.** Clean up all of the "finalv4final_thistimereallyfinalv2.jpg" files and everything else that's been thrown into random folders. Get consistent file names, file working versions separately from production versions, and archive your notes.

Client Revisions and Scope Creep

"Make it pop." "It needs to be edgier." "It doesn't quite feel right." "We love it, but…"

Revisions can hijack a project, drive it over a cliff, and set it on fire. Having your work picked apart can be painful. The natural reaction to criticism is to defend yourself instead of learning from it. Most of us would love for our exact vision to be left untouched and win all the awards. Winning awards, and impressing the blogosphere, isn't your job. Your job is to manage client expectations and meet their needs.

As projects progress and revisions pile up, you will run into scope creep. That means the scope of the project is slowly expanding as changes are made, and things are added. The leading cause of scope creep is unclear scope. To be specific, the more vague you are about the work being done and delivered, the more gaps there are for the client to fill in with revision requests and feature additions.

The best way to avoid unnecessary changes and scope creep is to research thoroughly the work up front and define how the feedback and review process works. The more questions you ask before you start, the closer you'll be to the client's expectations for the work.

How to Deal With/Mitigate/Tolerate Client Revisions

- **Communicate.** It's the first step in fighting off unnecessary revisions. Include the client from step 1 so that they know how things are going. The more feedback you're receiving along the way, the less you'll get when it's too late to make changes.

- **Count them.** Spell out what revisions are and how many are allowed in your agreements. For example, say, "five logo concepts, choose up to three to revise into two final concepts with one final round of revision on each before being presented with the final options."

- **Explain yourself.** Your client isn't a mind reader so you will have to spell out how the process works. Otherwise, they will assume it just goes on indefinitely until it's "exactly right" according to their standards. Tell clients as you present each phase what can change now and what will be locked once you move forward. If you don't tell them, they won't know.

- **Always ask, "Why?"** Be kind, but ask the client to explain the reasoning behind their request. Is it because they like red instead of purple or is it because purple has been proven to cause seizures with their target audience? The difference is articulating what's not working over what they don't like. Clients think they're being helpful by telling you exactly what they want, when what their project needs isn't top of mind.

- **Look for the "because."** Laura Kalbag noted that better feedback comes from asking clients to tell you more than the reason for change. They should add the word "because" to the end of the request and explain why they're asking for it.[2]

- **Don't get emotional.** How you receive feedback sets the tone for how clients will give it. Sure, you'll catch clients on a bad day or simply get hired by jerks, but you have the ability to set the tone for how revisions and feedback work with your attitude.

- **Only react to feedback from decision makers, but hear feedback from everyone.** A single person should handle deciding whether you should execute on particular feedback given; you should not take everyone's feedback and immediately act upon it.

- **Show your work.** Hiding the work in progress until it's done is the most surefire way to end up with revisions, often when it's too late.

- **Charge for revisions.** If a revision is outside of the scope of work in your SOW, then explain the costs associated with the revision to the client. There may be a battle of whether it should be free or not, but just by explaining the time and effort involved the client may be willing to accept an easier alternative that will save them money.

- **Use the timeline.** If the revision is going to affect the project timeline, your client may be willing to do without it. You may be okay with making the change, but not in the time left. If you explain that there will be a delay because of a change, a client is more likely to either pay for the revision or forego it.

- **Beware the CEO swoop-in.** That's when the boss comes in 90 percent of the way into the project and decides to "suggest" changes. It's going to happen; she's the CEO. The best way to avoid it is to include leadership as often as possible and solicit their approval before moving onto the next major phase in a project. Sometimes, it's unavoidable, and you have to play the charging more/take longer cards to get the CEO to back off.

- **Know the difference between compromise and concession.** There are times where you'll have to concede to survive. If you need just to get the project done and it's cheaper and faster to give the client all that they're asking, just do it. It's not worth losing sleep over. If, however, there are reasons to stand your ground, you may still have to compromise. That means you have to negotiate with the client regarding the revision. If all else fails, you can still say no.

- **Be okay with stopping work.** If a client is excessive in revision requests, you may have to stop work and walk away. Hopefully, you've tied your payment to time instead of deliverables, and there is an even balance between work completed and money received. Be willing to let a project go unfinished or be handed off to someone else if the client is excessive with revisions.

Clients can't fully understand how long a revision may take, or the work involved. They may see something as minor that is, in fact, very major. And the opposite, they may be afraid to make a minor request because it seems major to them. Always be in communication with your client as you go along, opening up the process to them so that they're able to comment on the work in progress.

Billable or warranty?

Sometimes a client makes a request to have something changed at the end of a project or after launch. They may not be willing to pay for the request because they don't see it as a revision, they see it as a warranty. This depends on the type of work you do, but any digital work such as web design or animation could be susceptible to this type of request.

Make it clear in your contracts what's covered after launch. You may agree to a post-launch review for a number of reasons, but you should set a cap on the amount of time or effort you'll provide. If the request is being made prior to launch, but will result in overages from your original estimates, it comes down to your pricing model.

If this is a project-based pricing agreement for a flat fee, it can be a matter of opinion. You'll have to decide how to proceed, but follow the steps outlined in the previous section to prevent miscommunication. If you're hourly, well then you're safe. If you're value-based, the same rules apply as project-based pricing. If you're on a retainer, then it's still hours.

You have to decide if it's best to lose a client or work outside of scope. Neither is right, and neither is fun, but you'll have to make a decision.

What To Do When the Client Is Wrong

Sometimes the client is wrong. If after reviewing the project goals, the market, and speaking with other stakeholders it's obvious that a revision or change is in the wrong direction, you'll be faced with a challenge. The key is to not make the defense about you or your opinion, avoid using the word "I." Focus on the effect the change will have on the project or business goals. Remind the client of the stated goals and ask them to explain how this will improve the chances of reaching said goals.

Never be afraid to kill a project. You may have to assert yourself as the expert and play the "you hired me for my professional guidance" card. You do need to make it clear that you know what you're doing, and the request is something you can't advise. You must be able to articulate that opinion with empirical research. It can't be "green is more popular" or "I like green better." It needs to be "green is the way to go here because of research done by this organization that determined X." If you don't have hard science or research, then you may have to tell your client that this is your call.

You can say that it's your professional opinion and that you can't move forward in good faith and let them make this mistake. You're putting yourself at risk, but at times it matters that much. You have to be willing to stop work and walk away. Maybe you can bring in a colleague for a second opinion or find other ways to make your point, but if it's worth standing up for, do it. And, sometimes, you're just going to have to put that picture of their dog on the home page and cry into your beer. Above all, never be afraid to kill a project. As we've covered before, always be in a position of power where you can hand the client their remaining money back, turn over the work, and end the relationship.

Copyright and Intellectual Property

When we work for a client, we're handing over copyright and intellectual property rights. The exceptions are typically for illustrators, photographers, and some designs used for reproduction. In those instances, an agreement for use and rights will be handled by an agent or attorney. For most creatives, you're creating something and handing it over to the commissioning client.

It's important to protect yourself by stating in all agreements with clients that they only own reproduction rights to the final work. They never get the rights to the process or have ownership of a particular style. The reason is that if you become known for a particular style, a past client could come after you for copyright infringement since you've turned that work over to them. You are in effect licensing your work to a particular client, not giving it to them, and your agreements should reflect that difference.

If you're publishing your work online, even on your blog or portfolio for viewing purposes, the assumed state is "all rights reserved." That is not copyright. You can file for copyright on your own, but most attorneys advise that it's best to get the help of a filing professional. You are putting your work in the wild. If it's important enough to protect, it's important enough to invest in that protection.

For work that is unclear on copyright, bad things may happen. It's important to do what you can to protect your work from non-payment, but beyond that, you're going to get screwed sometimes. My friend Jeff Fisher spends way too much time having to track down the illegal use of his creative work. People either rip off his logos as is or slightly adjust them. He sends letters from attorneys or himself and often has to take legal action, but when the violators are in foreign markets or simply don't respond, there isn't much he can do. To be frank, it sucks.

Copyright Defined

Copyright protects original works of authorship. A work of authorship includes literary, written, dramatic, artistic, musical and certain other types of works.[3]

As soon as a work is created, copyright is assumed. The work doesn't have to be completed or released to the public to attain copyright. It doesn't require paperwork to be attained, it only requires registration to enforce the copyright. You can use the © symbol without any paperwork and enforce it.

With the symbol and claim of copyright, you get these four exclusive rights:

- The right to reproduce the copyrighted work

- The right to display or perform the copyrighted work publicly

- The right to prepare derivative works based on the copyrighted work

- The right to distribute copies of the copyrighted work to the public by sale or other transfer of ownership, or by rental, lease, or lending

Smashing Magazine's Vitaly Friedman wrote an excellent piece that still holds up outlining the state of copyright on the web.[4] His points include:

- Copyright applies to the web.

- Your work is protected under copyright as soon as it's created and protected for your lifetime, plus seventy years.

- Copyright expires. When copyright expires, the work becomes public domain.

- Ideas can't be copyrighted, only the resulting tangible expression of the idea can.

- You may use logos and trademarks in your works.

- You may use copyrighted material under the "fair use" doctrine.

- You may quote only limited portions of work. You may publish excerpts, not whole articles.

- You have to ask the author's permission to translate his/her article.

- The removal of the copyrighted material doesn't remove the copyright infringement.

- If something looks copyrighted, you should assume it is.

- Advertising protected material without an agreement is illegal.

- You may not always delete or modify your visitors' comments.

- User-generated content is the property of the users.

- Copyright is violated by using information, not by charging for it.

- Getting explicit permission can save you a lot of troubles.

We often give it away without knowing

When you post your work online, you may be forfeiting your copyright protection. Take a look at the terms and conditions for sites that you use to share and submit your work to be sure that it cannot be used without your permission.

What Do You Do If Someone Steals Your Work?

You can start with a cease and desist letter telling them to take the work down. If it's an actual posting of your work, as in using your illustration on a t-shirt that they are selling for profit, you should get an attorney involved immediately. If it's a website that looks just like the one you designed, you probably won't have much recourse. It's common for people to have their entire source code, right down to the comments, copied and re-purposed for someone else's design. Again, you can send a cease and desist letter and threaten to sue, but you're likely dealing with an amateur or someone in another country where you'll have little success litigating.

Example Cease & Desist Letter[5]

Your name
Your address

Perpetrator's name
Perpetrator's address or URL

Today's date

RE: Cease and desist regarding (name of your work or product)

Dear (Perpetrator's name):

This CEASE AND DESIST ORDER is to inform you that you are using protected work without my authorization. You are hereby order to STOP USE IMMEDIATELY.

I will pursue any legal remedies available to me against you if your use of my work continues. These remedies include but are not limited to: contacting law enforcement to obtain criminal sanctions against you, and suing you for damages I have incurred as a result of your actions.

You have until (ten days from today's date) to send me written confirmation that you have removed my work. Failure to comply and send written confirmation via certified mail will result in immediate legal action.

This letter acts as your only final warning to discontinue use. No legal rights I have presently, or future legal remedies against, are being waived by sending you this letter.

To ensure compliance with this letter, and to halt any legal action I may take against you, you are required to fill in and sign the attached form and mail it back to me within ten days of your receipt of this letter. Failure to do so will act as evidence of your infringement, and I will immediately seek legal avenues to remedy the situation.

Sincerely,

(Your Signature)
(Your Name)

What If Clients Ask for Your Native Files?

A client may ask for the editable or native files of your work such as Photoshop or Illustrator files. The prevailing wisdom says never to agree to hand over native files. For one, you could be putting yourself out of a job if it's production work. For most good creatives, that's probably not the case since you're not creating cookie-cutter work that an untrained client can simply remix. The biggest risk with releasing native files is your complete loss of leverage in the event of a dispute. Once a client has your native files, they have everything they need to complete the work, even by hiring someone else or doing it in-house, without paying you.

Illustrators may be asked to hand over native files so that it can be resized or reformatted for final production. As long as you're being compensated appropriately, and your contracts cover what can be done with the files, you'll be fine.

If a client is paying you by credit card, do not *ever* hand over native files. Countless creatives have shared horror stories of clients getting native files and then disputing the credit card transaction. If the client must have native files, charge for it. Make it painfully expensive. You are opening up your tools and process to the client for their possible future use; they should pay for it. In case it's not clear, I don't commonly hand over native files.

Long-term Client Relationships

Getting More Work Out of Existing Clients

It's better to keep a client than find a new one. The time and effort required to acquire new clients far exceeds what it takes to maintain a relationship with an existing client, resulting in more work as you grow together.

You want to make sure that your existing clients know about all of your services. I had a graphic design client for two years who hired another firm to do their website overhaul. They never thought to ask me about the project, even though they were thrilled with my work because they didn't realize I built websites. That was on me.

So don't wait for your clients to beg you to take on more. If you see an opportunity to do more for them, whether it's an additional skill or service or more of the same work, then just ask. You have to find the right time to ask, so start with doing an excellent job with what you have. Be proactive by always sending your client interesting articles on their industry or challenges, and stay in constant communication with them about their business. Begin to use the phrase "we" instead of "you" when discussing their challenge/solution scenarios. Make yourself an indispensable partner.

Don't assume that your clients know everything that you do and don't be afraid to remind them. When you review your projects or retainers with your clients, ask them what else is going on in their department and if there's anything with which you can help.

It's hard to get more work out of existing clients, and it's not always a good thing

Just because you can do more for your existing clients, doesn't mean that you should. As we discussed earlier, you should never let a single client handle more than a third of your overall billing revenue. Some clients will gladly pile work on for you, so much that you have to hire additional staff. The problem is that you're growing at your client's pace instead of yours. You're also putting yourself in a position where the client has the advantage because they can significantly affect the health of your business. It can lead to irrational decisions or unwise compromises.

Client Size

The size of a client is relative to your business in many more ways than employee count or annual revenue. While Exxon and Wal-Mart may be your largest corporations on the Dow, it doesn't make them the biggest clients you can get. "Big" comes down to what it means for your relative growth. Working with a household name like Target or Sony may sound appealing, but you may only be making informational flyers for their transportation department and never speak to another soul in any of their thousands of marketing management roles.

In contrast, you may be working for a niche brand like Fat Tire Brewery or Lush Cosmetics and be on cloud nine simply making a single packaging label, but have the potential to do their entire website or marketing program as you continue to do good work. It comes down to what fuels you and pushes you closer to the kind of work you can get excited about that also allows you to grow.

Big clients also mean big work, as in entire product lines or a network of websites. It can mean working with a magazine editor who's in charge of all editorial illustrations, and you just became her favorite artist. It can mean getting connected to the department head for an event management company that puts on 200 trade shows a year and needs a trusted resource to design all of their booth art.

Can you keep working with them?

A good way to determine if a client is big or small is the potential for additional work. While working with the hottest restaurant in town could certainly bring you recognition, it's unlikely they'll need you to do much work for them on an ongoing basis. Working with a mid-size technology company that has to produce hundreds of micro-sites, email newsletters, and sales sheets will mean you'll probably have more work than you can handle without hiring a lot of help. While the restaurant website work may get you some cool referrals, the tech company is going to mean more to your bottom line over the long-term, so that's your bigger client.

Can you deliver?

The best way to keep big clients is to be reliable. It's likely that they are growing quickly, and they don't have time to micro-manage you. The more you anticipate their next move and ask for additional work to ease their burden, the more of a trusted partner you become. Failing to deliver on time or communicate openly will erode trust quickly. It's likely your direct contact has a boss to whom they've given the commitment to deliver on time, they are relying on you for that to happen. If you let that resource down, they can't keep using you.

Just don't go too big

The temptation is there, and succumbed to easily, to just keep taking work from the huge client that wants you to do everything. So much work may come in that you hire additional staff just to work on this client account. Agencies are certainly built that way, but it's dangerous territory. It's critical that you diversify your client base with both your big (repeat) clients and your small (one-off) projects.

When Things Go South

Not every client relationship ends amicably. It could be on you—you may get sick, have a family emergency, your computer may die the day of a critical deadline, or a file or deliverable may be completely lost or forgotten. It could be on your client—they refuse to pay, they go out of business, they never give you content or assets, they become demon-possessed, etc.

The typical causes are money and missed expectations. To beat a dead horse, communication is the absolute key to successful client relationships. But sometimes things simply get lost in translation. The way to fight miscommunication, and things turning sour, is with better communication. I know, magic! You have to face it head on and not give in to the tendency to stick your head in the sand.

I Drove the Bus Off the Cliff

Once, I was incredibly late with a project, weeks late. The client was very upset. I had gotten sick and was extremely overbooked, so the work was just late. I hadn't been letting them know what was going on, but they also had not been checking in with me. There was just silence on both ends.

I had been avoiding them, hoping they'd just be okay with it being late. I finished the work and needed the final payment, so it was time to deliver the work. I sent the work over with a detailed explanation of my process and thoughts and heard nothing but crickets. A week went by, and the client still hadn't responded. I worked up the courage to send over my invoice, and then I finally got a reply: "We're not paying this," the client said. That was it. I had completed the work to spec and delivered it, but what leverage did I have? The remaining balance and work completed were not trivial, it was thousands of dollars. I couldn't just walk away from that. I was the one who was in the wrong because I had failed to communicate. So I had to make it right.

I had to offer the client a significant discount to get them to pay, and I ended up doing a smaller project for them for free to get things back on track. They never hired me again, and they never offered a referral or testimonial. About two years later, I ran into the client at an event and he was very nice. He even commented on how effective the work had been. Our relationship was healed, but any trust that we had was eroded by my cowardice.

Don't Be an Ostrich

When you fail to communicate with clients from the moment things start going wrong, you are removing any leverage you have and causing the dispute to escalate. Clients are people, and they also have lives. If you're sick or simply overbooked, you need to tell your client the moment it becomes evident that you can't deliver. Provide alternatives such as delivering the work as is and sending a final invoice. Ask them if the delay is okay and what impact it may have. Find someone to finish the work for you and notify the client that you're bringing in extra help. Communicate!

Sometimes There's No Going Back

There will be clients with whom you simply can no longer work. They may be unethical, refusing to pay, or just too difficult to work with. It may be that you just can't handle them anymore due to your growth and their inability to keep up. They may be unwilling to go with you to higher rates and prices. The phrase thrown around pretty often is "firing" clients. While at times that's what you're doing—telling them to hit the road—firing comes from a place of judgement and contempt.

You can feel powerful, and mighty, firing someone. Letting go of a client shouldn't feel quite so grand. Something went wrong. That's not to say that it's your fault the relationship isn't working, but it is an opportunity to look at why things didn't work out. Even if the client was an insufferable ass from day one, what went wrong in your interview process to not allow red flags to pop up and tell you to pass on the project?

Let Them Go Carefully

Before you cut a client off, read your agreements. You need to understand where things stand regarding ownership of any incomplete work, any unpaid invoices, and intellectual property for information gathered. If you signed an NDA, are you still subject to its terms and unable to work with their competition? This has come back to bite many creatives who move on to a similar client.

If you're letting go of a client mid-project or mid-retainer, you may negatively impact your cash flow. As much as you may want to get away from a client, the financial implications may be too much to bear. Unless you have a full book of business, you probably want to have replacement revenue lined up. If it's a one-off project, are your forecasts adjusted to account for the lost revenue no longer coming from this client down the road? Can your business bear the loss? If red flags continue to pop up with a client, make it a priority to focus on replacing their revenue before jumping into letting them go.

How to End It

If the client is local, it's best to handle it face to face. I know that sounds absolutely terrifying and you'd much rather send them a box with their stuff in it via courier. The honorable and professional way to do it is face to face. If it's a client that you have an actual problem with, as in non-payment or a legal dispute, face to face isn't really an option. The severance will probably be self-evident and handled through your attorney. But most clients that you're letting go of for "not so bad" reasons, such as a wrong feel for one another, can be handled with civility. At the very least, do it by phone and not by email.

Never publicly complain about a client. Even if you're in litigation with them, don't go on social media or blogs and publicly air your grievances. It doesn't matter how right you are, it makes you look unprofessional. The initial separation of agreement isn't always the end of the relationship. Anything that's public or in writing could come back to bite you down the road if you end up in a dispute with a client.

You Lead, They'll Follow

Any commissioned project is a collaboration. As a creative professional, you are working with your clients to accomplish a shared goal. Clients may think they're designers, and at times they may actually be, but we can't expect them just to know how this works. Your process is different. Each creative has their way of working. You need your feedback, revisions, and documentation in a way that differs from others. So it's up to you to let clients know what's working and what isn't. If no one speaks up, then nothing productive is being said. It's up to you to establish the methods, channels, and tone of communication from the start. Frequently communicating with your clients, openly and honestly, leads to a much more enjoyable collaborative process.

Notes

1. http://www.eyemagazine.com/feature/article/bob-gill.
2. http://alistapart.com/column/i-dont-like-it.
3. http://pvd.library.jwu.edu/friendly.php?s=images.
4. http://www.smashingmagazine.com/2007/07/07/copyright-explained-i-may-copy-it-right/.
5. http://thompsonhall.com/cease-desist-trademark-infringement-template-example-sample-form/.

CHAPTER 7

DONE IS BETTER THAN PERFECT

DOING the WORK

GOALS!!!!
- ☐ SAVE 4 Rome
- ☐ 3 gallery shows
- ☐ MFA app
- ☐ learn hip hop dance

SKETCHBOOK

Mon
- ☐ Paint 3 hrs
- ☐ email MOMA
- ☐ Practice hip hop (20 min).
- ☐ Create monthly budget

Tues
- ☐ hip hop prac.(20)
- ☐ paint
- ☐ start app

Wed
- ☐ invoice
- ☐
- ☐
- ☐

"A professional distances herself from her instrument. The pro stands at one remove from her instrument—meaning her person, her body, her voice, her talent; the physical, mental, emotional, and psychological being she uses in her work. She does not identify with this instrument. It is simply what God gave her, what she has to work with. She assesses it coolly, impersonally, objectively. The professional identifies with her consciousness and will manipulate it to serve her art. Does Madonna walk around the house in cone bras and come-fuck-me bustiers? She's too busy planning D-Day. Madonna does not identify with "Madonna." Madonna employs "Madonna."

Steven Pressfield[1]

The Work

The work is what you do for your clients and yourself. It is the outcome of your effort, the fruits of your labor, and the tangible result of intangible thoughts and ideas. Your work, however, is not you. As creatives, we tend to merge our personal identity into our work and take our entire lives into the hole with us. The grind of running and growing the business can become so involved that you ultimately lose sight of the work and it becomes this dark cloud that sits above you 24/7.

You can go too far into the business mindset so that, sometimes, the business side of creativity becomes so engrossing that you stop doing creative work altogether. For some, that's a natural progression. For others, they can't imagine letting go of actually creating and doing the work. For me, that was never an option. I love to create more than anything. I don't ever want a business that is so involved that I can't actually work with clients any more.

As you mature in your business, you'll have to find ways to ensure that you have the time and energy to get the work done. Otherwise, the growing demands of your business will take it all away from you, and you'll be far less involved in the work. In Chapter 9 we'll dive deeper into growth and what you can do to find your ideal size and situation, but that process takes time. The realities of running a creative business colliding with growing a creative business are in front of you right now; growth isn't happening overnight. We're going to focus on running your creative business while still doing work that you enjoy.

Here's what we'll cover:

- Deadlines
- Just ship it
- Impostor Syndrome
- Procrastination

- Scheduling and time management
- Delegation
- Side projects
- Staying inspired

Deadlines—Just Ship It

Deadlines

I remember a particular week in 2009 when I had seven deadlines in four days. That may not sound too bad, but let me tell you how much work was left: forty-six hours. And that was my estimate. As Paul Wilson says, "things take twice as long, cost twice as much, and bring half the rewards that you anticipate."[2] So in reality, I was looking at ninety-two hours' worth of work. You may ask yourself, how did I get here? How did I end up with such a ridiculous amount of work due at the same time? This is not my beautiful house … anyway.

Well, the whole truth is that three of the seven deadlines had already been shifted to that week because I had missed them in weeks prior. One of the other deadlines was moved up a week because I needed to spend the following week on site with a client in planning meetings. None of these projects were last minute. In fact, most of them had been weeks or months in the making. I was the problem. I had spent excessive amounts of time on research, sketching, planning, and who knows what else. I had procrastinated and delayed getting any designs done because nothing "felt right." Needless to say, I was screwed.

"Work expands so as to fill the time available for its completion." Parkinson's Law

I made four of the deadlines and finished two of them on Saturday and Sunday. I worked no less than fifteen hours each day and slept no more than four hours any night that week. I mostly fell asleep on the couch downstairs. The three deadlines I missed were all for existing clients, no one new, and I was able to talk my way out of any repercussions. But, I still had the planning meetings the following week. So now I had to work ten-hour days with one client and then go home to work all night catching up on the three remaining deadlines. I slept four hours a night that following week.

I found myself in this situation over and over again. I had to do something, but reading productivity books and ignoring the lessons learned wasn't going to save me. I learned about procrastination, time management, and sticking to my schedule. More importantly, I also learned about "good enough" and managing inspiration overload. That's where we're going in the rest of this chapter.

"Something that is often overlooked with creatives is time management and getting shit done. You can be the most talented designer in the world but if you don't follow through and get stuff out there, it doesn't matter ... Following through and finishing things is one of the most important things you can learn. One of my favorite quotes is "Done is better than perfect." That doesn't mean making crap—I believe you should always strive for the highest quality you can— but you have to finish."

Ben Barry[3]

Done Is Better Than Perfect

In a University of San Diego study,[4] subjects endured a battery of experiments both hypothetical and actual to determine whether exceeding expectations (going above and beyond promises) was symmetrical with disappointment (breaking promises). The study concluded, quite handily, that "Breaking one's promise is costly, but exceeding it does not appear worth the effort." To be blunt: people remember when you screw up, they tend to forget when you go all-out.

When it comes to creative work, clients always remember vendors who are late or miss the mark. They quickly forget those who go above and beyond the expected requirements. Rarely are the exceptional remembered for their work, rather, they're remembered as being on time and budget. Work that was "good enough" would have produced the same results.

"Do you think miners stand around all day talking about how hard it is to mine for coal? They do not. They simply dig."

Cheryl Strayed[5]

It's Hard to Make Great, So Make Good

Head of Creative & Design at HubSpot, Keith Frankel, shared a simple guide to recognizing when a deliverable can be considered "good enough" in a 2014 blog post:[6]

- It successfully solves the problem, addresses the need, or conveys the message intended.

- It is clearly and distinctly on brand.

- The quality of work is consistent with or above the level of previous work.

- It has been thoroughly yet objectively scrutinized by other qualified individuals.

- The final decision of preference had been left in the hands of the creator.

Just freaking ship it. You will always look for reasons to hold back or delay, but if it meets the client's needs or does its job, it's ready to go. It's likely you can iterate on your work at a later time, so get something out there. And if your work is more permanent, like illustration or photography, having something out there is better than nothing. You can always do better next time.

Impostor Syndrome

" For the things we have to learn before we can do them, we learn by doing them."

Aristotle[7]

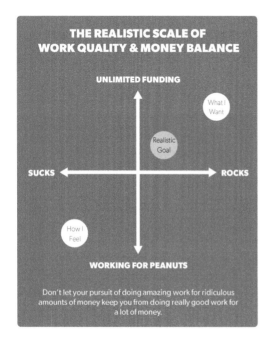

As I sit here, writing this book, I have no clue what I'm doing. I am learning as I go along, and I'll never get it right. It will ship; you're reading it so unless you're inside my brain or have stolen my computer, it shipped. My work is out there and the world will keep spinning. Yet no matter how well it does and how much you love it, I will always feel that I didn't deserve to be asked to write a book and tell you how all of this is supposed to work.

Seeing the work of a seasoned professional, it's easy to feel insecure. You say to yourself that you'll never be that good. Even worse, seeing the work of an 18-year-old designer whose work is better than anything you've ever done makes you want to set your computer on fire. Then, one day, something you've made gets recognized or admired. You wonder if people see all of the flaws. Then you get asked to talk about it, and people want to work with you. You get better, but you never get "good." You feel like you're pretending and that people will find out you're a complete fraud. Well, we are all pretending, even the most accomplished creative in your industry is pretending. We learn enough to get by, but we never know all that there is to know.

"It is not your business to determine how good it is nor how valuable nor how it compares with other expressions. It is your business to keep it yours clearly and directly, to keep the channel open. You do not even have to believe in yourself or your work. You have to keep yourself open and aware to the urges that motivate you. Keep the channel open. ... No artist is pleased. There is no satisfaction whatever at any time. There is only a queer divine dissatisfaction, a blessed unrest that keeps us marching and makes us more alive than the others."

Martha Graham[8]

Creative culture is being crushed under the weight of inspiration overload. You can spend your entire day looking at what everyone else is creating without doing anything yourself. There is a paralysis that strikes when you start a new project and feel the need to find out what everyone else is doing so that your work fits with what's out there. You spend so much time comparing your unborn project to finished works that you then wrap yourself in despair before taking the first step.

"Nobody tells this to people who are beginners, I wish someone told me. All of us who do creative work, we get into it because we have good taste. But there is this gap. For the first couple years you make stuff, it's just not that good. It's trying to be good, it has potential, but it's not. But your taste, the thing that got you into the game, is still killer. And your taste is why your work disappoints you. A lot of people never get past this phase, they quit."

Ira Glass[9]

Thanks to the abundance of online galleries, conferences, blogs, and social media, we get to compare ourselves to the work of everyone around the world, not just our local competitors and colleagues. But we're comparing our outtakes to someone else's highlight reel. Most creatives only feel successful when their work is better than everyone else's. No matter how good it is or whether it accomplished your client's goal, if it's not as good as the work it's compared to, we feel like it's not good enough. And comparing your client's goals to someone else's completed outcome could derail your project. There is so much inspiration out there that you can get sucked into poor solutions for your work to look like, or better than, everyone else's.

"A few years in I had to stop looking at other illustrators, because if you want to be like them at that point, the best you can be is second best."

Yuko Shimizu[10]

As your career advances, you may find yourself surrounded by more and more talented individuals. The tendency to always compare often results in feeling inadequate. The expectations to "arrive" and "succeed" continue to stack up and Impostor Syndrome gets worse as your career blossoms.

"The genuinely untalented, meanwhile, probably have no idea that they're no good—because they're too untalented to realize it. (This is the "Dunning-Kruger effect," inspired by the tale of an incompetent bank robber who thought rubbing lemon juice on his face would make him invisible on security cameras.) In short: if you're worried you don't measure up, that could well be a sign that you do."

Oliver Burkeman[11]

So guess what? Someone is always going to be better than you. They'll do work that you simply can't and they'll win awards for it. You'll hate them, and then fall in love with them. Maybe you'll meet them at a conference and realize that they're just as insecure as you are. When you see something that inspires you and makes you want to be better, view it as an aspiration rather than a comparison.

"Our deepest fear is not that we are inadequate. Our deepest fear is that we are powerful beyond measure. It is our light, not our darkness that most frightens us. We ask ourselves, Who am I to be brilliant, gorgeous, talented, and fabulous? Actually, who are you not to be? You are a child of God. Your playing small does not serve the world. There is nothing enlightened about shrinking so that other people will not feel insecure around you. We are all meant to shine, as children do. We were born to make manifest the glory of God that is within us. It is not just in some of us; it is in everyone and as we let our own light shine, we unconsciously give others permission to do the same. As we are liberated from our own fear, our presence automatically liberates others."

Marianne Williamson[12]

Hopefully, you'll embrace your craft and realize that everyone suffers from Impostor Syndrome. If they don't, they're likely a psychopath. Our work is subjective and its success is largely determined by the approval of others. If it accomplishes your client's goals, you likely had to make compromises. Working within constraints isn't an excuse. All that you can do is create the best work you've got in you and get it out there.

"Impostor Syndrome is the domain of the high achiever. Those who set the bar low are rarely its victim."

Margie Warrell[13]

Procrastination

We self-sabotage through procrastinating. Psychologists have theorized that we, in our current state, see our future selves as a completely different person. From skipping the gym to getting a questionable tattoo, we fail to see the consequences for our future selves any more than we would for a separate person. The result is most of us may choose to procrastinate and let the "future me" deal with the problem.

One of Seth Godin's most famous pieces concerns our "lizard brains." Our lives are filled with contradictions. We say we want a creative life, to make something, but we fail to start. Godin quotes Steven Pressfield, who calls this "resistance." Godin says,

"The resistance is the voice in the back of our head telling us to back off, be careful, go slow, compromise. The resistance is writer's block and putting jitters and every project that ever shipped late because people couldn't stay on the same page long enough to get something out the door. The resistance grows in strength as we get closer to shipping, as we get closer to an insight, as we get closer to the truth of what we really want. That's because the lizard hates change and achievement and risk. The lizard is a physical part of your brain, the pre-historic lump near the brain stem that is responsible for fear and rage and reproductive drive."[14]

We are wired to stall, to fear starting so that we may avoid risk. Godin continues, "The lizard brain is the reason you're afraid, the reason you don't do all the art you can, the reason you don't ship when you can. The lizard brain is the source of the resistance." You will never be able to stop procrastinating; it doesn't go away. The greatest productivity expert on the planet still has a lizard brain.

We waste so much time on things that have little value, much of it is procrastination from the things that can bring us so much value. Marcus Aurelius wrote, "Stop whatever you're doing for a moment and ask yourself: Am I afraid of death because I won't be able to do this anymore?" Do you have that level of commitment to making progress every day?

Fighting Procrastination

What we can do is fight the disease through tactics, constantly at war with our own selves. Heidi Grant Halvorson, an expert on motivation, shares three key reasons we procrastinate and how to overcome them for the *Harvard Business Review*.[15]

Reason #1—You are putting something off because you are afraid you will screw it up

Solution: Adopt a "prevention focus." What you need is a way of looking at what you need to do that isn't undermined by doubt—ideally, one that thrives on it. When you have a prevention focus, instead of thinking about how you can end up better off, you see the task as a way to hang on to what you've already got—to avoid loss.

Reason #2—You are putting something off because you don't "feel" like doing it

Solution: Make like Spock and ignore your feelings. They're getting in your way. Somewhere along the way, we've all bought into the idea—without consciously realizing it—that to be motivated and effective we need to feel like we want to take action. We need to be eager to do so. I really don't know why we believe this, because it is 100 percent nonsense.

Reason #3—You are putting something off because it's hard, boring, or otherwise unpleasant

Solution: Use if–then planning. Do yourself a favor, and embrace the fact that your willpower is limited, and that it may not always be up to the challenge of getting you to do things you find difficult, tedious, or otherwise awful. Instead, use if–then planning to get the job done.

"The work you do while you procrastinate is probably the work you should be doing for the rest of your life."

Jessica Hische[16]

As a creative business owner, you have more opportunities to procrastinate than most because you wear so many hats. You're able to procrastinate on client work, marketing, operations, admin, personal errands, general tasks, and your health and well-being. You have all the options! The grind gets to us and it's much easier to just check a few more websites or reorganize our desk again. If you work from home, there's laundry to be done and dogs to be walked; work can wait!

Jessica Hische has mastered the art of "procrastinatiworking" by turning her attention to interesting side projects while she's supposed to be doing client work. The results have become some of her most successful endeavors. The reason, she believes, is that she was so focused on not doing client work that she had intense focus and freedom of thought in her procrastiwork.

Scheduling and Time Management

As frustrating and cliché as it seems, the single most important step you can take for balancing your work and your business is to manage your time effectively. Administrative tasks can take up as much time as your actual client work. If you're allowing errands, unexpected interruptions, and lingering conversations and meetings to rule your day, you will never get any work done. The result is that you end up working during what should be your down-time.

There is No Nine-to-five

You work when you need to work. Burning the midnight oil is so normal for creatives that it feels odd to stop at a consistent time and be "off" for the rest of the evening. Working odd hours and having a flexible schedule is a big draw for our industry. However, boundaries sort of go out the window when it comes to scheduled hours and most of us end up working far more than our nine-to-five counterparts. There will always be times when you're going to work eighteen hours straight to get a project out the door. That's part of the adventure and the push and drive to finish something. But it shouldn't be the normal way you go about your business.

So, how do you get a "normal" schedule while running a not-so-normal creative business?

Work in Bursts

The pomodoro is the tomato-god of time travel that will save your life. If you're not familiar with pomodoro techniques, it was invented in the early nineties by web developer Francesco Cirillo. He named it after the tomato-shaped timer he used while he was a student to track his time. Cirillo broke his time down into short intervals of twenty-five minutes that he timed with the little tomato. For the duration of the timer, he focused on a single task, then took a break of five to ten minutes. He would repeat this throughout the day, often in sets of three or four before longer breaks such as coffee, lunch, an afternoon walk, and dinner.

It has been proven in countless studies to increase focus, attention, and efficiency. The best part of this technique is that it works no matter where you are and no matter what you do; all you need is a timer. You can use your stopwatch on your phone, an egg timer, an hourglass, or get yourself a cool tomato timer. You can get apps to help you understand pomodoro and keep up with your performance.

Don't Waste Your Best Hours

Many time management books and blog posts will tell you to become a morning person and start at 5am. While that's a habit many creatives have found useful, myself included, it's not for everyone. You have to lean into your strengths and do what works for you. If you work best at 2am, then build your schedule accordingly. Just have a plan and stick to it. Make your schedule public with the people it affects including your family, clients, and colleagues. Set office hours. Your office hours don't have to be nine-to-five, but you should have a regular time period when you're actively working.

What is important is to use the hours at the start of your work day to do your critical work. If you check email and Twitter first thing, someone else is now dictating how your day will go. Start your day by getting the most important thing done, that way it's over with. Mark Twain called this "eating your live frog." We're most creative in the morning. Again, "morning" is a relative term depending on your lifestyle. Whenever you get up, that's your morning. Our prefrontal cortex is the most active during and after sleep.[17] Successful creatives use their first few hours to invest in themselves and the deep thinking required to do the work.

Your Schedule Is Your Life

You can't separate your work schedule from your personal schedule, so don't try to. We'll break this down a bit more with time blocking. No matter what method you use for your schedule, you have to keep your personal and professional calendars together. You'll have errands, appointments, and interruptions that come up in the middle of the day. The benefit to making your own schedule is that there is no paid time off or vacation bank to work from; you're the boss. The downside is that you don't have strict guidelines forcing you to schedule doctor appointments or trips to the salon on the weekends like everyone else. While this is great for getting the appointment you want, it can blow up your work day.

I carve out a set block of time on Friday mornings each week for appointments and other personal errands. I take advantage of being my own boss and staying out of weekend crowds, but I don't let appointments pop up at random times.

Kill Multitasking

The fastest way to rot your brain is to multitask incessantly. Psychologists have conducted countless studies and concluded, with certainty, that there is no such thing as multitasking—it's simply task switching. To clarify, you actually can't focus on two things at the same time, one of them is being done with limited brain capacity.

The solution, and alternative, to multitasking is Time Blocking. Cal Newport of Study Hacks has popularized Time Blocking as a way to overcome the impossible pile of tasks and deliverables most knowledge workers face each day. We can choose to ignore tasks or leave them incomplete. If we have any hope of completing them all without frying our brains, the only sustainable solution is to plan every minute of your work day.

As horrible as it sounds, planning every minute of your day is actually far more freeing that simply floating around to see what happens. It's been proven that people who develop the habit of strict scheduling, such as Time Blocking, have more free time and enjoy it more. Newport says that a "40 hour time-blocked work week, I estimate, produces the same amount of output as a 60+ hour work week pursued without structure."[18]

Use Time Blocking

Entrepreneur and Business Coach Kate Matsudaira took Time Blocking to the next level with her Spark Notebook, something I've bought into completely. You have probably tried dozens of productivity apps, task managers, and systems to get a handle on your schedule. The app store is home to more productivity apps than *Angry Birds* games. You may have found an app or system, such as Wunderlist or OmniFocus, that does the job. But the time it took to put everything in an app just never worked for me.

Planning your schedule is thinking time, not doing time, and you should do it away from your computer and phone. Getting it into a hand-written notebook and forcing yourself to take the time to think through it drives focus and keeps you from checking email and social media. Forcing an analogue process into your digital workflow can do wonders for attention to detail.

Kate defines Time Blocking as "just a method for planning your day. And the reason why it works is because it forces you to focus on your top priorities for an amount of time that reflects their importance."[19] Using a notebook or other tool, you break your day into morning, afternoon, and evening. In blocks, you write down the things you need to get done and put a checkbox next to them. When you do them, check them off and move onto the next thing. It's simple, yet extremely powerful. The key is to put everything in there. Even if it's as simple as "go get coffee" or "text mom," put it in your time block. Put a number next to it for how long you think it will take.

How you can use time blocking

When you estimate how long something is going to take, don't lie to yourself. Be honest about knowing how long it will take you, not how long it should take anyone else. If you know you're prone to procrastinate with certain tasks, then you need to build in some of that time. You can't change your habits overnight. Add an extra fifteen minutes or half hour and then work as if you don't have it; try to finish early. The more buffer time you have between blocks, the less stressed you'll be. Use a time-tracking tool religiously and even look into Rescue Time or Slife, a tool that monitors all of your on-computer activity. You can't improve what you don't measure.

Kate's tips on sticking with Time Blocking include:[20]

- Focus on a single task; close everything else including email and social media. If you can, put your phone on do not disturb.

- Find your rhythm for getting the hard work done. For most, it's early in the morning when you have the most willpower. Don't use your best focusing time on low-quality tasks like email and busywork.

- Always front-load your week with more than you think you can get done, especially on Mondays. It's easier to push hard earlier in the week and move things back than to play catch-up as your week goes on. This helps with procrastination and, if you finish things early, you could just take off on Fridays.

- Break projects and features into very small pieces. It helps you to start on something small vs. looking up at the mountain of work that encompasses the entire project. It also makes it easier to be productive in fifteen minutes when your schedule shifts; you can still get something done.

- Your personal schedule and work schedule are the same. You work for yourself so that you can go the doctor or salon on a Thursday when it's easier to get an appointment, and that affects your schedule. Likewise, if you are running errands on the way to work or working out in the middle of the day, it needs to go in a time block.

"In the context of work, uncontrolled time makes me uncomfortable. If you're serious about working deeply and producing high-end value, it should probably make you uncomfortable as well. Using your inbox to drive your daily schedule might be fine for the entry-level or those content with a career of cubicle-dwelling mediocrity, but the best knowledge workers view their time like the best investors view their capital, as a resource to wield for maximum returns."

Cal Newport[21]

Location shifting

Time Blocking works best when associated with triggers, and one of the most powerful is location. When you're at your desk, you work, and when you're in your favorite chair, you relax. It can be taken to the next level by actually breaking up your work day by location.

An example may be starting your day at the coffee shop to journal and plan. Then, move to your desk for mid-morning creative work. Then go to lunch, then back to your desk, and then a walk, and then maybe another shift to somewhere else in your home or office, then the gym, and so on. By setting your triggers for tasks to locations, you are limiting your time and resources to accomplish the task. It pushes you even further to get things done in the fixed window of time.

Meetings About Meetings

Meetings can hurt your flow and slow your productivity. Even if you stay solo, the volume of business development, project status calls, and "check-ins" that come along as you fill your book of business can consume your entire day. When people ask me why I left a comfortable corporate job to start my own business, my first answer is always, "I had too many meetings about meetings." Communication is critical for a business to survive, and online channels such as email and instant messaging can consume just as much of your time as meetings. But meetings typically involve travel to and from the venue, someone being late or going over, and small talk that can add a full half hour.

Meetings cost creatives more. People who make things have a different schedule from those who manage them. For example, a writer can't set aside an hour to write; she needs an entire afternoon or evening to get into her flow and work out the piece. A manager, conversely, has meetings all day and is used to switching from one conversation and task to the next. They are each wired to work a specific way. For the creative business owner, you wear both hats: maker and manager. It can take a toll on your creative output.

Getting control of meetings

While avoiding meetings altogether isn't possible, you can control them. At my agency, we have all of our full-staff internal meetings on Tuesdays. No other internal meetings are held any other day of the week unless they are absolute emergencies. The first half of Tuesday and Thursday, and the entire days of Wednesday and Friday are banned from meetings. We encourage the team to take this further, me included, by turning off notifications and chat during these windows. On non-meeting days, we set aside two designated times at mid-morning and late afternoon for project check-ins.

Meetings can be successful, and there are ways you can get the most out of them when they have to happen:

- Always question the meeting. Can this be handled with an email or can someone else take care of it? Can it be delegated?

- Always look for an alternative. How about a call or a quick stand-up discussion?

- However long you think you need for a meeting; cut the time in half. Set a timer for that amount of time and when it goes off, the meeting is over.

- Only include people who have to be in the meeting; don't even add them as optional to the invite.

- Take notes and post them for everyone else to view if they so choose.

- Have an agenda and stick to it; send it ahead of time. If you can't prepare an agenda, then it's not a meeting; it's a one-to-one conversation.

- Make meetings online or by phone whenever possible, use chat tools or set up a conference call so that people can return to work as soon as the meeting is over.

- Combine face-to-face meetings with other tasks such as lunch, breakfast, or exercise. Get people to walk or work out with you instead of just sitting around a table.

Delegation

Outsourcing expert Chris Ducker created an exercise to help you find what you should move off your plate and onto someone else's. Make a list of the things you don't like doing, can't do, and shouldn't do. Then, find someone else to do those things for you. When you get this stuff out of the way, it helps you have more time to do what you like doing and to get your work out there.[22]

At some point, you'll have to let go of some things that you do like doing and get help. Either employees, freelancers, or virtual assistants will be doing tasks that you wish you had the time to do. You are your own worst enemy when it comes to delegating interesting work. Something I learned is that the better I am at delegating tasks, the more time I'll have to work on at least *some* of the tasks I enjoy. If I am not effectively delegating, I'm scrambling to get things done and I end up doing more work because we're behind.

How to Delegate

You are not the only one. Despite my Neo complex, I am not "The One." There are others who are better than me at certain tasks. I should hire those people to complete the tasks for me.

They aren't you, so they won't be perfect. They may do a better job in the eyes of the client, but others won't do exactly what you would have done, so you may not be "happy" with the work. If the work meets the client's goals and all other criteria, it's good enough. Just ship your delegated work.

Don't Like Doing	Can't Do	Shouldn't Do
Sending Invoices	Writing PHP Code	Loading Blog Content

Over-explain. You can't give too much information, but you can give too much direction. Supply as much background as you can and let your employee decide what to do with it. However, don't tell them exactly how to do the work if they have their own process. Sometimes their methods may be better for their workflow.

Set boundaries. While you shouldn't tell them how to do it, you should still be specific on parameters. Employees will go as far as you let them or do as little as possible. It's not based on personality either, it's based on the expectations you set. Tell them if the client is a huge deal and expects top-notch work or if the client is low-priority and will be fine with "good enough."

Check it, correct it. Have set check-in times where both you and your employee are prepared to review the status of work in progress. They are in a question and feedback mindset and you are in an answer and correction mindset. Review the work thoroughly and provide constructive feedback whether there are changes or not. Let them know what they did right that they can continue doing in the future.

Let them screw up. If you dig them out of every hole, they won't learn. If it's work going directly to a client, you have to fix it. But you can allow your employees to make mistakes and correct them before shipping off the work. Don't fix it for them; fix it with them.

Teach a man or woman to fish. Show them how, not just what, to do. Let them know how you do it and then they can decide if it's the right process for them. Let them take the lifecycle of the work as far as possible up to and including interfacing with clients.

Increase over time. As people show promise, increase their responsibilities.

When to Delegate

- You're out of time, and the project has to ship.
- It's a task that you don't want to do.
- It's a task that you enjoy, but shouldn't be doing.
- It's a task that you should be doing, but someone else can get it done faster or cheaper with similar results.
- You're out of money, and you can outsource to get things done cheaper.
- You need another perspective or idea.

Side Projects

It's good for the soul to do something different. The best way to branch out is to experiment with side projects. You may learn you're great at something, so good you may even start offering it to clients. Or, you may learn that it's good you aren't making your living at a particular skill or in a certain market. Otherwise, you might be flipping burgers soon.

Side projects can be revenue generating. Some of the most popular apps and services on the web started out as side projects including Basecamp, MailChimp, and Flickr. The goal of side projects shouldn't necessarily be revenue. Otherwise, they're just another project, but it's perfectly okay to think about a financial future for the work as you go along.

Do Stupid Stuff

Side projects should be stupid. Keep things simple and don't take it so seriously. When you're working with clients, there's a lot on the line, so you can't be too laid back. When it's a side project, you can let go of much of the pressure and just enjoy the ride. It can be daunting because you're the client, so you have no boundaries or deadlines holding you back. It's easy just to let it go because no one is watching.

Break Out Of Your Comfort Zone

Side projects certainly don't have to be an extension of your primary creative role. If you're a writer, your side project may be a clothing line. If you're a developer, it may be a board game. It just needs to flex your creative muscles (and maybe even your physical ones). Side projects should be far enough away from your work to feel like a break, but not so far away that it's a hobby. They can be as simple as a personal website or tutorial, but it's important that they still feel a bit like work. The biggest takeaway should be learning. Whether it's learning a new programming language or design style or building something with your hands instead of a mouse, it's about finding new ways to think.

They Can Shift Your Perspective

The best part about side projects is that they allow you to see your day-to-day work in a new light. They may help you to fall back in love with your craft if you're feeling burned out. They may show you that you enjoy something else more and can push you toward a new endeavor. The important part is just to start; it's just a stupid side project.

Stick With It

Meaningful work and sustainable growth stem from learning to work on your business instead of just in it. Don't let your operations and client communication tasks stack up. On a weekly basis, work on your business and step away from client work. Set aside time for uninterrupted work and don't allow the daily grind to infect your creative time.

Whether it's hiring professional services such as accountants or bringing on employees and contractors, it's unsustainable to do all of the work yourself for the long-term. Asking for help and allowing others to do some of the client work while you're working on marketing, operating, and improving the efficiency of your business is hard to do, but it's necessary. Regardless of your company size, one or a hundred, only by setting boundaries and clear goals can you free yourself to continue doing the work that you love.

Notes

1. Steven Pressfield, *The War of Art: Break Through the Blocks and Win Your Inner Creative Battles*, p. 86.
2. Paul Wilson, *Calm at Work*.
3. http://99u.com/articles/7118/facebooks-ben-barry-on-how-to-hack-your-job.
4. http://www.chicagobooth.edu/capideas/magazine/winter-2014/dont-bother-doing-more-than-you-promised.
5. Cheryl Strayed, *Tiny Beautiful Things: Advice on Love and Life From Dear Sugar*.
6. http://blog.hubspot.com/marketing/good-content-creation-design.
7. Aristotle, *The Nicomachean Ethics*.
8. Agnes de Mille, *The Life and Work of Martha Graham*, p. 264.
9. http://nprfreshair.tumblr.com/post/4931415362/nobody-tells-this-to-people-who-are-beginners-i.
10. http://99u.com/articles/29941/yuko-shimizu-make-your-own-path.
11. http://99u.com/articles/32985/nobody-knows-what-the-hell-they-are-doing.
12. Marianne Williamson, *A Return to Love: Reflections on the Principles of "A Course in Miracles"*.
13. http://www.forbes.com/sites/margiewarrell/2014/04/03/impostor-syndrome/.
14. http://sethgodin.typepad.com/seths _ blog/2010/01/quieting-the-lizard-brain.html.
15. https://hbr.org/2014/02/how-to-make-yourself-work-when-you-just-dont-want-to.
16. http://www.humblepied.com/jessica-hische/.
17. http://www.publicationcoach.com/best-time-to-write/.
18. http://calnewport.com/blog/2013/12/21/deep-habits-the-importance-of-planning-every-minute-of-your-work-day/.
19. https://popforms.com/how-to-do-time-blocking/.2https://popforms.com/how-to-do-time-blocking/.
20. http://calnewport.com/blog/2013/12/21/deep-habits-the-importance-of-planning-every-minute-of-your-work-day/.
21. Chris Ducker, *Virtual Freedom*.

CHAPTER 8

The ART of DISCOURSE

COMMUNITY, COLLABORATION and SHOWERING REGULARLY

The doorbell rings and you rush downstairs, leaping over the dog and crashing through the hallway. You fumble with the lock but manage to get the door open in time. He's walking away, you yell after him, "Jeff, how's it going?" "Good Steve, nice out today," Jeff the FedEx guy replies. "So, uh, did you see the game last night?" you reply. "Yep, we're looking good. I think this is our year!" Jeff says. "Gotta run buddy, full truck today," Jeff shouts as he jumps back into his truck. You wave sadly, forgetting the cookies you'd baked for him as you slowly close the door.

Sound familiar? Yeah, you may need to put on pants and get outside.

Here's what we'll cover:

- Building relationships by getting out there and networking

- Building an audience by sharing your story

- Building bridges by connecting with other creatives and mentors

- Building collaborations by working with vendors, partners, and collaborators

Avoid Isolation

The creative life can get lonely. Even if you don't work from home, we tend to be hunched over a laptop or sketchpad most of our day. You can start to feel like a hermit. Even if you work in a busy office or have a vibrant social life, you can still feel isolated if you're not around others who have similar jobs. We need to vent and commiserate over industry jargon and client horror stories. Branching out to connect with others can go a long way in bolstering your love of your work.

Lisa Kanarek has a wonderful blog called workingnaked.net which captures the highs and lows of working solo. For many people, the appeal of working in pajamas is a perk of the job; as is avoiding unnecessary commutes and office politics. The downside is that you're on your own, a lot, and unless you're friends with other people who have done or are doing the same thing, you are going to feel isolated.

Preparing yourself for the solo mindset is one of the hardest parts of the job. There is no way to practice for it and after a few weeks or months, it hits you that it's not quite the land of complete, pants-free freedom you'd envisioned. Working alone means you can do whatever you want, whenever you want. That's the appeal for many of us. But it also means you can do whatever you want, whenever you want; no one is going to tell you when to stop or when to start. One of the biggest mistakes made when people start out is a lack of boundaries. You squeeze in a couple of extra hours here and there. You skip the gym to make that deadline since you're not getting out of the house that day. Before you know it, you've gained twenty pounds, and you only own t-shirts and sandals. Independence is awesome, there is no doubt about it. But you have to understand that it's easy to forget you're running a business when no one is watching.

You'll probably find your greatest sense of community with others who do exactly what you do. Often, they are your competitors. Our industry was built on sharing and collaboration, and you can be a part of continuing that tradition. So don't be afraid to take a shower, put on pants, and get out there with the other creatives!

Build Relationships

Find Your Tribe

Networking will help you build your tribe. Going to conferences, meet-ups, being active on Twitter, and just staying connected will help you find the people that you will carry along throughout your career. Think of collaborations in the film industry: Martin Scorcese and Leonardo DiCaprio, Tim Burton and Johnny Depp, Christopher Guest and his gang dating back to Spinal Tap. It's just as common in music, theater, art, and so on. Once you find people that you trust and enjoy working with, you will carry them with you no matter where you go.

I found my first tribe in 2008 at the first Creative Freelancer Conference, which is now a part of HOW Design Live. There I met eight other young designers, at varying stages in their careers but all still sorting out what the hell to do, and we immediately bonded over breakfast. As we spent the next several days together eating, drinking, and sharing ideas, we found common bonds that carried far beyond Chicago. Relationships formed that transcended geography and industry to create lasting bonds that still hold up today. When a referral, recommendation, or congratulations are needed—we're still there for each other.

"Find a group of people who challenge and inspire you … Spend a lot of time with them, and it will change your life … Listen, say yes, live in the moment, make sure you play with people who have your back, make big choices early and often. You never know what is around the corner unless you peek. Hold someone's hand while you do it. You will feel less scared. You can't do this alone. Besides, it is much more fun to succeed and fail with other people. You can blame them when things go wrong."

Amy Poehler, Harvard Class Day Address, 2011[1]

That tribe morphed into another in my hometown of Atlanta. I attended a few events with our local Atlanta Web Design Group meet-up and got to know a few people who just happened to sit next to me or be next in line at the bar. Over time, the bonds formed with about a dozen core colleagues that I still carry today. One of them is my current business partner and one of my closest friends. My staff, my vendors, my clients, and my office location were all driven by the bonds formed with my tribe. When business has been down, I've turned to my tribe first for referrals and freelance work. When business has been too much to handle, I've turned first to my tribe to find vendors and freelance help.

Your connections make you necessary. When people are excited about your work and what you're doing, regardless of what it may be, it's because they're excited about your involvement—they're excited about you. After you, your network is the most valuable asset of your business.

"Go find your team and get to work." Leslie Knope[2]

How to Meet People and Ask Them for Things

Connecting with a complete stranger—whether it's a prospect, industry pro you admire, respected local professional, or your personal hero—is terrifying. What will they say? Will they publish my letter online and write a scathing "how dare he!" takedown of my naive request? Or if you were to call them, would they scream at you and hang up the phone, proclaiming that you'll never work in this town again! Admit it, I'm not being hyperbolic, this has gone through your head. The truth is you'll either be ignored, acknowledged, accepted, or embraced. Any of the four can happen, and the outcome is out of your control. Some people are welcoming and generous, some are busy yet understanding, some are simply too busy to be bothered, and some are a bit full of themselves.

What you can control, however, is how you talk to them and ask them for things.

Be brief

You don't have to dance around or give every reason and justification. The most important thing is to make sure you're asking the right person. Find out if they can make the decision to help you and that they'll be able to help. If it's an email or social media connection invite, keep it short. It's an unsolicited message from a stranger, so they're not going to read the whole thing.

Be specific

Be very up front on what you're asking for, e.g. "I want to work with you" or "I'd like to ask for your help with X" or "I truly admire your work and I'd like some mentorship." The vague request to "pick their brain" or "get to know them" is going to either be ignored or met with an "I'm too busy" response. If possible, ask for something to which they can respond with a simple "yes" or "no." Ask to meet for coffee for thirty minutes on X date at Y time, ask for a fifteen-minute phone call on X date at Y time, or ask to meet them before or after an event you are both attending. Don't be vague and say words like "sometime", "whenever," or "if it fits your schedule." Don't be afraid to tell them point-blank how they can help you.

Use your elevator pitch

You need to state who you are and what you do; they may look you up later, but it needs to be in the conversation or message. Keep it to two sentences and try to denote any connections you have such as shared acquaintances, brands you've both worked with, proximity, or same school attended.

Be positive

Be the kind of person with whom others want to talk. You should commiserate with other creatives over horrible client stories, but make it fun. Don't be a downer, be the magnet. People should be in a better mood after talking to you than they were before.

Turn awkward into awesome

Since you're a creative, you're probably a little quirky. You aren't the type to fall into line and do what everyone else is doing. Embrace your awkward quirkiness and use it to your advantage. When you meet people, don't feel like you have to talk about the weather or economy. You can start the conversation with quirky statements like "do you think the bar in this place has good whiskey? Because I need whiskey to get through what's left of today." Feel free to use that one, it's my go-to.

Do your research and connect beforehand

If the event you're going to has a list of attendees, "stalk" a few before you go. Just use your pre-research/stalking for good. When you meet someone or email them, quickly state that you admired a recent blog post, that you saw them speak at an event, or that you enjoyed a particular aspect of a recent design project. If you know a bit about a person, it's easier to make a connection. Follow them on Twitter or send them a LinkedIn request before the event and mention that you'll both be there and you'd like to connect. Taking the initiative to set up a conversation can help you skip the small talk and get straight to talking shop.

Embrace serendipitous encounters

You never know who you're sitting next to at the bar. Striking up a conversation and sharing what you do could result in your next great adventure. I just met a young woman who was stocking towels at a resort. She would have casual conversations with guests about what they do and how their day was going. A particular guest noticed how hard she worked and how pleasant she was. After finding out about her creative background, he offered her a job on the spot. She could continue working from home and at the resort while building a creative career. If she hadn't been prepared to talk about her pursuits, that job never would have happened.

The Art of Coffee Meetings

The ultimate networking wet fish handshake is "let's grab coffee sometime." The coffee meeting is often the most unproductive meeting in the world, doing nothing for anyone involved other than the $2 tip the barista got from each of you. However, it's unbelievably powerful if you put your back into it and use them for good. Likewise, if you've reached out to that complete stranger and gotten them to commit to coffee, you can make it worth their time.

"The coffee meeting is the Swiss Army knife of networking. It's a low-risk way to meet new people, swap advice, and lay the foundation for a more substantial relationship."

Sean Blanda[3]

The coffee meeting is the most common way to form relationships with referral partners, potential clients, and colleagues. Here's a few tips on getting the most out of them.

Do your homework. Only meet with people you've researched. If you've scheduled a meeting, spending forty-five minutes learning everything about each other means you have to have at least a second meeting to get anywhere. Do your research on their background and current endeavors and start the conversation by asking "tell me more about what you do" instead of "tell me about what you do." That way you can spend your time together on specific actions and asks.

Pay. If you made the invite then you should offer to pay. You're not putting the person in debt to you, it's just common courtesy.

Be early. Starting the meeting in a rush is never a good idea. You're going to a coffee shop, which is a place where some creatives spend their entire work day. Getting there early and getting some work done isn't a stretch.

End on time. If the conversation is going great, stop five minutes before the agreed upon time (typically thirty minutes or an hour) and ask your guest if they need to wrap up since the scheduled time is coming to an end. I set a vibrate alarm on my phone to go off five minutes before; you don't want to be looking at your watch while the other person is talking. If they decide to continue, and you can do so as well with your schedule, then it's okay.

Mentorship

Mentorship, the concept of having a wise old soul show you the ropes and take you through a montage, is dead. Likewise, the idea of being the next executive in waiting or replacing your boss after she retires is dead. It used to be normal for people to work at one company for their entire career or at least for decades. Now, it's expected that people will stick with a particular job for no more than two or three years. In fact, people under thirty-five who are in the same job for ten years are now considered abnormal. The idea of being mentored by someone a generation older than you isn't even possible for most creatives since only a handful of people were in creative business a generation ago. Mentorship now falls to people who are further along than you, but they may be younger and less experienced in life as a whole. It's likely you look up to, and would love to learn from, someone who is in reality your peer. Getting them to guide you is typically something they welcome, as long as you ask the right way.

They may not accept your invite or may never respond at all. They may reply that they'll be glad to connect online and stay in touch. They may agree to a brief call for a few minutes. Make the most of what they give you by being sincere with your ask. If they do accept the meeting, they have already agreed to provide assistance and give you a part of their day, so make it as easy for them by making it the best meeting possible.

Finding the right mentor

- **Speakers.** If someone is taking the time to share their knowledge with strangers, they're more likely to share it with friends. If you can build a relationship with conference speakers you enjoy, they could be an excellent resource for mentorship.

- **Community leaders**. Your mentor doesn't have to be a creative, but they should be in a leadership role. It doesn't mean they head up a company of thousands, just that they've taken the initiative to engage with the community.

- **Educators.** If they can teach a classroom, they can teach you as well.

- **They're successful.** I would rather have advice from someone who's doing well than someone who is failing.

- **They have a clear interest in you.** Sometimes a relationship becomes a mentorship without intention. If someone who is further along in their career takes the time to answer your questions and chat with you regularly, you may be forming a mentorship organically. You should ask to make it formal and let them know you intend to learn from them.

Build an Audience

Building a website and printing business cards isn't enough; you have to connect with other creatives and engage. If you build it, they won't necessarily come. Even if your website and portfolio are amazing, you have to share them with industry publications or on social media for people to hear about them. No one goes to Google and types in "awesome graphic designer" and has your hidden website pop up. I've met many talented creatives over the years of whom no one has ever heard. I've also met some pretty average creatives that were very famous. The difference between the two is exposure. The more people know about you, the more people will see your work. The quality of the work isn't always as important as the personality of the individual. It sounds simple, but so many creatives neglect to sell themselves.

I believe one of the biggest reasons people aren't promoting themselves is that they feel it's "pushy." They don't want to seem like attention addicts. That feeling doesn't go away. If you don't have some reservations about self-promotion, you're probably narcissistic. But you can overcome your fear of self-promotion and build a valuable audience.

Gain Exposure

When you're selling good creative work and have a solid process worth sharing, you're not taking advantage of people; you're making their lives better. You're helping your clients stay in business so that they can provide for their families. You're making things easier or more enjoyable to use. You are making the world a better place, even if you're designing direct mail pieces for used car lots. By bringing a professional attitude to creative work, you're making it more valuable. If you have something to add to the conversation, then you're doing the creative community a disservice by keeping your mouth shut. You are helping people by giving them your knowledge and perspective. You have something unique to say, and others would like to hear it.

Getting to a place where self-promotion feels right can be done with a simple change in mindset. Don't look at it as promotion. Look at it as evidence of your value. To put it another way, it's not about fame, it's about traction. Traction means that you have clearly identifiable momentum and progress. You're going places. When people see that you're headed in the right direction, they're more likely to work with you. No one wants to climb aboard a sinking ship. Those who have an audience and recognition are perceived as being in demand. Thus, the more traction you have, the more likely you'll find clients and get to keep working.

Get Social

The lowest-cost and lowest-friction way to build an audience is through online networking and social media. Leverage the tools on the web to connect with people across the world who share your interests. It's not about posting every waking moment of your life or twenty selfies a day. It's about showing who you are and what you do.

You don't have to have a separate presence for your "personal" network and your "professional" network. You can create an online persona if you like or keep certain networks to only friends.

- Facebook and Twitter are best suited for two-way conversations. You connect with your audience on a more personal level and share thoughts and images throughout the day. You may share what you're working on or what you find interesting.

- LinkedIn is better suited for one-way conversations where you share content periodically and engage in limited bursts within groups.

- Pinterest and Instagram are visually oriented, so they're more about showing off your work and your process. You can engage with your audience through comments, contests, and giveaways.

- Chat apps and real-time connection tools such as Snapchat, Periscope, and whatever else is hot right now allow you to open up your life to your audience. You can talk to them in real time and allow them to see who you are and how you work.

Tips on better use of social media with your audience

- **Quality over quantity.** Focus on building the right audience for your goals. If you're an illustrator who would like to work with more magazines, then you should target your social efforts in the magazine publishing industry. Follow editors, art directors, and other illustrators.

- **Don't try to be everywhere.** Pick the platforms that are right for you and focus your energy there. You can have a presence across all major networks, but find the one that makes sense for your clientele and do it with excellence. If you're a highly visual creative, look at Instagram as your place to work. I've noticed hand lettering and illustration are huge on Instagram and certain creatives have hundreds of thousands of followers. Needless to say, if they're selling their work or speaking at events, they've got quite the reach.

- **Engage your audience.** Don't just post out things for people to consume, actually interact with your audience. Create members-only groups or private email lists. Hold Q&A sessions or meet up with people in chat channels. Let your audience know when you'll be at an event and plan real-life meet and greet time.

- **Go with your audience's pace.** Don't post everything, but don't let yourself be forgotten. If you're process-oriented, then show your works in progress. If your work is more suited to showing off your finished product, then build a posting schedule that makes sense for when your audience is online. You'll have to track your performance to see when people engage. Tools like Buffer and HootSuite can give you powerful data on when social posts are successful.

Share Your Process

Keeping your ideas to yourself means you're robbing the world of your contributions. You never know if what you're doing is exactly what someone else has been trying to do for years. By writing a tutorial or simply posting a video of you working through your creative process, you may be educating the next great creative.

You don't have to create forty-hour tutorial programs or a video blog. But you can take snapshots of work in progress, add your thinking to your case studies, and share the challenges you face as you work through projects. For digital creatives, Dribbble and Behance have become great places to show your work as it progresses and get feedback along the way.

Those who teach often have the largest audiences. Chris Spooner and Chris Coyier, no relation, have built massive audiences through teaching. They both do great work, but they aren't standing out because of their finished products. They stand out because they constantly teach. They open up their processes to those on the web and engage with their audiences regularly.

Tell Your Stories

People love to hear your story and find common ground. If you're a single mom photographer, you'll be amazed when you find other single mom photographers who want to connect with you and talk shop. The stories behind the work are often more fascinating than the finished product. It's why art museums are far more enjoyable than simply looking at the work in a book. When you hear from someone who knows the struggle behind the work, or even the artist herself, you have a newfound appreciation of the art.

It's up to you to join your creative community. We're lucky to live in the time of Twitter. You can connect with your heroes and icons throughout the world and, if funds allow, go to conferences and meet them. Even if you live in a remote town with no other creatives nearby, you can build thriving relationships with others who share your struggles and victories.

Build Bridges

Professional Associations

There's no VA or Masonic Temple for creatives, but there are still a lot of ways to join the club in person and online. Groups like the AIGA, Graphic Artists Guild, ASJA, CHI, and others are actual clubs for people with particular job skills. From holding regular meetings and lectures from industry professionals to hosting portfolio shows and workshops, they can provide multiple outings in a given month to get you in conversation with your colleagues. These associations are also your advocates with government and industry officials when it comes to your rights and needs. They're perfect for mentoring, finding interns or employees, fostering partnerships, and sharing war stories.

Community Organizations

Local Chambers of Commerce are where small business owners connect. Here you will find prospective clients, competition, partners, and drinking buddies. Some people may end up holding more than one of those titles. The best way to get a return on a

Chamber membership is to attend networking events regularly and become known. Don't be afraid to connect with people regardless of their profession, you never know to whom they may be able to refer you.

Invest your time and money wisely

Professional associations cost money, typically an annual fee of a few hundred dollars plus per-event costs, so you have to choose carefully. They also take up time. You can't get heavily involved in more than three organizations, and two is probably the realistic limit. Ideally you should choose one professional guild or association for your craft and one for business development such as a Chamber or open networking group.

Organizational leadership

Volunteering for board positions and event committees can pay off. Get plugged into the organization and look for ways to help. Joining and then showing up to random events to stand in the corner is a waste of your time and money. When you're visible as a leader in your community, it immediately increases your perceived thought leadership among your peers. I'm an owner of the Atlanta Web Design Group where we have thousands of members and our own event space. The visibility and credibility that come from my involvement with speakers and community leaders have done wonders for my business.

Conferences

Attending conferences is one of the best parts of being a creative. I've had years of experience working with trade shows and professional conferences for non-creative industries and I can tell you that creatives are unparalleled in putting on praise-worthy events. While the typical insurance or sales conference in Vegas can certainly end in life-altering debauchery (and tattoos), creative conferences are the right kind of fun. Sure, a lot of us are huge nerds and weren't exactly kicking off the fast dance at prom, but getting together over drinks and talking about design theory or the latest Medium post can be surprisingly cool.

Some of my dearest friends are conference pals. There are people who live in my own city whom I'd never met until we both attended a conference on the other side of the country. Seeing your colleagues and competitors outside of the office can change your perception of them drastically. The camaraderie that comes from breaking bread together away from the office is special. Most conferences you'll attend will be for your skill, such as a design conference or a photography workshop, so you're naturally going to be around your competition. Making friends with them is one of the best things you can do for your career: more on that in a bit.

Getting the most out of conferences

Getting the most out of a conference goes far beyond attending the talks and workshops. While you're there to learn, the real connections happen at after parties, around the lunch tables, and going out to dinner with your new-found friends. Seeing a new city with new people is a sure-fire way to get out of your routine and find a new sense of adventure. You don't have to go wild or do anything uncomfortable, it may just be going to a nearby restaurant to take over a corner and chat late into the night. You'll hate yourself for a few minutes when you have to get up for the next day's sessions, but you'll be glad for the connections made.

Conferences are a great way to find mentors as well. Standing around after they've given a lecture in your hometown to briefly speak with them is great, but they're there for one purpose: to give their talk. You're between them and their hotel room where they can call their family, grab a drink, and catch up on emails. Meeting someone you admire at a conference means meeting them out of their element. They have to eat, drink, and decompress. If you're able to join them for that downtime, you're no longer an admiring person looking up to them, you're a peer joining them for a bite.

Choosing wisely

Conferences can be expensive, so it's important to choose wisely and ask others about conferences that they've enjoyed in the past. You don't have to attend the big ones that everyone goes to. In fact, I tend to enjoy the events with fewer than 500 attendees. Try to target new prospects in cities where your conference will be held, or meet with your existing clients already there, and schedule meetings or lunch with them. There will be times when you really can't afford to go to a conference, but you know you need it. It's a business expense and it's part of your growth; it's worth foregoing a purchase or taking on a little extra work to make a good conference experience happen. I've never regretted making that call. We actually budget for conferences in our shop rate calculation.

Non-creative conferences

Attending conferences for your vertical market, such as a healthcare or construction conference, is a great way to network with prospects. You can go so far as to buy a space and set up a booth. There's value if you have a product or service that you can quickly discuss with people on the conference floor, but the expense may be better utilized in buying a few key prospects dinner or drinks over the course of the conference. This requires pre-research and contacting the prospect to find out if you can connect, but if you're there at their industry conference to learn, it certainly says a great deal to your prospect about your commitment to their industry. It's worth a shot.

Public Speaking

If you're an introvert but you want to attend events, a solution is arranging to be the speaker. There's a difference between introversion and shyness. You may be more comfortable on a stage rather than having small talk with a few people you've just met. When you're the speaker, people approach you, and there's a ready-made topic of conversation. Presenting your ideas to a small group of peers in your office is an excellent way to develop your skills and form relationships.

Thought Leadership

Speaking at conferences will move you closer to thought leadership. When you've been selected by organizers to share your idea, you've been given a vote of confidence by your peers. Other creatives want to learn from those willing to share their ideas, process, and lessons learned. You don't have to come up with your own original idea or some earth-shattering process. And you most certainly don't have to have clients of a certain size or be in charge of a big company. Some of the best talks I've ever heard have been from young, solo creatives without a single client I've ever heard of. The key is being open and willing to share, preparing as best as you can, and making yourself available after your talk to connect with anyone interested.

The best speakers are those who are truly there to share something. Putting the time and effort in to get a talk right can equal a full two weeks of client work. You will sacrifice free time and income to prepare. Speaking isn't easy, but it's well worth the effort. Check out recommended resources on developing your speaking practice on the book website.

Build Collaborations

At times, you will have to work with creatives who diminish the quality of your work, drive you insane, or ruin the entire project. Instead of being forced to work with others who aren't at your level, you can build your own network of collaborators that you bring to all of your projects.

It makes you better

Psychologist Kevin Dunbar studied the workings of four prominent microbiology laboratories for insights into how new theories are developed. What he found was that the majority of creative insights and great discoveries actually occurred during regularly scheduled lab meetings, where individual researchers revealed their latest findings and shared their most difficult setbacks.[4]

Sometimes simply talking about your work with others will help you find new solutions and ideas. By breaking the cycle of isolation and deep thinking, you can spark creativity. Where these conversations happen is up to you. a you're solo, you have to seek out events and group settings. If you're part of a team, you have to foster a culture of collaboration by sharing your work in progress. If you're the leader, then you should open your books and show your work in progress as well.

Making Friends With Your Competition

There's more than enough work to go around. Even if you're in a small market with only a few businesses, you aren't limited to your potential client pool. If you're good at what you do, and you provide value to your clients, you will find work as long as you market effectively. It doesn't matter if there are twenty others going up against you for every job or just two, you will get work. Living in fear of competition and holding your ideas close to the vest isn't going to help; in fact, it hurts.

Some of the best friendships you'll develop over your creative career will be with your direct competition—people with your same skills, vying for the same clients. We are in a unique industry, one where people freely give away their ideas, processes, and tools to people who can use them to make money. Most of us, myself included, wouldn't have this job if it weren't for the work of others. From online tutorials to friends handing me clients they didn't have room for, working with the competition has made a creative career possible.

Viewing your competitors, local or remote, as a threat will only make you paranoid. There are jerks out there, sure, and someone may try to tarnish your reputation to get their next client. That's on them; life happens. You can choose not to be the problem and always take the high road. You'll never regret being the bigger person. Be larger than a single client or individual employee when developing relationships with your competition.

It's likely you won't be doing the same thing for years and years; you will change your craft. As you do, your competitor may go in a different direction or close up shop altogether. They may need a home for their clients or a place to work. The more allies you have, the more likely you'll be to get the next generation of talent and the clients you need.

Having repeat partners for complementary skills can do wonders for your business:

- Partners get different referrals and leads. If you commonly need one another, you essentially have two teams doing full-time business development for your next client.

- Partners can be marked up in cost, so if you choose to be the face of the entire project to your client, you can add a cost on top of your partner's fees and make a profit for simply managing the work.

- Partners make it easy to establish routine practices for project management, file sharing, and communication. If you're working with the same people over and over again, you won't have to re-learn or reestablish these systems each time.

- Partners can make your business look bigger to your clients. If you're offering more than your own services to your clients, your business appears bigger to them, and they could consider you capable of even greater responsibility.

- Partners can become great friends and colleagues. Your partner may grow much faster than you, but if you've established trust, they can grow your business for you by getting you on board with bigger clients who have bigger budgets.

- Partners give you the confidence to go after more work. If you know someone has your back for bigger tasks or skills you don't have, you're more apt to go after an RFP or reply to a prospect.

How to Find Partners and Collaborators

Partner with people who share your skills

It may be that one of you does a particular aspect of the job better than the other or that you simply like working together. Regardless, partnering to the power of two can make the job more fun. Often it's because a particular project is too much for you to handle on your own, but you want to do the work. Partnering with a like-minded creative or agency to get the work done as a team is better than not getting the work at all.

Partner with people who complement your skills

Unless you have a very particular skill that clients can use in a vacuum, you'll have to partner with others who have complementary skills. It may be a web designer and developer, writer and marketer, or photographer and advertising designer. Some sell easier than others or have a larger client base. By attaching yourself to people who have a service that has a shorter sales cycle or higher volume, you can get more business.

Partner with people who share your interests

The market or client you wish to work with may be out of reach for you, at least when on your own. You may be able to break through with individual prospects when you partner with someone else. It could be combining more than one agency into a single proposed services package for a large client. You're building a relay team to tackle something that larger groups may be able to handle with individual in-house departments. This approach can also help you develop long-term collaborations for complementary skills.

We're All in This Together

A 1920 study showed that a group of people working on individual tasks but at the same table performed better. They weren't collaborating or competing; they were simply working near one another. It's why we enjoy working at coffee shops or co-working spaces. It's one of the reasons we find ourselves stopping in the middle of important work to check social media. The energy of other people can act as a substitute for a creative team even if we're working solo.[5]

There's no reason to hold your ideas or process so close. Remember that ideas are worthless and execution is everything. We're better together, even when we're competing for the same clients. The cream rises to the top, and your colleagues and teammates can help carry you with them as they rise. As each of you improves, and shares, you'll be far better off than working in a vacuum.

Notes

1. http://news.harvard.edu/gazette/story/2011/06/2011-harvard-university-class-day-speech-by-amy-poehler/.
2. http://www.imdb.com/title/tt3748226/?ref _ =ttep _ ep13.
3. http://99u.com/articles/19678/10-steps-for-an-awesome-coffee-meeting.
4. http://99u.com/articles/7187/why-sharing-your-work-setbacks-struggles-breaks-creative-blocks.
5. http://99u.com/articles/16850/everything-youve-ever-wanted-to-know-about-teams.

CHAPTER 9

NO TIME LIKE THE FUTURE

GROWING YOUR CREATIVE BUSINESS

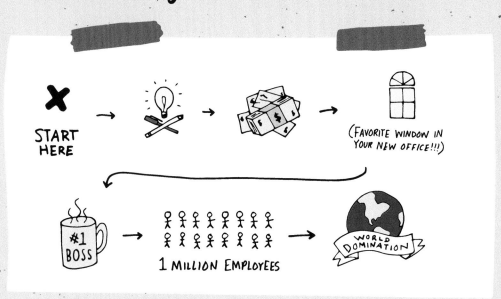

START HERE

(FAVORITE WINDOW IN YOUR NEW OFFICE!!!)

#1 BOSS

1 MILLION EMPLOYEES

WORLD DOMINATION

As you grow, you may do less and less of the creative work you set out do. If you're a designer, you may design less as you get more clients and larger invoices. The majority of your days will be meetings, messages, planning, and operations. There may come a time when you have to decide who you are: creative or business owner. That line in the sand is what divides freelancers from business owners in the minds of many.

Freelancers are business owners in every sense of the word and deserve the same respect as the principal at a 100-person agency. There is no right path, but for many creatives there will come a time when you must choose. You can only do so much work in the time you have. Raising your rates has limits. There are designers, artists, and writers who can command large fees for their work and they deserve it. You can be one of those artists if your skills and connections converge in the marketplace. Others run the risk of pricing themselves out of their market, so they have to scale or cut back on growth. That's the balancing act we're going to cover.

In this chapter, we'll break down the steps you can take to manage your growth.

- Handling growth
- Freelancer vs. employee
- Managing freelancers
- Hiring staff, apprentices, and interns
- Scaling your business
- Partnerships and mergers
- Specialization or generalization
- Getting office space
- Passive income
- Failure and letting go
- What does the end look like?

Grow or Plateau

Eventually, you'll want to make more money for your time. That means you have to charge more, hire help, and find more ways to be profitable. You have to scale. Ben Chestnut, the founder of MailChimp, shared the gritty details of his company's decision to move from services to a product in 2007. Ben shared how chasing large clients puts you at tremendous risk for falling very far and very fast when things go wrong. By shifting their focus to smaller, yet large in number, clients vs. single large clients they were much more profitable and able to weather ups and downs.[1] As a solo creative or a small team of three or four, your risk increases along with your rates. Once you become accustomed to a certain income or lifestyle, it's hard to go back. Whether it's staffing up, moving to a product or agency retainer model, or taking hold of value-based pricing, you will have to make a move.

It's common for creative business owners to get so far away from the actual creative work that they take a full-time job or allow themselves to be acquired simply to get back to the craft. That's not failure; that's freedom. If you're willing to walk away from the business you've built to get back to your creative roots, that's a choice you will most likely be happy with. For those who stick with business ownership though, growth can be tough.

Small isn't "small"

Staying small or solo and never growing into a large business isn't Peter Pan Syndrome. You can choose to remain freelance, a solopreneur, or two-person shop your entire career. Some of the best and most admired creatives in the world are solo practitioners who work from home. Conversely, some of the biggest charlatans in the creative industry are at the head of 500-person agencies. Growth doesn't mean adding people or getting bigger offices, it simply means always to be headed forward. Moreover, some people go back to going solo after heading up massive agencies for years or decades. Small isn't "small" when it comes to talent, billing practices, or quality clients. You have to find what's right for you and your lifestyle; don't let anyone else define growth and success in your business.

Freelancers vs. Employees

Freelance Contractors

- Operate under a business name
- May have their own employees
- Invoice for the work done
- Have more than one client
- Set their own hours
- Pick their clients & projects
- Advertise their business's services
- Own and use their own tools

Employees

- Operate as individuals
- Are paid a salary or wage
- Work for only one employer
- Work as dictated by the employer
- Are given specific training by the employer
- Use tools provided by the employer

Walking the thin line between freelance contractor and employee has gotten much more dangerous in the past few years. With healthcare reform and service tax changes, companies continue to find creative ways to get around additional expenses. As companies are unsure whether they need a full-time designer or writer, they want to test the waters with contract work; even more so with programmers and developers who work with rapidly changing technology.

Don't Mess Around

You can receive penalties and fines for not handling contractors properly. If you have to re-classify someone, you will have to reimburse them for overtime pay, any missing wages between their salary and actual hours worked, backed taxes, health insurance, and so on. There are entire organizations attempting to unionize and organize contract workers against unfair employment practices, so it's unwise to ignore a contractor who may be getting close to the line. If a complaint is filed, tax authorities such as the IRS are the first to investigate. Your entire business can come under scrutiny, which isn't something you want.

How to Tell the Difference

For you the individual or you the business owner who is hiring contractors, there are a few key questions to ask the person who's doing the work to determine how to classify them:

- **Do you perform the same work for other clients?** If so, then you're a contractor.

- **How are hours set?** Is the time that work starts and stops being dictated? For example, is a rule in place that states work must be conducted between 9am and 3pm on Tuesday and Thursday every week? As you dictate more than half of a person's working hours, you are effectively controlling their schedule and acting as an employer.

- **Where can you work?** Are you required to arrive at a particular office? While contractors can work on-site, combining location requirements with time requirements edges the relationship away from freelance toward employment.

- **Is overtime a requirement?** If the work to be completed requires more than a standard workweek, the schedule has been dictated and is therefore employment.

- **Are you using your tools or supplied tools for the job?** If the work is being done on your own equipment with your own software or tools, that's typically freelance. If equipment is being supplied and required, that's more in line with employment. Additionally, if the manner in which the tools are used is being dictated, that isn't really freelance.

- **Are you performing tasks that are also being done by employees of the company?** If you're a copywriter and five other copywriters work there as full-time employees, you probably can't be a contractor for more than a temporary period of a few weeks or months. If, however, you perform a job that no one else there does you may be able to be a contractor indefinitely.

The circumstances, duration of work, and many other factors make it even more gray. You also have to consider which is best for you. As your business grows, and you need to add staff, you'll be tempted to keep people freelance as long as possible. There will come a point when it's cheaper to hire someone and pay them a salary vs. paying them hourly, so the decision may be made for you.

Managing Freelancers

When you are following the rules, use freelance help as long as you can. The biggest benefit to having freelance help is that you can comfortably remove or replace them if things aren't working out. It's easier to budget for freelancers than it is when you need to hire someone. You only have to consider their rate and the time they will work instead of insurance, taxes, equipment, and so on.

Hire freelancers with the same standards as employees. While they are easier to get rid of if they don't work out, a bad contractor can still ruin your office and make your life hell. Make sure they're a cultural fit. If they're providing a critical skill for a key client, you may be forced to hire them if the work sticks around. If you've brought on someone who isn't a good fit, you've just disrupted your culture. So don't just hire them for skill, hire them for fit.

Be open about your structure

Don't lie to your clients if they ask about freelancers. You don't have to put a giant freelancer stamp on their forehead or in their email signature, but if a client asks you directly if someone is an employee or contractor, tell the truth. You can get them an email at your company domain name and even have them add you to their LinkedIn profile. But as the client works directly with them it will become apparent that they aren't full-time and then it diminishes your credibility.

Protect ya neck

Put your freelancers under contract just like a client. Define the scope of work, timeline, budget, and expectations with them in writing. If there is a scope change from your client, your freelancer will have a scope change, and you'll need to deal with it in writing. Be specific in your agreement on what's covered such as materials, software, stock images, travel, etc.

Get a Work for Hire (WFH) agreement

You must get it in writing that any work created for your company by the freelancer is your property. Otherwise, you cannot legally hand it over to the client under your ownership clause with them. Agencies have been sued by freelancers who weren't told that the work was being transferred in ownership and found their illustration on a t-shirt or their design in a book that was resold.

Treat them like employees when you can

Keep freelancers in the loop. Don't lock them out of client communications; make sure they can interface directly with the client. Too much can get lost in translation while trying to protect your company's image; it's better to hire freelancers you can trust to communicate directly with your client. It's likely they'll often be remote, so use chat tools, video meetings, and standing conference calls to make sure they are involved in the discussion.

Make them feel like part of the team; don't treat them like they aren't "real" employees. Make sure they get invited to the office parties and lunch outings. If someone continues to do a great job, try to hire them when it makes financial sense. If you can't hire them, take an interest in helping them find a good job. You never know if they'll end up working at a client you'd like to have down the road.

Hiring Help

The fastest way to profitability is to have people who work for less than you charge. For example, you pay someone $40 an hour, and you charge the client $80 an hour. You are, in effect, making $40 for nothing. Of course, it's not that simple. For every billable employee, such as a designer or writer, you're going to have ¼ of a non-billable employee such as a project manager or account executive. So for every four creatives, you have to hire at least one non-billable employee. That is unless you want to manage eight or twelve people by yourself or with only one other person helping. You could do that, but that means you would most likely do zero creative work going forward.

Office space, equipment, insurance, and taxes also factor into an employee's cost and your margin, so making a clear profit on staffing up requires significant scale. It means creating middle management—such as creative directors, art directors, and producers—who will command a higher salary and generate less profit.

How to Hire People

If it's clear you do need staff, here are the steps I recommend for finding the right fit for your team.

Test the waters

If at all possible, have candidates work with you as a contractor on a project first. See how they work and communicate. I have personally had top-notch candidates whom I was ready to hire to work with me only to find out they were a terrible fit. This has saved my life so many times. Even if they have a full-time job, see if they'll do a small project or quick weekend job with you. You can take this even further. For my junior creatives, they all contract with us for three months before we will hire them full-time. We want to see how they handle the small business world on their own.

Hire for culture, not skill

You can teach people to use your software or tool of choice, but you can't teach them to be nice. Look for raw skills such as inquisitiveness, exploration, self-motivation, a love of learning, strong communication skills, attention to detail, and good meeting etiquette. You can teach the rest; we all had to learn at some point. I'd rather have a creative who isn't a rock star that I can trust with clients over a diva artist. I can contract the diva when I need him.

Let them do the talking

You don't need to sell your company; this isn't Silicon Valley startups. Let them tell their story and sell you on them. We love to talk about what we do in our shops, and we end up doing all of the talking in interviews. Be silent and listen.

Don't hire your friends, hire people with whom you'd like to become friends

Don't hire someone you consider a peer outside of work to be your subordinate. It rarely goes well. If they're a peer, find a way to partner with them. Making someone your subordinate who doesn't see you as an authority figure is going to make things tough. Instead, look for people who can become your friends if you so choose and consider them for leadership roles.

Use the layover test

If you were stuck overnight with this person, and only this person, in an airport, could you handle being with them? If not, then don't hire them. You're going to travel with your employees and be with them at after-parties and events. If they drive you crazy, why would you hire them?

Find the money or find the person

If you have the right person but you can't afford them, find the money. If you have the money, but you can't find the right person, take the best cultural fit for now and find a way to fit in a good person when they are ready to come on board. Pay less now, invest in training, and teach them up.

Apprentices and Interns

The best way to test the waters is to take creatives who haven't been corrupted by the Sith Lords of agency world and mould them into creative thinkers. You can find raw talent that's a cultural fit at a low cost and low risk. If you work with someone you love, you can build rapport with them and have them come aboard early in their career.

There are two types of education-level hires you can make: apprentices and interns. They're similar but different in a few key ways.

Apprentices

Longer-term hires that commit full-time. Working and learning at your business is their only job. The apprentice works under individual employees on your team for extended periods of time and will interface with clients. They tend to make more money than an intern and can even be a full-time hire and receive benefits. The key is that their employment agreement has a defined end that protects you from having to explain their release. It's clear from the outset that they are there for a limited time to learn and will be released when a predefined period is up. You have the option, but not the obligation, to hire them.

Interns

Shorter-term hires and typically in a full-time education role such as college or graduate school. They work for a much shorter period, typically the summer or one semester. They can be unpaid or paid very little at an hourly rate. They aren't employees and are paid through either a staffing agency, their university or school, or a third-party provider. They are there to learn about the industry more than a particular job skill. They typically aren't hired after an internship and there is no obligation to do so.

How to treat Apprentices and Interns

- **Pay them**. I believe interns should be paid and work on constructive projects, not making coffee runs. They need to pay their dues, and that will sometimes be busy work, but they are there to learn, and you should compensate them for the help they'll provide. They aren't a burden; they're a blessing to the industry.

- **Train them**. Give them hands-on experience instead of a classroom environment. Constantly let them see how you and your team work and let them pick the process apart. Show them, don't tell them.

- **Give them homework**. Tell them what you're reading and let them do the same. Discuss the books, blogs, and studies you share. Assign essential reading and tools for them to explore in their own time.

- **Invest in their future**. Help them build relationships with agencies or companies that may hire them. Pass along your knowledge and save them any headaches you can.

- **Let them leave**. Don't feel obligated to hire them, even if they're a fit. The best thing for some is to let them go out and work in a bigger firm or in a different environment. The experience could help them be more adaptable in your environment if you hire them later on.

- **Hire them only if you have room**. Don't feel obligated to bring them on. Never promise or hint that a job may be open if you're not positive it will be *and* you expect to consider them seriously for it.

- **Give them honest feedback, but make it constructive**. Tell them what to improve and how to do it. Don't just tell them what's wrong or what's right; show them how to get better.

Good Employees Leave

Talented creatives will leave your business. That's part of it; we all start somewhere and then we grow into our own. You're moving from player to coach, and players graduate. It hurts to lose people you've invested in, but never make employees sign ridiculous non-compete agreements that keep them from moving on to the next destination in their career.

And let them take the work they've done for you with them. Sure, they need to credit your business for the work, but don't block them from telling the stories to their future clients or employers.

Scaling

The Speed of Growth

Growing too quickly can stretch you too far. In my first two years of business, I went from being solo to having five full-time employees. As we added clients, we added staff. Over a matter of months, not years, our clients' needs changed but our skills didn't. The biggest failure was a massive website project we took on that called for one particular type of development. No one on my team had any idea how to work with this particular technology, but we still took on the client.

I had two developers on my team with nothing to do and a subcontractor eating up 70 percent of the project budget. This wasn't the last time I made this mistake and I ended up with a team that couldn't do the work I was selling. In retrospect, this was what destroyed my small business and took me all the way back down to a solo practice. That's not a bad thing, but it wasn't my plan at the time.

The second time around, after the incidents in 2010 and 2011, I took the lessons learned and grew at scale. I hired freelancers for specific skills or projects. I layered in complementary services and subcontracted it to partners at a profit. After a while, I would transition them to full-time hires. Some of my most trusted "employees" are small development shops and illustrators that I continue to partner with today. They either weren't interested in becoming full-time employees or they weren't doing enough work with me on a monthly basis to justify making them a part of the team permanently. Eventually, I merged my company and took on a partner. Our skills complemented one another's, and we had the right mix of capabilities between our respective teams. I believe we've grown the right way.

The process for hiring that we just covered in our hiring help section has worked well. We're now a dozen salaried employees but have up to thirty people working at any given time on projects we lead. We're able to serve clients who would typically hire forty-person agencies without the hassle of running a forty-person agency.

The Scale of Growth

There are two simple ways to grow: charge more for each project or increase the amount of projects. There are also two ways to go about it: retention and acquisition. Getting repeat business from existing clients (retention) is usually easier than generating new business from new clients (acquisition).

Retention and higher cost

This means you are keeping your same clients, or at least the same amount of clients, but charging them more for each project. You're either raising your rates for hourly billing/retainers or going up on the price of your work. Switching from commoditized pricing to value-based pricing is the most logical step. This is harder to do with existing clients because they're used to your same talent at lower rates.

Acquisition and higher cost

You take on more clients at a higher cost. You may have to build a mix of clients on your old rates and new rates and slowly replace your existing clients with new ones who are paying the higher rate. You can decide whether to keep your existing clients (retention) and have them step up to your new rates. Some will, some won't. My largest client of over six years hit a ceiling on what they would pay, despite my contributions to their success. I didn't have any hard feelings, they simply couldn't afford me anymore. I had to find another client of similar size at a higher rate, which took over a year.

Retention and more volume

Keep the same clients you have, but add more work. You have to ask for the work, and ensure that it's work you want to do. The most common scenario I've seen is a design shop taking on coding and development work. It could mean a static design shop taking on animation or video. You may not have to expand your services, you could scale laterally. If you have a client at a large corporation, you may be able to expand into additional departments. I have a large client who has creative teams scattered throughout numerous divisions of the company. After doing good work with one division, I was referred to other divisions. That's borderline acquisition instead of retention, but semantics matter little to me when I'm getting new business.

Acquisition and more volume

You're taking on more clients and more work. It means you'll have to staff up both operationally and creatively. Each new client needs project and account management, not just creative work. It can be very profitable because you have a mix of clients and billing practices. You can grow what works and drop what doesn't. However, this isn't sustainable for a solo creative or tiny team; you'll have to grow in size. It's also the highest risk way to grow because your overhead increases as your team grows.

Scaling Costs

You've got to spend money to make money. It's not just hiring people; you'll have to buy things and find places to put those people and things. You have to be smart about what you buy and sell. The best way to go about it is to scale costs, layering your time for dollar services with profitable endeavors.

A layered approach means adding in complementary services and offerings alongside your core. If your core service is graphic design, then adding in web template design makes a lot of sense. You don't have to be a top-notch web designer to sell it to your existing clients. For many small businesses, they just need design direction on a drag and drop website builder. If your core service is web design, you may add in web development and subcontract the development work to a partner or freelancer. Yes, you can add more volume with your core service and sell more of the same. But I've found that adding in complimentary services that you can scale at their pace doesn't force you to increase your staff as quickly.

A simple way to scale costs

Your income should grow at least 1.5x faster than your overhead. For example, if your current overhead is $10,000 and you need to make a hire of $5,000 per month including all operating costs, your overhead is now $15,000. Only when you can have your income at a consistent $17,500 should you consider making the hire. That means that you have to make an additional $7,500 a month to justify spending another $5,000 a month. This is a very basic guideline and not at all an economics master class. If that new hire needs a new computer, a new desk, and new software that costs $3,000 in total, you can choose to break that up over a few months at $1000 a month (meaning you have $16,000 in overhead and need to make $19,000 a month) or save that up before making the hire as a one-time purchase.

No Rush

Some shops won't have the luxury of waiting; they have to hire as fast as they can find the talent. This type of growth isn't always bad, but it's a bit like speeding down a highway. Your risk of crashing increases as you accelerate. One bad apple can spoil the whole bunch, and it's hard to get rid of the bad ones. Here's a few quick tips on dealing with fast hires:

- **Use staffing agencies to protect yourself**. You will pay a fee to hire them if they work out, but it may be worth it. The last thing you want is an unfit hire that you can't remove. By going through a staffing firm they can get benefits and other full-time job perks, but you can still let them go without reason if they aren't working out. It also protects you if the pace of growth suddenly slows and you don't need all of the help you had brought on.

- **Use freelancers**. Again, this is how I scale. If someone can't possibly freelance for us because they want to go from full-time job to full-time job, then we won't hire them in a hurry. I'd rather pass on top-notch talent than rush a hire.

- **Go part-time**. See if you can get someone to come on part-time with you while they are still working with their own clients. Have them work three days a week or every other week.

- **Try to stay project-based**. The smartest way to grow is to do it with each client or project. Hire people as you need them to complete work. Get long-term agreements from clients and hire people under those same agreement timelines.

No Means Grow

One of the signs of a healthy creative business is commonly saying "no" to an RFP, an actual request for work, or when an existing client asks you to take on additional tasks. If you're in a position to pick and choose who you work with and what you work on, your business is probably healthy.

My friend Greg Hoy, head of Happy Cog, said in an article for *A List Apart*, "I used to think the hard part was 'getting to yes,' but over time, I've learned that the hardest part isn't closing the deal, but figuring out which deals are actually worth closing. It all begins with taking a hard look at the prospect you're talking to, and keeping an eye on early behaviors that all too frequently lead to problems."[2]

What's in a Name?

To some, this may sound trivial, but what if your business is "you," as in your business is called John Smith, Incorporated? There have been heated debates over the need to change the name once you have partners or lots of employees because being named after a person makes a business seem small. If being "small" does bother you, then you can always just shorten the name to Smith, Inc. Likewise, if you have a partner, such as Smith-Williams, Inc. and Williams leaves, changing to Smith, Inc. may not be appealing. Rebranding can be good, especially if you've significantly changed, but it's okay if you want to stick with your name forever. You've hopefully established yourself as a thought leader, so why not be recognized for it?

Change in Lifestyle

If you grow beyond just yourself, the lifestyle shift is significant. Working from home, whenever you want, and however you want, is why many creatives started. As you grow into more meetings and more team members, this tends to go away. There's something about having even a single partner or peer that completely changes the dynamic of how you work. You feel an obligation to work a bit more, have a stricter schedule, or take less time off. You can fight that by creating the right culture, but there is a tendency to test one another out at first to see how loose things will be. It's up to you to set the tone for how you and everyone on your team works. So set the tone and culture that you want; there is no right or wrong at any size. If your goal is to build a few websites here and there and also teach yoga a few nights a week, you probably want to stay solo.

You'll Lose Some Control

You're going to give up control as you grow. Whether it's taking on partners or having to hire administrative staff, you won't be able to manage every aspect of the business if you grow beyond work that you can execute on your own. That may be appealing or terrifying, it depends on what you envision for your business. If you have a product or have gotten large, you may even need investors who aren't creatives. They're going to want a return on their investment; they're not philanthropists, and you're no charity, so it will change how you work.

Taking the layered cost–profit approach means you may have to diversify your offerings. It's tough to do one thing, such as editorial illustration, and do it at scale for more and more clients. You can charge more and be more profitable, but if you want to grow in the traditional sense of hiring staff, you'll probably have to offer additional services, which you may not want to do. It also means you'll be working in areas where you're less competent and rely on staff or partners. I never felt more out of control than when my business was delivering solutions that I couldn't produce myself.

You Won't Only Be Hiring Creatives

Adding more creatives means they have to be managed and need operational support. So it's not just about adding another writer or designer, it also means adding project managers and sales people. The more you have non-creative staff on board, the less your company feels like a creative endeavor. Finding this type of talent isn't as easy as finding creatives. It's hard to review someone's project management portfolio. You do have to hire based on experience and recommendations for these roles. They can still be brought on by staffing firms or be freelance, so if that's an option you should take it.

Small Batch

You can stick to the "boutique" or "craft" style business. This simply means you're a single location, small-batch business that limits the amount of output (client work) done in a given period. Just like craft whiskey or high fashion, boutique businesses can demand much higher prices and drive demand.

People line up to work with the best tattoo artists, illustrators, and songwriters. Top-notch solo creatives can't scale themselves. What they can do is sell their work as a product, share their secrets and process through workshops, or hire apprentices to work in their studio. When you hire these high-end creatives, you pay a premium to get them to work on your project instead of one of their employees. It could allow you to charge high rates, sometimes $500 an hour or more. People will pay it because you're price anchoring or price bracketing inside of your business. They see the benefit of getting the best person and are willing to pay for it in comparison with the lesser known talent. You can also fill up your work pipeline for quite some time this way because people are willing to wait to work with the master creative.

Specialization and Generalization Without Intention

Vertical and horizontal marketing are a big part of your growth strategy. As we covered in Chapter 3, there are risks and rewards. As you grow, you may not realize you're specializing until it's too late. You might have also fallen into generalization if you layered in far more complementary services than you intended.

The good thing about scaled growth is that you can cut off any parts of your business that you don't like. If you've gotten into a vertical niche that you aren't enjoying but you're diversified in your client base, you can grow the other clients and reduce your commitment to the niche. If you're doing the same highly specialized task for several clients but you have a large team, you can leverage other skills from your team members to experiment in new horizontals and sell those skills.

Passive Income

Making money while you sleep or while lying on the beach sounds great, right? While hiring staff and delegating work will free you up to a degree, you're still responsible for managing it all. Passive income is simply a product or service that you've created once and can sell to multiple buyers over and over again without your involvement.

Unless you build a product that reaches critical mass, it's probably not going to replace your services business. But it can supplement your income enough to allow you to take on fewer clients or say "no" a bit more often.

The fastest way to develop products is to reproduce one or more of the services you are already offering. For example, if you conduct a workshop with clients, hold it as a group event and record the audio or video, then sell the recordings online. If you're a designer who makes brochures, create basic templates for everyday customers like flower shops or boutique hotels and sell them on creative marketplaces and stock sites. Or if you tend to do some concepts for clients but only use one, resell the concepts on marketplaces or stock sites.

Even if your skill set can't be reproduced effectively for resale, you can leverage your knowledge or process into informational products that can sell at scale.

- If you've developed custom tools for your workflow, such as templates or code, you can resell it.

- Document your process and research and turn it into paid writing gigs.

- Write an eBook or guide, even if you give it away it can serve as a lead-generation tool.

- Teach an online course or tutorial and charge for it.

- Develop a blog or website that has advertising space that you sell through a marketing network.

Partnerships and Mergers

Taking Your Talents to South Beach

You've run the business long enough on your own, and you long for someone to help carry the weight. It may be time to look for a partner. You may be consistently partnering with another business that you want to join forces with or you may make or receive an offer to acquire or be acquired by another business.

Taking on a partner isn't something you'll take lightly. If you've built the business on your own and had total control, the idea of giving up that autonomy will probably make you nervous. You've always been your boss, doing whatever you want, whenever you want, and now someone else will be there. Even though they'll be your peer, the idea of having someone else looking at the bank account (and some questionable purchases), the way you work, and what you've actually been doing all this time is a bit like opening up your underwear drawer or journal.

Only partner with someone that you would go on vacation with and share a house or hotel room. First, because that'll likely happen due to the cut in pay you're both about to take so that you can save money when you travel. You're going to be talking to this person at 3am about your sick kid and a fight you had with your spouse. They're going to know about your debt, your health, and your habits. You're sharing bank accounts and tax bills. You'll have to agree to hire and fire people and which clients you'll take. They will make decisions that affect you and your family.

Just like a personal relationship, you'll want to partner with someone who complements you and isn't your clone. You'll need shared interests and a similar outlook on important issues, but you want to be different enough that you can be yourselves. It may be someone with your same skills, such as two web designers, or it may be a designer and developer. It may be that you're the creative, and she's the business brain. It may be someone who's coming from a corporate or agency job and bringing a client base or set of connections to the small business world. Whoever it is, make sure that you have enough differences to not get sick of each other but are similar enough to be able to understand one another.

What partners should agree on

- **Clients**. The type of clients, industries, and individuals you want to work with

- **The lifestyle you want**. Time off, travel, family time, etc.

- **All hires**. Never hire someone that you both wouldn't hire on your own

What partners should differ on

- **Attitude and demeanor**. If you're both laid back, no one is ringing the alarm but if you're both alarmists, the office is constantly stressed.

- **Outside interests, to a degree**. My business partner and I have a lot of shared interests, some we've developed together, but we differ enough that we have some friends and interests outside of work that we don't feel the obligation to include one another in.

- **Key skills**. Even if both of you are illustrators, each of you should be stronger in one area than the other, and lead with it. If a lot of work is coming in that's only suited to one partner, then the other partner should pick up the slack on business development.

Mergers

If someone wants to acquire your business and fold your team in with them, you've got a lot of choices to make. You're likely giving up the freedom you set out to build when you started. You'll be moving offices, changing your schedule, and working with people you didn't get to choose. It's not all bad, and many people have been thrilled with this decision.

Tips on mergers:

- **Involve attorneys.** No merger should be done without attorneys involved that represent each party. Do not use the same attorney. There are entire books and websites dedicated to this process, so if the time comes, check the website for resources.

- **Involve accountants.** There are serious tax and operational implications of mergers. You have to have someone determine your individual tax basis, your cash contributions, and your percentage of ownership. Things are rarely as simple as half and half ownership of a business. Someone has to lead in some capacity financially.

- **Date before you wed.** Work together on projects if you can before you jump into bed together. If you're being acquired by a large agency, try to work with them on a project to determine if it's where you want to work.

Office Space

You may never need a "real" office. There are people who have been very successful for decades who continue to work from home or co-work. Your reasons for getting office space are your own. There are solo creatives who work in 1,000 sq. ft. by themselves and love every minute of it. There isn't a magic formula for when you should get space or how much you can afford. In Cameron Foote's *The Business Side of Creativity*, he gives the general guideline of 500 sq. ft. per three or four employees. Even still, with today's varying footprint needs depending on your role, there's no way to know.

Take It Easy

Be willing to ease into your office; don't feel the need to compete with agencies you see with these amazing lobbies and game rooms. While it's fun to work in a place like that, the overhead can cause tremendous stress. My first office was featured on numerous websites for cool workspaces and clients were blown away when they came in. Did it get us one more client or close a deal that wouldn't have otherwise? No. So was it worth it? No. The reason you should invest in impressive office space is for your people so that they have a working environment that they love. Place your focus on amenities and features that help your team more than trying to impress your clients.

Get Help

Hire a leasing agent or realtor that is property-agnostic. Don't ever rely on the realtors assigned to you by properties you may be interested in; they are not in the business of protecting your interests. Whether you should buy or lease is a subject worthy of its own short book. It depends on what you can do with the space and where you believe your company is headed. Always give yourself plenty of space to grow; choose a space larger than you think you need and be willing to bring in another creative firm to split it with you if you can't fill it up.

Share the Burden

Partnering with a complementary creative or agency, or someone in an entirely different line of work such as accounting or insurance, is an excellent way to get your space. Maybe you have a friend or family member with their own small business in need of space, but neither of you wants to take on your desired location on your own. Partnering with someone to share space can ease some of the burdens and make you appear larger to visiting clients.

Take a Hybrid Approach

Our company has always taken the hybrid approach: we keep a permanent space at managed office spaces such as co-working and incubators. There are downsides such as privacy and access to certain resources, but the benefits heavily outweigh them. The lower risk of not having a long-term lease, the support that comes from someone else managing the property, and the connections made with others in the building are well worth any shortcomings. Best of all, you're sharing the things that typically make an office cool like video games and lounge areas without the expense.

Failure is an Option

There may come a time where your business simply isn't working. You may need to stop and give up. There is no perfect answer for "when" as far as time or revenue. When struggling business owners ask Gary Vaynerchuk when they should consider giving up, he responds by asking them "how continuous is the pain?"[3] What Gary means is that we'll all have ups and downs as our businesses grow. But if you've constantly been in a state of stress and anxiety about cash flow or sustainability for years, what you're doing may not be working.

I'm glad that Gary says years and not months when handing out this advice. There are entire books on the "two-year rule" or the "five-year rule" when it comes to hitting your stride as a business. The window of success, where you arrive on the treadmill of growth and enjoyment, does tend to fall in between two and five years. It's extremely rare for it to fall within the first year or a matter of months. The first year or two is going to be hard. Money may not be the issue; you may be overworked from too much business. Either way, stress and anxiety are completely normal for the first few years.

You May Never Be Able to Charge What You're Worth

You may reach a point in your creative career where your income isn't commensurate with your skills. You may be such a good designer or writer that there is no way to find enough direct clients, and manage them, to pay you enough. The sales side of things just never worked out for you. So, you continue to get job offers, and they start to look attractive. If a job offer seems perfect, and it's something you'd like to try, then it's okay to walk away from your business and give it a shot. You can always go back to your creative business. Keeping it open requires a few tax and corporation filings each year, and you'll probably do a side project here and there. It takes just as much courage to stop as it does to start.

How You Can Let It Go

If the time arrives where it's clear you need to move on, what should you do? First, take care of your clients. If you still owe them work, then you need to either find a way to refund their money in payments or find a way to finish the work. If they're depending on you for upcoming deliverables, it's best that you help them find a replacement agency. If you have employees, giving them as much notice is possible is the right thing to do. That may only be a matter of days; just don't end a relationship with a text message. Also, work with your accountant and attorney to make sure everything has been done correctly. You may have obligations to address such as a lease, bills, or equipment that no longer has a home. That will take the time to sort out. I sold my office off piece by piece out of my garage.

Exit with grace. Don't burn any bridges, do the right thing, and keep the door cracked for future opportunities. You may not shut down your business, you may just downsize to yourself or just your leadership team. I've been offered full-time jobs with amazing brands numerous times and it has crossed my mind to take my business all the way back down to a side hustle. I can't say that I won't take that chance if the right one comes along. There is no right and wrong when it comes to a creative life, only what brings you closer to your goals.

How I Let It Go

My first creative business, at least the iteration I'd set out to create, didn't survive. I had to let everyone go and sell almost everything but my laptop and chair. I like to call it my 98 percent downsizing to life support. I had to pay my remaining lease off over the next two years, take on the business credit card debt in my personal name, and pay backed payroll to my ex-employees out of my own earnings on future freelance projects. It wasn't pretty.

I'm glad I didn't completely shut down my business, and that may be where you can land. Maybe it's a 98 percent downsizing for you as well instead of an all-out stop. Maybe it means taking a contract position or full-time job for the next year while you try to rebuild your business on the side. Maybe there's an awesome opportunity to work full-time with a brand you admire, and you can't pass up the chance. Whatever your circumstances may be, just remember that it's okay to stop.

When You're Sixty-four

"Designers don't retire. We die." Jeffrey Zeldman[4]

Once Spiderman was bitten, he was Spiderman for life. He may hang up the mask and web shooters, but he'll always be Spiderman. Once you've been bitten by the creative bug, the infection never goes away. You may move beyond your creative business and go live on a farm, but you'll always be a creative. There is no single trajectory for growth. In fact, no two creatives have the same trajectory. We're not lawyers or stockbrokers; there are no standard paths our parents took before us.

Growth simply means to increase and spread; the metric isn't always company size or wealth. If you're enjoying what you do and can continue making a living, then you're growing. You're flat and stagnant when you stop learning and stop taking chances. There is no gold watch at the end of most creative careers; you simply stop making money for your creative work. I don't think that means you stop creating. Honestly, I don't know how I'll ever stop. Maybe the same holds true for you.

Notes

1. http://tinyletter.com/ben/letters/whale-hunting-or-scale-hunting.
2. http://alistapart.com/article/getting-to-no.
3. https://medium.com/the-entrepreneurs-journey/enough-is-enough-when-should-you-give-up-on-your-idea-6dd5720272c4.
4. https://twitter.com/zeldman/status/232183026296168448.

CHAPTER 10

YES
🍕
PLZ

BE SOMEBODY
YOUR CAT
LOOKS UP TO

TAKING A BREAK FROM ALL YOUR WORRIES

This Creative Life

INSPIRATION
IS GOOD

SYNERGY
★ ⚡ ★

ROCKS

WORK
HARD
Y

SUCCESS
☆ ☆
$ $$
$

MY OTHER COMPUTER
IS A MAC TOO, LOL

TODAY
S A DAY

yay

Your creativity is your life; there is no such thing as work/life balance when you choose a creative career. If you are pursuing work that you love, there is no way to turn off your desire to keep going. We started with the phrase "follow your passion, fall off a cliff." I hope it's evident that you can create a business you love, but only if you walk with your eyes open.

We've covered taking a hard look at your structure, marketing, pricing, operations, communication, and working strategies. Now it's time to take a look at what runs underneath it all. Without realizing, you may begin to dread your work, to resent your clients, and even envy people who have stable jobs. The feeling doesn't last long, but it's poisonous enough to alter your taste, and desire, for your work. You can lose that loving feeling when the grind gets to you.

To wrap up, let's learn to put ourselves first above every client, task, deadline, and anything else that may seem more important. If we don't, all of this is for nothing. The work we create is impermanent, our lives are eternal. When you choose to forego sleep or food to get work done, it shouldn't be because of the money or the deadline, it should be because your creative spirit simply won't let you stop. We've covered ways to mitigate risk and keep the grind to a minimum, but it never goes away. Remember, this shit is tough. We will break ourselves down at times. It's just part of the creative life.

Your Business Is More Important than Your Client's Business …

You're useless to your clients if you're always stressed out and can't focus on the work. If you're in a daily routine of transferring money between accounts and figuring out which credit cards to split your order at Starbucks between, you're likely not doing great creative work. If you're neglecting business development, paying bills late, and failing to set money aside for a rainy day, then you're setting your future self up for failure.

Rather than reacting when your business screams for attention, set aside time at the start of your day to work on the business. Block out a big chunk of one routine day each week to focus even more. Don't wait until late nights or Friday afternoons to work on marketing and operations. Once you've been in business for a while and had your marketing machine in place, careful planning can prevent most of the stress on your end, leaving you more energy to deal with client challenges.

… And You Are Your Business's Greatest Asset.

I almost died running my creative business. I've been an athlete my whole life and am still in great shape. Being sick and tired isn't something I enjoy. I ran myself into the ground trying to keep my business going. I made poor decisions because I put my clients' needs over my own. I've learned to care for my mind and body as I care for my finances and my equipment. Without proper care and maintenance, they will break down. Care for your mind and body so that you can keep going in your creative career for years to come.

Mind

Cultivate a Love of Learning

Learners win. Those who always want to learn more, to expand their horizons, and push into new territory are the ones who succeed. Learning breeds freedom, especially as a creative because you can change your course at any time. As you learn, you may find a deep desire to pursue something new that you've learned as your craft. It may take you longer to make the turn as you have more responsibilities. But you're still in a field that is easier than most others for a career change.

For creatives reliant on technology, such as web designers and developers, the sheer volume of new information and techniques launching each and every day is deafening. You can spend your entire day, and career, learning new languages or tools and testing out new techniques without ever building anything tangible. Balancing the desire to learn with the fear of falling behind can be overwhelming. The best response is just-in-time learning. That means learning new things as you need them.

For any technique, it's difficult to learn it in the abstract. You need an actual goal or project in front of you. That doesn't have to be for a client, but learning for the sake of learning when it comes to creative craft doesn't fit into your schedule. If it's a new design style, find a project where you can do a variation and incorporate the new techniques. If it's code, look for small side projects or personal projects where you can try it out. Musicians call it noodling, just playing around without any pressure to see where things go. You're only going to retain most information if you use it for a purpose.

You will feel like younger creatives coming behind you know more than you. The fact is that they do when it comes to certain techniques. You are unlearning just as much as you're learning at times, which takes up half of your processing power. Creatives who aren't having to unlearn old ways or methods get the full processing power. Not to mention that you probably have greater responsibilities and commitments, so hacking away at a tutorial for eight hours on a Tuesday night isn't in the cards for you.

For most creatives, you will seek mastery over diversity. Great violinists may know enough about the cello to pick it up and play a bit, but they're going to call on a cellist when it's time to play together. Everyone on a major league baseball team can probably throw a decent fastball, but only a few guys are going on the mound.

The most important thing to remember is that you'll never know everything. As you grow, you'll need to learn what's new and what's changing so that you can do your job. That doesn't mean you have to learn every new language or style out there. It means you can partner with others who do know it or hire them to work for you. It means being the best at what you do know and using your wisdom to apply it to current problems.

Here are some tips on building a lifetime love of creative learning:

- **Reverse engineer.** Take apart other people's work. You may be apprehensive and ask about originality, but there is little left when it comes to originality. To learn about a style, method, tool, or trend, reverse engineer the work of others. Try to deconstruct their process and actions and recreate their work. See how they got there and try to learn along the way where you can adapt their process to suit your needs. By no means am I suggesting that you steal the work of others or label it as your own. It's for your consumption, learning, and instruction.

- **Get personal.** Learn a new piece of software by doing a personal project, such as designing a poster in something other than Photoshop and Illustrator. Right now, the trends are Sketch and Affinity Designer.

- **Change your tone.** Write in a different voice or genre than you're used to. If you're a mystery writer, try historical fiction.

- **Look into your crystal ball.** If you have a particular market you focus on, such as healthcare, think about where the industry may be headed and ways that your services can fit into future trends. Even if the demand isn't there yet, start working on ideas for how you'll service that niche.

- **Sketch**. It doesn't matter what you do, if you're a software engineer you can benefit from sketching your ideas. Instead of creating a document, try spelling out your idea as a cartoon strip.

- **Use your hands**. Build something, even if it's out of Lego instead of a Raspberry Pi. Find a way to push yourself beyond your comfort zone when it comes to making physical objects. Try wood carving or making your own soap.

- **Scratch your own itch**. You'll hear this often because it's priceless advice. Some of the best ideas out there came from someone making an item or process they needed that simply wasn't available. It could be a tangible product, like the bacon bowl, or a service, like Uber. Don't be afraid to prototype and test the idea.

Write

You may not be the type to blog or write a book or even post original thoughts to social media. But you're not writing for others, you're writing for yourself. One of my greatest regrets in my early creative career is how little detail I have to look back on. The lessons learned, the way I felt at the time, and the relationships made are often lost when they aren't recorded. I treasure the journals, notebooks, and random scraps that I do have. They're of more value to me than any book or blog post written by anyone else.

It doesn't have to be elaborate or formal. It doesn't have to be in an app or even one central place. Find a time each day, and keep it consistent, to write down what's going on and what happened. Your future self will be incredibly thankful. If you can work up the courage, publish it online. Blog as often as you can. James Altucher says that he doesn't publish a blog post unless he's scared to hit "publish." He finds that the more scared he is, the more meaningful the post is.

Meditate

Meditation doesn't have to be cross-legged incantations and floating above the floor. Thanks to apps like Omvana and Headspace, you can learn to meditate and focus in just a few minutes a day. Guided meditation through an app, audiobook, or in courses is the best way to start; it's tough to learn the art on your own. It will help you learn to center yourself and focus on your work. Learning to meditate can decrease your reaction to thoughts and stimuli, which builds the ability to have more control over reactions outside of meditation. The medical benefits are still up for debate, though I see them myself, but at the very least it's worth your time just to breathe and learn to focus.

The biggest benefit of meditation is you'll learn to cope with stress. Taking a moment to think before you act can be the difference between fixing a client issue and lashing out, losing the relationship. Saying the wrong thing the wrong way to an employee or freelancer can have lasting damage, so learning to control your emotions even a tiny bit more is well worth the effort.

Look Up

Even if you're not religious or spiritual, finding something bigger than yourself can do wonders for your work and perspective. Steven Pressfield refers to his Muse throughout his writing. You can call a higher power whatever you want, and whether you believe it or not, this world is bigger than you and me. Get involved with a charity or non-profit that has you doing something outside of your skills. While it's great for a web designer to volunteer her web design skills for a local non-profit's website, it's better for her well-being to do something out of her daily routines such as make house calls or mentor job seekers.

Be Satisfied

You can always take one more client, one more call, or one more meeting. More is better, or so we like to think. The drive to be the best and to be paid handsomely for it is good and positive. But you have to turn it off at some point in the day and week. Your bank account could always be bigger, and your trophy case could always be more full. It has to stop somewhere, and you have to learn to be satisfied with what you've done. At the micro level, this is about just shipping a design or article when done. Don't keep toying with it incessantly and making yourself sick. Your day should be satisfying. You worked hard, you put your mind to it, and now it's time to rest and be done. Your week, your month, and your year should do the same. Take the time to reflect and be satisfied with the hard work you've put in.

Say "No"

"Saying "no" has more creative power than ideas, insights and talent combined. "No" guards time, the thread from which we weave our creations. The math of time is simple: you have less than you think and need more than you know. We are not taught to say "no." We are taught not to say "no." "No" is rude. "No" is a rebuff, a rebuttal, a minor act of verbal violence. "No" is for drugs and strangers with candy."

Kevin Ashton[1]

What are we missing when we say yes? Ask yourself that question again, "what are we missing when we say 'yes?'" Life is filled with fear of missing out. A favorite phrase is "dude, you should've been there!" It's not just the always-on age we're in with devices and social media, it's the busyness and awareness that the modern world forces on us. People who choose to sit at home all day and not continually accept every social invite are considered boring and anti-social. If you constantly reject others in your industry who just want to "pick your brain" you're considered "self-absorbed."

You are not a jerk for saying "no." You are too creative, too driven, and too focused to say "yes." Every time you say yes, you are saying no to your work, your business, and your health. When you say yes to someone else, you are valuing their time and their feelings over your own. You are putting someone else's priorities higher than your own. You're worried that they won't like you anymore or that they'll judge you. Separate saying "no" to the request from saying "no" to the relationship. You aren't rejecting the person; you're denying their request. The two aren't necessarily connected.

Will the person you said "yes" to pay your bills when your business folds? Will they give you the opportunity to show your work or speak in front of an audience when your work is less than it could have been? Will they give you back the sleep you missed so that you could stay up late finishing a project because you spent the evening with them?

Despite the cult of online personality, the creative life isn't a popularity contest. Sure, you need readers and viewers, you need clients, and you need connections. But saying no isn't going to keep that from happening. In fact, saying no to things that aren't important empowers you to say yes to the things that will make you, your work, and your reputation stronger.

That doesn't mean say no to everything in life and just work all the time, quite the opposite. What it does mean is saying no to the unnecessary, the overwhelming, and the extra requests. When you only say yes to what matters, you are more fulfilled. When you say no, you have margin in your schedule to say yes to the spontaneous. Things like random dance parties with your kids, unplanned escapes with your partner to a beach, and just knocking off for an entire day and seeing five movies at the theatre and eating four buckets of popcorn.

Saying no doesn't have to be said with the word "no." You can say "later," "another time," or other alternatives. If someone asks for a meeting, offer a phone call instead. If they want to interview you, offer to have them send questions via email and you'll answer them in writing. If they want you to take on a project that doesn't fit, give them names of others they can call instead.

Body

Take Time Off

Sick days, vacation, and help when you're overwhelmed all come at a cost out of your pocket. I've worked from a hospital bed, my child's delivery room, beaches, weddings, funerals, and my own birthday party. I've learned to draw boundaries, and I'm able to take time off now, but it took a long time to get there. Learning to turn it off when there's one more email or one more prospect or one more pixel is tough.

You have to schedule your time off and commit to it and if that means booking hotels ahead of time with non-refundable rates, then do so. Force yourself to travel and spend time with others. Make it impossible to avoid.

Sleep

All-nighters aren't solving anything. You only have so much willpower and unless you actually have a morning deadline that you're going to miss, you're far better off getting six to eight hours of sleep and working furiously in the fixed amount of time you have the next day. Sleep deprivation is thought to cause serious health problems including heart attack, stroke, Type 2 diabetes, premature aging, and obesity. The most notable effects that I experience are irritability and clouded judgment. Those two side effects alone are enough to tank your business if you're experiencing them regularly.

Hydrate

Keep water by your desk and drink tons of it. Coffee is lovely and being your own boss means you can drink alcohol while you work. The additional benefits for your skin and circulation aside, you should drink lots of water every day; your brain needs it to stay focused.

Eat

It shouldn't have to be said, but you have to eat. We get so engrossed in our work that we starve and binge. Don't just eat healthily though. Eat on schedule and snack smart. Keeping junk food at your desk or in your home will slow you down and ruin your keyboard. Snacking is fine, it's good brain food, but you should eat a regular breakfast, lunch, and dinner away from your work. Take a lunch break and use the time to meet with others, go analog, or just be outside.

Exercise

Your physical health can easily suffer when you're in a creative career. Most of us don't have the clear separation of working hours that allows us to go to the gym at regular times. Our schedules can get erratic, and there's always that "one more thing" we need to get done, and then we'll work out after that. For the last few years, I've practiced yoga. It has made a tremendous difference in my health and overall well-being. As someone who had scoliosis as a child, and still needs monthly chiropractic adjustments to keep from leaning to one side, Yoga keeps me centered, literally. Sitting, or even standing, in front of a computer for an entire work day can ravage your back, hands, wrists, and knees.

It's important to make physical activity a priority every day. It isn't me telling you to eat your vegetables, though you should; rather it's a hard truth that the healthier you are, the better your work will be. Find even seven minutes on one of the hundred fitness apps to get some physical activity in your day.

Stand and Stretch

Never sit for more than forty-five minutes straight without taking at least ten minutes to stretch and walk around. Use your Smartphone to check emails and do it while standing or walking. Anytime you have calls, take them standing up and pace while you're on the phone. If you can dictate or generate ideas on your notebook on a counter top, stand and work whenever possible to keep from sitting all day.

I'm a life-long weightlifter and former competitive runner. I still participate in some physical activity six days a week plus I'm always wrestling with my kids. Research has shown that working out at the gym in the morning or evening, even if it's every day, isn't enough to counteract the effects of sitting all day. You have to counteract the effects throughout the day to offset the damage. A standing desk won't fix it either, even though I do use one. While a standing or treadmill desk is a good idea, you can just as easily form bad habits standing and be just as sedentary. You have to move around.

Stop Being Busy

"Hey Brad, how's it going?" my friend asked. "Busy, Bob, super busy," I replied. That's the standard method of operation in creative life—we're always busy. At least that's what we think. The truth is that we aren't busy, we're fragmented. We're constantly switching between tasks and commitments and shrinking our brains in the process.[2]

We fill our lives up with so much to do that we have no room to do anything meaningful. So stop being so damn busy and give yourself a break.

How to Stop Being Busy

- **Write all of your worries, to-dos, and ideas down every day.** Dump everything out in the morning and at night on paper. Try to avoid using an app. Write it down and organize it loosely into what needs to be done, and when.

- **If you don't prioritize your life, someone else will.** Use the Eisenhower Matrix, Time Blocking, an app, a paper planner, or whatever system works for you to get all of your priorities in order. It's as simple as deciding what's most important and doing that first.

- **Sprint and group similar tasks.** Task-switching from one mode to another, such as writing to paying bills, expends energy. The more time you can spend working the same way, such as designing similar items at once or answering emails in batches, the less time you'll spend resetting between tasks.

- **Turn important recurring tasks into habits.** Habits take up little willpower. Tasks take up a tremendous amount of willpower. Transferring the same action, such as tracking your timesheet or writing in your journal, from task to habit can give you time back. Habits feel automatic, and they're hard to forget. Tasks product friction and breed guilt when they're ignored.

- **Handle things once.** Don't stack things up or shove them into folders to do later. If it's a bill that needs to be paid, don't open bills until you're also prepared to pay them. If it's an email that requires a reply, don't check emails until you're also prepared to craft replies.

- **Stop multitasking.** Do one thing at a time, limit the amount of time you'll spend on it, and stop doing it when that time is up.

- **Schedule your time off and commit to it.** If you have to, book non-refundable flights and hotel rooms or prepay for all-inclusive cruises. Do things that force you to take your vacations and leisure time as seriously as a client deadline.

Burnout

Burnout doesn't go away if you take a week off or work with fewer clients; it's not simply exhaustion or having your schedule overfilled. Burnout is a feeling, a state of being, that isn't tied to a particular illness or ailment. It's not depression, it's not exhaustion, and it's not stress. It's something much more, and it can linger for years. The way it's often described is feeling "off" or "bad" all the time. You just aren't enjoying your work or your life anymore. You may have days and even weeks where everything seems fine, but you find yourself drifting into negative territory regularly.

It doesn't mean you're overworked or even have too much going on, it just means you're burned out. Burnout happens to almost all creatives who stick with it for a while. It varies in intensity and frequency and isn't even tied to success or failure. There are creatives who are constantly in need of more clients who are burned out.

According to the Association of Psychological Science, there are three types of burnout[3]:

- **Overload:** The frenetic employee who works toward success until exhaustion is most closely related to emotional venting. These individuals might try to cope with their stress by complaining about the organizational hierarchy at work, feeling as though it imposes limits on their goals and ambitions. That coping strategy, unsurprisingly, seems to lead to a stress overload and a tendency to throw in the towel.

- **Lack of development:** Most closely associated with an avoidance coping strategy. These under-challenged workers tend to manage stress by distancing themselves from work, a strategy that leads to depersonalization and cynicism—a harbinger for burning out and packing up shop.

- **Neglect:** Seems to stem from a coping strategy based on giving up in the face of stress. Even though these individuals want to achieve a certain goal, they lack the motivation to plow through barriers to get to it.

Recognizing Burnout

Developer Kent Nguyen, in tandem with Lifehacker author Adam Dachis, created a list of signs you're experiencing burnout:[4]

- A generally negative attitude, often paired with the feeling that nothing is going to work out.

- Inability to concentrate.

- General apathy towards your work, chores, and other tasks.

- Feelings of stagnation.

- A lack of interest in social activities and being with others.

- Difficulty with healthy habits like exercise, diet, and regular sleep.

- Feeling like you're never doing enough.

- Neglecting your own needs (and putting the needs of others ahead of your own).

- Personal values and beliefs lose their importance.

- Short temper.

- Constant exhaustion.

- Feelings of inefficacy.

- Feelings of detachment from people and things you care about.

- Frequent boredom.

- Psychosomatic complaints, such as headaches, lingering colds, and other issues with a cause that's difficult to identify.

- The denial of these.

- The work you do keeps having issues for several consecutive days.

- What you expected to be a simple task has dragged on for days.

- Completely consumed by work you forget to pay bills or forget your date(!).

- You lose track of time; it was Monday yesterday and it's Friday tomorrow.

- You work long non-productive hours and you wish to be efficient as you used to be on some other days.

How to Beat Burnout

In "Go the Fuck Home," Pam Selle says,[5] "if you can't name two things you're regularly doing outside of work, you're spending too much time there." Most people get burned out because they aren't finding inspiration and joy outside of work. Their entire identity is built around what they do instead of who they are. They've lost sight of who they are.

When I experienced severe burnout, taking a sabbatical wasn't possible. I have a family and a mortgage, I'm not the type of creative who can afford to just stop taking clients. But I could cut back, I could make changes, and I could charge more. Only through finding outside interests again, and seeing work as part of my life instead of all of my life, was I able to let go of total control and settle into better business practices.

The root cause of burnout is being unable to do what you love. You are frustrated because your time and life are being wasted. Fighting burnout starts with you getting back to what you enjoy, what you truly want out of your day and your work. The tendency is to blame others—your clients, your employees, your family, or your colleagues. While outside factors can cause burnout, it's up to you to face it head on and make a change.

It can get to a point where you have to change careers or sell everything you have and start over to get back to your love, but you can't will yourself out of the burnout state by saying "get over it." The best way to avoid burnout is to schedule and structure your day rigorously. Then take a look at what's important at the smallest level possible. If not hourly, then daily. Consistently check with yourself to see how things are going.

- Ask yourself what you'll regret not doing, not what needs to be done. The difference is crucial.

- Take time for yourself first thing every day, which means don't check email or messages as soon as you get out of bed.

- Take vacations every quarter, even if they are camping or just lying around binge-watching Netflix. Build in time off and schedule around it.

- Go to lunch and stop eating at your desk, get away from your work in the middle of the day.

- Learn to live with "good enough" and just ship it.

- Journal, and focus on the positive; write down what you've done instead of staring at your half-finished to-do list.

- There will always be more to do; be okay with leaving things undone.

- Last, and most important, learn to say "no."

"A 'no' uttered from the deepest conviction is better than a 'yes' merely uttered to please, or worse, to avoid trouble."

Mahatma Ghandi

Embrace the Ups and Downs

We're passionate people. We may become pragmatic and learn to walk with our eyes open, but our wiring will always keep our temperature rotating between sub-zero and boiling. The worst thing you can be is lukewarm or apathetic. At times, you will have more work than you can handle and feel high as a kite. Conversely, you'll fear for your financial future and drink a little more than usual. The treadmill of a strong business and stable personal life still requires motion. Embrace the back and forth, the up and down, and learn to recognize where you are. Never settle, but don't panic. Just keep going.

- Being a creative is hard and will never be free of challenges, but a creative life is the best life and is always worth the challenges.

- You may produce work that sucks, but you can make things you want to show your mom.

- You may fail and completely miss the client's expectations, but you can blow a client away with a problem solved.

- You may fail to listen and do something completely wrong, but you might be high-fived for borderline mind-reading.

- You'll probably be late on a deadline, for a meeting, or for your child's recital, but you'll learn to let it go.

- You'll stay up all night to make a deadline but look back on it fondly.

- You may be fired by a client, and you may fire a client and feel like a boss when you do it.

- You'll hate most of the work you did more than three years ago, but you'll look at an old project and be in awe of how far you've come.

- You'll get older and may lose touch with other creatives, but you'll be shocked at how much younger you always seem than your nine-to-five counterparts.

- You will change what you do more often than you like, but you also get to change what you do and where you do it.

- You will break things, and you'll be glad you broke that thing.

- You'll likely have a client fail to ever pay an invoice, but you'll be so glad for the lesson learned.

- You will be outbid for a project, then see the work your competitor did and thank God for dodging a bullet.

- You may work with someone you can't stand and end up being best friends.

- You will fall in love with a client, and they will break your heart when they leave, or you'll break their heart when you have to let them go.

- You will work more hours in a day, week, month, and year than you thought possible and want to do it all over again.

- You will use the word "synergy" and then make fun of people who use the word "synergy."

- You will have to spend money you don't have, yet know you are in control of making as much as you want to pay it off later.

- You will suffer from Impostor Syndrome more than once, but pretend you're a famous in front of the mirror.

- You will be frustrated by how much better someone half your age is at your job, then see someone half your age do incredible work and mentor them to the point of adoption.

- You will panic, and then learn to stay cool under pressure and have no idea how you did it.

- You will lose hope and think about changing careers more than once. But you'll love every single minute of your career and wish you could start over and take the ride again.

About That Courage

The risk never goes away; you will always have to be courageous. No matter how many clients you have, how much money in the bank, or awards on your mantle—insecurity always lingers close behind. Your work and you the person are forever intertwined. To be creative is to be vulnerable and adventurous. There will be highs and lows, days you need a drink just to get by and days you need a drink because there's nothing to do but celebrate.

The greatest truth any creative can learn is that this life never gets easy, it only gets harder. You may grow to the point that you're not struggling to find clients or income, but you'll fight to manage your time. You may be the most admired creative in your craft, but you will always wonder if your work will die with a trend and be forgotten. You may build a product with millions of users, only to fear that someone will build something better and cheaper. There is no security, there is no net, there is no retirement. A creative is a creative for life, no matter what you do next.

It's up to you to go head first into the fire, to love what you do, and make a life with the gift that only you have been given.

"Be yourself; everyone else is already taken." Oscar Wilde

Go and Grow

Stoke the fire the fire and keep the creative spark burning, but always take a hard look at the business. Don't be afraid to walk and talk like a business owner. You can still be creative, but try to be pragmatic and learn from your past experiences.

Take good notes and always be learning. Try to fall back in love with your business every day, especially on the days when it seems easy. The hard times can seem fun, at least they were for me, the worst is when you're indifferent. Guided passion is rocket fuel for a creative life worth living.

You don't have to love everything that you do, but you can love the business you've created. If you've learned anything from this book, realize that it's never too late to start over or rebuild. You can start today with any new habit or system; it's your business, and there is no box or mould.

Go out and build valuable relationships that will last far longer than any work you create. Even if you're creating print or physical work, it has a shelf-life. Strong relationships with clients, referral partners, colleagues, collaborators, and friends can last a lifetime.

Make the money you want; don't worry about what you deserve. Go out and build the life for you and your family that will keep you excited about going to work each day. Live where you want, work where you want, and do what you want.

Stand your ground, know you're valuable, and never compromise your integrity. Feel free to walk away from any client or situation that isn't helping you grow. Guard yourself and do what's necessary to care for you and your business first.

Be honest and open with everyone you work with. Ask for help, say what you mean, and don't be afraid. If you're transparent and consistent, the worst thing that could happen is you lose money or a relationship. It's never worth losing your sanity or integrity.

Do the work, hustle, and show off when you succeed. Know that you can't manage every single aspect of your life. Someday, you may shut down your business and return to the world of the employed. Losing control of your entire schedule and time will be hard. So don't be so hard on yourself when you are in control.

Work with your competitors; it's likely you'll end up friends. Share your secrets, open your books, and tell the most embarrassing stories. You'll be better for it. And spend the money on conferences and events; they're worth it.

Grow the way you want and stay as small as you like. Get a building with your name on the side and fill it with people who work for you. Work solo on your front porch and in your favorite coffee shop until you're ready to retire. Build a business, and then sell it or shut it down and go work somewhere. You do you.

Until Next Time

I wanted to quit in March of 2010. I had no hope and couldn't see any light ahead. For almost two additional years, I struggled and held on, never knowing why. I now know that something deep inside—that spark—wouldn't die. It remained through the burnout, the failing health, and the financial struggles. Something bigger than my circumstances held it all together, and I'm lucky to have an ongoing story worth sharing.

I have one life, but I've had several creative lives. They're held together by a single red thread that stretches to all of those who've helped me along the way. I hope that my story and lessons learned have helped you in some small way. As you learn and grow, pass it on to those around you and make the creative life that only you can.

"I may not have gone where I intended to go, but I think I have ended up where I needed to be."

Douglas Adams[6]

Notes

1. https://medium.com/@kevin _ ashton/creative-people-say-no-bad7c34842a2.
2. Brigid Schulte, *Overwhelmed: Work, Love, and Play When No One Has the Time.*
3. http://www.psychologicalscience.org/index.php/news/minds-business/burnout-comes-in-three-varieties.html.
4. http://kentnguyen.com/personal/getting-rid-burnouts/.
5. http://thewebivore.com/go-the-fuck-home-my-ignite-talk/.
6. Douglas Adams, *The Long Dark Tea-Time of the Soul.*

Index

Printed and bound by CPI Group (UK) Ltd, Croydon, CR0 4YY

24/10/2024

01778610-0001

—